The Emergence
of Mexican America

CRITICAL AMERICA

General Editors: Richard Delgado and Jean Stefancic

Recent titles in the Critical America series include:

*Legal Education and the
Reproduction of Hierarchy:
A Polemic against the System,
A Critical Edition*
Duncan Kennedy,
with commentaries by Paul Carrington,
Peter Gabel, Angela Harris and
Donna Maeda, and Janet Halley

*America's Colony:
The Political and Cultural Conflict
between the United States and
Puerto Rico*
Pedro A. Malavet

*Alienated: Immigrant Rights,
the Constitution, and
Equality in America*
Victor C. Romero

*The Disability Pendulum:
The First Decade of the Americans
with Disabilities Act*
Ruth Colker

*Lawyers' Ethics and the Pursuit
of Social Justice: A Critical Reader*
Edited by Susan D. Carle

*Rethinking Commodification: Cases and
Readings in Law and Culture*
Edited by Martha M. Ertman
and Joan C. Williams

The Derrick Bell Reader
Edited by Richard Delgado
and Jean Stefancic

*Science for Segregation: Race, Law,
and the Case against Brown v. Board
of Education*
John P. Jackson Jr.

*Discrimination by Default:
How Racism Becomes Routine*
Lu-in Wang

*The First Amendment in Cross-Cultural
Perspective: A Comparative Legal
Analysis of the Freedom of Speech*
Ronald J. Krotoszynski, Jr.

Feminist Legal Theory: A Primer
Nancy Levit and Robert R. M. Verchick

For a complete list of titles in the series,
please visit the New York University Press
website at www.nyupress.org.

The Emergence of Mexican America

Recovering Stories of Mexican Peoplehood in U.S. Culture

John-Michael Rivera

NEW YORK UNIVERSITY PRESS
New York and London

NEW YORK UNIVERSITY PRESS
New York and London
www.nyupress.org

Library of Congress Cataloging-in-Publication Data
Rivera, John-Michael, 1969–
The emergence of Mexican America : recovering stories of Mexican
peoplehood in U.S. culture / John-Michael Rivera.
p. cm. — (Critical America)
Includes bibliographical references and index.
ISBN–13: 978–0–8147–7557–8 (cloth : alk. paper)
ISBN–10: 0–8147–7557–8 (cloth : alk. paper)
ISBN–13: 978–0–8147–7558–5 (pbk. : alk. paper)
ISBN–10: 0–8147–7558–6 (pbk. : alk. paper)
1. Mexican Americans—Ethnic identity. 2. Mexican Americans—
History. 3. Mexican Americans—Cultural assimilation. I. Title.
II. Series.
E184.M5R58   2006
305.868'72073—dc22   2005035676

New York University Press books are printed on acid-free paper,
and their binding materials are chosen for strength and durability.

Manufactured in the United States of America

c 10 9 8 7 6 5 4 3 2 1
p 10 9 8 7 6 5 4 3 2 1

Contents

Acknowledgments   vii

Introduction "How Do You Make the
Invisible, Visible?": Locating Stories of
Mexican Peoplehood   1

1   Don Zavala Goes to Washington:
Translating U.S. Democracy   24

2   Constituting Terra Incognita:
The "Mexican Question" in U.S. Print Culture   51

3   Embodying Manifest Destiny:
María Amparo Ruiz de Burton and the
Color of Mexican Womanhood   82

4   Claiming *Los Bilitos*: Miguel Antonio Otero
and the Fight for New Mexican Manhood   110

5   "Con su pluma en su mano": Américo Paredes and
the Poetics of "Mexican American" Peoplehood   135

Conclusion: Recovering *La memoria*:
Locating the Recent Past   165

Notes   177

Bibliography   189

Index   205

About the Author   211

Acknowledgments

This book began and ended with people in mind. Within and outside the margins, the people I have met cast their influence upon every thought and inspired me over the years to complete what I thought would never end. Ten years ago Nicolas Kanellos guided me to a life of thinking. For his caring, his wisdom, and mentorship, I will be forever grateful. In Houston, I also began what has become a wonderful friendship with José Aranda. In periods when I thought I would never continue, his belief in this project over the years has been helpful beyond words. I also thank my dissertation advisors and especially Shelley Fisher Fishkin, an erudite scholar who amazes me with every conversation. I offer a very special thanks to my mentor and dear friend José Limon. I would not be a professor if it were not for him, and I aspire to become a person of his kindness and merit. In the last few years, the University of Colorado at Boulder has giving me the support and time to finish this project. At CU, Patty Limerick has been a great friend and introduced me to Jean Stefancic and Richard Delgado. All of these people believed in this project in its early stages, and I thank them for their help over the past five years. I also thank Eric Zinner and Emily Park at New York University Press for giving me the opportunity to publish this work.

Thanks also to my chair John Stevenson for having a wonderful vision and being very supportive. To my compadres Adéléké Adéèkó, Fred Aldama, Cheryl and Dan Higashida, and Will West, all of whom have helped me through their friendship. I offer my gratitude to my dear friends Anna Brickhouse and Vincent Woodard : Anna read every page of this manuscript a number of times with care and a critical eye; Vincent, whom I have known since graduate school, read with skepticism and helped me fine-tune ideas in this book and in my life. To my *tia*, Emma Perez, who inspired me twenty years ago to go to Berkeley and later to get a Ph.D. To my dad John Rivera and my mother Yolanda Perez: in their own ways both of them have given me the ability to write these pages; I love them dearly. And finally, to the two people who guide my every word, my every thought: my wife Rhonda and my daughter Elyse. With laughter and love you have both helped me write this book but, most important, filled my life with story. This project found its voice two weeks after my daughter was born. This book and Elyse grew together over the last five years, most of the times she growing faster than the amount of pages I managed to write during her naps. I dedicate this book to them.

The Emergence
of Mexican America

Introduction

"How Do You Make the Invisible, Visible?" Locating Stories of Mexican Peoplehood

My story of the Mexican past in the United States begins with a story of the Mexican present. During a long drive from Los Angeles International Airport to the high desert of Lancaster, California, in the summer of 2004, I saw a billboard that would haunt me for days. In bold black letters, the billboard simply stated: "Mexicans Are Leaving on May 14th." What did this mean, I wondered? My question quickly went from intrigue to concern. Who produced the large billboard? Was it a new anti-immigrant group trying to prepare the public for a xenophobic proposition denying Mexicans the same rights as other American citizens, a reactionary position informed by the fact that Mexican people now make up over 50 percent of the population in Los Angeles? Or had the new California governor, Arnold "The Terminator" Schwarzenegger—who seems to have taken it upon himself to legislate Mexicans out of the state—sponsored it? Was the billboard a political call for a modern "repatriation" of the entire Mexican people? This was, after all, California—a state that had been trying to "legally" get rid of its Mexicans since the Gold Rush and the signing of the Treaty of Guadalupe Hidalgo in 1848. "Are all the Mexican people really leaving on May 14th?" I asked my wife in half-jest and half concern. Sardonically, she replied that what really bothered me was that I hadn't received the invitation. She was right. I'd been away from California too long.

It would be days before I found out that this controversial billboard was promoting the release of Mexican director Sergio Arau's movie, *A Day without a Mexican* (Figure 1). On May 14th, in fact, I did leave my home, and, along with hundreds of thousands of other Mexicans across the country, went to the theaters to watch this poignant and modern story of Mexican peoplehood. The film evokes important historical questions about the political and racial location of Mexicans in the United States.[1] Part satire, part social drama, the basic plot of the film develops when a mysterious fog surrounds California, and, in its wake, the Mexican people of the state literally disappear from the landscape. In the scenes that follow, the film shows the varying political, economic, and cultural losses that result from the mysterious disappearance of millions of Mexicans. Arau's film, then, is a paradoxical story. Despite the literal disappearance of Mexican people from the screen, it is, in the end, a story about the ideological processes in white America that inform the marginalized, modern position of Mexicans in the United States and the normalizing factors that influence the symbolic and real disappearance of Mexican "people" as political actors from the stage of democratic culture. That is, it reveals the colonial project hidden within the discourses surrounding the liberal concept of "the people." In this way, *A Day without a Mexican* is a self-reflexive meditation on the colonial logic that has historically constituted Mexicans as political nonentities, personae non gratae, which has led to a modern ambivalence surrounding Mexican collectivity in the United States.

In *The Emergence of Mexican America*, I set out to recover important cultural works that emerged in nineteenth- and early-twentieth-century U.S. democratic culture[2] that constitute what I am calling "stories of Mexican peoplehood."[3] Building on the foundational work of Critical Race scholars Richard Delgado and Carl Gutiérrez-Jones and political philosopher Rogers Smith, I argue that "stories" in democratic cultures inform the productive and reproductive logic of political "people-making" itself (Delgado 1989; Gutiérrez-Jones 2001; Smith 2003). Stories of Mexican peoplehood, then, are cultural narratives that represent the norms and ideals associated with collectivity in democratic nation-states. By telling their stories, the Mexicans of this study enter the public sphere and transform the very contours of democractic culture that had affected their constitution in the United States as personae non gratae.[4] My study of nineteenth- and early-twentieth-century stories of Mexican peoplehood is not only an archival recovery of the early emergence of Mexican cultural narratives in the United States but also an examination of the people-making endeavor that works in relation with the development of Mexican cultural production in the national public spheres from 1821 to 1939.[5] I am interested in cultural works that facilitate Mexican peoples' self-understanding as a racialized and political collective within and against a

Figure 1. Movie poster for *A Day without a Mexican*, 2004

white democratic culture that excludes them as full members of the majority political collective. This book, therefore, is a study of the representative works that reveal the poetics of Mexican democratic collectivity and the early formation of what political philosopher Cornelius Castoriadis calls the "social imaginary" in Mexican America (3–43). To this end, I argue that stories of Mexican peoplehood are fundamental to understanding not only the contradictory logic of American democratic culture but also Mexican American cultural production and the ambivalent location of Mexicans as citizen-subjects in the United States.

Like Sergio Arau, the director, the Mexicans of this study engaged the concept of "the people" because it was so fundamental to emergence of

U.S. democracy. Serving as the cultural framework of democracy, "the people" have historically become a discursive site that fostered both igalitarianism and egalitarianism, exclusion and inclusion.[6] To this end, defining who counts as "the people" reveals the contradictory logic of democratic nation-states and the ways in which rhetoric about the people facilitates democratic legitimacy and power for the majority population in the United States. As members of a minority group, the Mexicans of this study entered these debates through their stories of peoplehood in order to transform the colonial rhetoric surrounding their own political identity as a group. Of paramount concern to these cultural workers was the desire to transform the imperialist discourses that had predicated them as personae non gratae into *personae designatae*—subjects who are visibly included in a political and legal category that recognizes them as full and equal members of the body politic.

A *Day without a Mexican* displays this strategy well. Interviewed about what had become a highly controversial film in the national public sphere in the weeks after its release, Arau explained that he had made the movie in order to explore a fundamental question of Mexican peoplehood in the United States: "How do you make the [Mexican] invisible visible?" In effect, he was asking how we recover Mexican people from historical and political obscurity and make them a recognizable and equal part of society. Embedded in his question and the film's leitmotif of invisibility, moreover, is the paradox of locating a material and tangible conception of "the people" in democratic culture. By focusing on the invisibility of Mexican peoplehood he is implicitly calling into question the nebulous nature of actually locating an entity of people who come to understand their collectivity as Mexicans in the United States. In this way, Arau's film and the questions it generated ask us all to contemplate a fundamental question of political philosophy: How does a minority population conceived of as a racialized group of individuals come to constitute itself as a collective of subject citizens within a democratic culture that desires cohesion and conformity to the majority? In other words, how do Mexicans become a sovereign people in a nation-state that has historically relegated them to the discursive margins of "We, the People" of the United States? Answering this question, the film captures the ways in which Mexicans have become one of the largest and most intangible minority peoples in the United States, at the same time that this country has discursively marked their status through ambivalence and invisibility.

Ironically, it is Arau's cultural narrative about Mexican invisibility itself that makes visible the material and political conditions of Mexicans as a collective in the United States. Mexicans become a tangible collective through the thematic logic of absent presence. To this end, the film seeks actively to transform and, in the end, consolidate Mexican peoplehood at the turn of the century.

At the same time, Arau's film suggests the fundamental role that narrative plays in people-making: individuals come to understand their location as part of a given people through varied cultural forms and active narrative engagement in the public spheres. Stories of Mexican peoplehood, therefore, produce the terms by which individuals come to understand their "Mexicanness" as more than an autonomous designation of selfhood and begin to see themselves as a part of a collective constituted as "Mexican."

Reading a number of representative cultural works, in *The Emergence of Mexican America* I excavate the embedded narrative dynamics involved in becoming Mexican in America, and, in doing so, I conceive stories of peoplehood as the self-authenticating mediums that govern and produce the collective logic behind seemingly autonomous individual statements of racial or ethnic identity (Calhoun, "Nationalism and the Public Sphere" 132). What complicates this is when a given subject-citizen must negotiate his or her self-proclaimed or constituted peoplehood according to a bifurcated logic of belonging (Mexican American, African American, etc.), and must negotiate (or deny) a split and at times antithetical designation of peoplehood that resulted from historical factors such as racism, slavery, genocide, and imperialism.

Arau's story of Mexican peoplehood and the "Mexican Question" ("How do we make the invisible, visible?") that emerges from the screen is in fact rooted in the stories of a long line of cultural workers who have struggled with the logic of Mexican people-making in the wake of U.S. imperialism since the nineteenth century. It is significant that *A Day without a Mexican* premiered at a contemporary moment when the politics surrounding the democratic inclusion of the Mexican people in the United States were of particular importance to American public culture. Indeed, the irony is that Arau released the movie in a period when Mexicans were beginning to transform a number of crucial ideological questions about the democratic landscape of the United States. In fact, their visibility in the United States had become a hot topic in the public spheres before September 11th, following the release of the 2000 census numbers.

In 2001 the U.S. Census Bureau published a special atlas titled *Mapping Census 2000: Geography of U.S. Diversity*. Within this visual document, the government's cartographers mapped the populations of ethnic peoples, visibly marking what were once predominantly white American spaces of the United States into ethno-landscapes (Figure 2).[7]

Of particular importance in today's public culture is the large section of the atlas representing Latino population changes. Thirty-seven million Latinos now reside in the United States. In its shades of grey, the map visually represents a new demographic reality on the landscape of the United States: Latinos, and specifically Mexicans, are now the largest minority and soon will perhaps take over the map—a "brown tide is rising."[8] The abstract numbers of the census had been transformed into a material and political reality.[9] The visible signs of the map created a range of pressing concerns in mainstream white America, now forced to question if, in fact, the Mexican people were literally taking over the national landscape. A majority Mexican population meant that white America could no longer control Mexican culture by eating the occasional fast-food burrito at Taco Bell, nor could they walk the multicultural tightrope and "go native" by feasting upon "the authentic" at the Mexican restaurant on the other side of town. Instead, they had to deal with growing Mexican demographic numbers; now Mexicans lived everywhere. In this context, interestingly, *A Day without a Mexican* reveals how Mexicans themselves have engaged in asking questions about Mexican peoplehood at moments when their very existence has been scrutinized in the national public spheres, moments when their visibility becomes a concern in white America. *A Day without a Mexican* is trying to take control of the rhetoric in the public sphere that, like the symbolic fog in the film, surrounds the largest growing population in the United States, Mexicans.[10]

Indeed, the film's leitmotif of Mexican disappearance and invisibility is ironically embedded in the visual subtext of the 2000 census maps. In the census's cartographic elaboration of the Mexican population residing on U.S. territory lurks something that this map elides and naturalizes in its representations: the emplacement of Mexicans and the historical and cultural location of their collective bodies in what is now the United States. For in its representation of the present and future place that Mexicans will hold in the United States, the map temporally locates Mexicans within the here and now of the body politic; the "browning of America" is a contemporary phenomenon. Buried under the landscape, however, lies the transcontinental period of expansion that led to the U.S.-Mexico

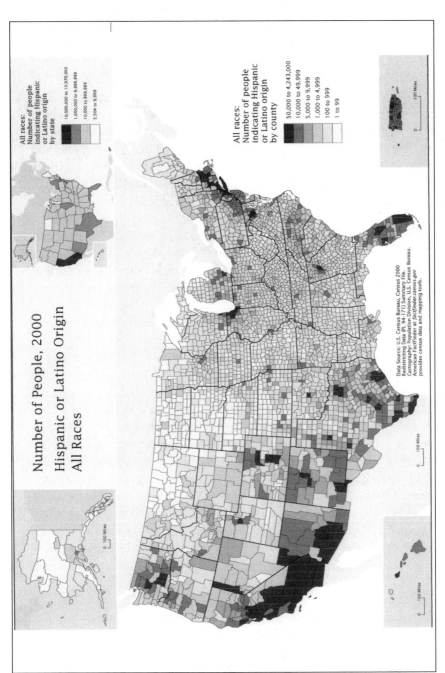

Figure 2. "United States Census Map of Latino Population 2000," in *Mapping Census 2000: The Geography of U.S. Diversity*

War of 1846–1848 and to the signing of the Treaty of Guadalupe Hidalgo in 1848, which, in theory, constituted Mexicans as Mexican Americans, seceded millions of acres of lands, and (re)defined the borders of all U.S. maps thereafter.

In fact, Arau was aware of the historical and geopolitical amnesia that led to the invisibility of the Mexican people in the United States. In September, he released yet another controversial ad campaign that stated: "On September 17th, Mexicans will be leaving Austin, Texas, Florida, and Colorado." This second installment of the ad expanded to all areas where Mexican population numbers were growing. The ad spread its symbolism across the country and countered the expansionist ideology that white America used to incorporate and colonize in the nineteenth century. As the film spread from theater to theater, Arau hoped to raise historical awareness about the place of Mexicans in the U.S. political culture since the nineteenth century—that Mexicans have indeed been part of the United States since its inception as a nation.[11] Arau is aware that the historical amnesia of Mexicans in the United States has contributed to their modern disappearance.

It is not entirely surprising that one of the first documents to "incorporate" the Mexican population of the United States[12] and to perpetuate an expansionist rhetoric in the public spheres is another census atlas, the Walker Atlas of 1870 (Figure 3), which was based on the first major U.S. census after the U.S.-Mexico War. Published in the "American Progress" section of the atlas, this map is particularly important in U.S. history because it is the first to visually and demographically mark the Manifest Destiny of a country that found progress through the geographic expansion of democracy. But, again, something is missing in the map. The west is unpopulated; it is space, not place, it is terra incognita.[13] In the nineteenth century, Mexican and Native American bodies are invisible; therefore, they do not mark a color on the landscape of the map. At the time the Walker Atlas was drawn up, Mexicans were not full citizens; they were represented in public culture as "semicivilized" subjects of the state (Almaguer 3–9). Of course, the problem with this is that at the time the United States commissioned the map there were nearly 175,000 Mexicans in the southwest, and by 1900 there were nearly half a million. In the end, progress must elide both the genocide of Native Americans and the imperial acquisition of Mexican lands.

This book begins with a contemporary story of Mexican peoplehood to show that the cultural and political history of Mexican invisibility in

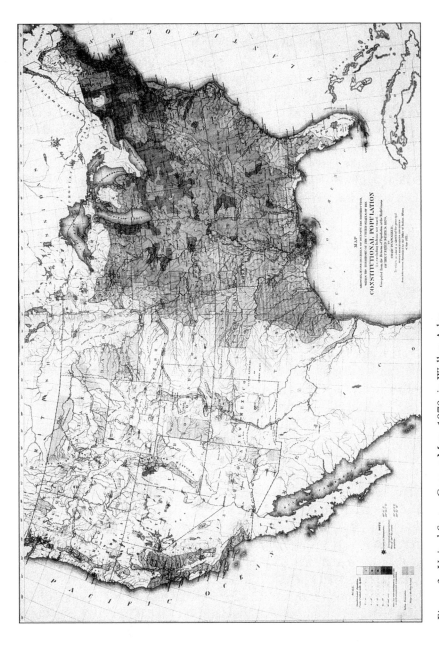

Figure 3. United States Census Map, 1870, in Walker Atlas

the United States finds its impetus in the ambivalent political and racial inquest that emerged in nineteenth-century public spheres; this debate concerned the early incorporation of Mexican people into the democratic nation-state. I use the subjugated knowledge of the maps to draw an atlas of Mexican political peoplehood in the United States—a geography that recovers a new history of Mexican America that begins in the nineteenth century. In this way, I propose to remap and explore how Mexicans first entered the political landscape now defined as the United States, and then how Mexicans in the United States would forever change its prevailing national narratives through their stories of peoplehood. Arau's film works as a springboard for this "topospatial" cultural history, which encompasses the cultural emergence of Mexicans in the United States and their asymmetrical and at times invisible relationship to the constitution of the U.S. body politic (Saldívar, *Border Matters* 79).[14] This is a story of their lived experience within the natural landscape and their search for place and belonging through what I call "stories of peoplehood."

Since the early years of American expansionism—not coincidentally the period when the very notion of "We, the People" was such a contested term—stories of Mexican peoplehood have engaged democratic statecraft. By locating representative stories of Mexican peoplehood, I recover the bodies that lie buried within the landscape of the above maps, unearthing their histories. Despite their ambivalent position in U.S. culture, Mexicans were always on the western map, fighting invisibility and creating a literary and cultural history. I follow feminist political philosopher Catherine Holland and Latino cultural critic Kirsten Silva Gruesz and ask: How is the figurative past sustained within the political present? How does the figural past operate, and by what mechanism does the past come to be elided or erased even as it is reconstructed within the American political imagination (Holland 2–6)? According to Gruesz, this allows us to theorize "a new relationship between the past, present and future that avoids the pitfalls of both an antiquarian historicism and the denial of their past that is so visible in the present progressive focus of Latino peoples" (Gruesz, "Utopía Latina" 57).

My contention is that American public culture has asked a fundamental question of democracy that endures over the history of U.S. culture: What should the United States do about Mexicans, and what are their democratic rights and racial status in our democracy? Although this question may seem new to an American public that has only recently turned its attention to Mexican immigration, following the 2000 census and the release of Arau's film, this inquest is historically rooted in a long line of political thinking about U.S. democracy's understanding of itself as a sovereign nation-state, its transnational relationship to Mexico, and its capacity to incorporate Mexican people in the United States into the political landscape. This "Mexican Question"—what are the rights and status of Mexican people in U.S. democratic culture?—inevitably found its discursive roots in the geographic body of the nation itself: in the nation's geographic imagination. Buried within the rhetoric of this rather simple question, therefore, is a complicated inquiry into the relationship between America's geographic imagination as a (trans)continental empire and the political rights and racial status of Mexicans as an identifiable collective group who reside both within and outside the maps shown here. Deeply tied to the Mexican Question are two fundamental questions of U.S. democracy: Who is represented as American citizens, as an included people on U.S. soil, and what are the rights and status of collective minority groups that, in theory, became included in the body politic under colonial conditions?

The discursive roots of Arau's question began growing in the nineteenth century, when stories of Mexican peoplehood first appeared. Indeed, 150 years before Arau created his film, another Mexican looked at the California landscape and began an inquest into the invisibility of Mexican people in the legal spheres. Writing in the California newspaper *El clamor público* just seven years after the signing of the Treaty of Guadalupe Hidalgo in 1848, Californio, newspaper editor, and political philosopher Francisco P. Ramírez astutely questioned the new racial and political position that the Mexican people in the United States found themselves in:

The United States' conception of freedom is truly curious. This much-lauded freedom is imaginary. Civil Freedom is the right that links all citizens to society so that they can do as they please when it is not to the contrary of the established laws. But here in this fabulous country, he who robs or assassinates most is he who enjoys freedom. Certain people have no kind of freedom—this freedom, we say, is that which the courts deny to all individuals of color. It is enough that these institutions are unique in a country that tries to consume everything due to its "Manifest Destiny." . . . The latter is that which affects our Californian and Mexican population directly. They particularly distinguish us by the title Greasers. (Ramírez 109–110)

Sardonically addressing the foundational ideals of American democratic culture—"freedom," and the "right" to equality in U.S. civil society—Ramírez wrote that American democratic culture's "imaginary" presuppositions did not truly represent its Mexican constituents precisely because their connotations did not fully consider the materiality of the racial ideologies that developed from Manifest Destiny. For Ramírez, the racialization and political constitution of the "Californio" Mexican people developed because of the profound contradiction resulting from the geopolitical effects of "Manifest Destiny," which spatially affected the "rights" and the representations of Mexicans in the United States.[15] American democratic culture's belief in the expansive rhetoric of Manifest Destiny resulted in an irresolvable tension between European American stories of racial otherness and the modern political system of representative democracy that espouses universal freedom, equality, laws, and "natural" rights for all the nation's people. In this way, Ramírez was one of the first Mexican cultural workers to locate the inextricable contradiction between the United States' land hunger, the spatial logic of democracy, and the racialization of Mexicans as "individuals of color" who, by negation to the white *demos*, ultimately make up a collective political group (Ramírez 35; Honig 4–32).[16]

Contesting the founding sentiments of Thomas Jefferson, Thomas Paine, and John Adams, Ramírez's comments are located in a long line of political thinking about democracy's ability to include minority and racial subjects within a representative democracy that emerged through imperialist acquisitions.[17] However, unlike those political thinkers' desire to locate and normalize a white "virgin landscape" for a collective Anglo-American body politic, Ramírez revealed that democracy's expansive logic produces an internal contradiction when concerning the theoretical inclusion of bifurcated subjects (Mexican American) within a democratic nation-state, as political people who are both citizens and racial others. Ramírez emphatically noted that discourses of land expansionism like Manifest Destiny led to political and cultural representations of Mexicans as "greasers" who are "not fit for democracy."[18] What Ramírez captured in this and many of his editorials is that the cultural and political practices of representing Mexicans as racialized greasers were in fact central to the norms of U.S. democracy and the discursive ideal that defines its modern ethos, "We, the People."[19]

Ramírez's comments suggest that Mexicans are democracy's representative "other" precisely because of the racial logic of U.S. democracy and its desire to incorporate minorities according to asymmetrical relations. Here, then, it is worth unpacking the basic premises of democracy and the racial contours that define its "inclusive" logic. As many democratic theorists have argued, American democracy is a great political system of inclusion because it entails rule and representation by the *demos*, the people. In theory, democracy lives or dies on the premise that every person will have access to democratic norms and ideals such as citizenship, rights, freedom, and the law and that the state will represent and guarantee these interests. Although degrees of difference marked liberal or republican brands of American democracy in the nineteenth century, for both, a strong democracy develops through the state's ability to represent the democratic voice for all of its constituents and to guarantee rights. Democracy in America not only includes liberal ideals such as rights, freedom, and privacy of its people; it also presupposes a state that allows people to voice their rights, self-autonomy, freedom, and associations. Hence, the idea that U.S. democracy emerges through associations among the people implies a democracy that allows for the recognition of a given people in the first place and, as a people, critiques the state and enacts their rights of privacy and freedom through public sphere access.[20]

However, if the warrants of democracy entail political equality, representation, and freedom for its entire populace, the basic question of who represents "the people" in a founding American democratic phrase like "We, the People" is also ironically fundamental to its contradictory logic of inclusion. Does the majority group always rule, and, if so, how do racial ideologies inflect this normative question? These questions reveal that it is precisely the democratic constitution of "the people" that creates a tension within democracy's inclusive ideals. To be sure, the people of a democratic state are split into two distinct categories: that which the Greek language and Western political philosophy calls the *demos*—the collective universal group that stands as the norm of democratic rights—and the *ethnos*, the people as particular racial or ethnic types.[21] In early democracy, white propertied males represented the *demos*. The constituents of the U.S. *demos*, for example, were able to abstract themselves as a racial group by racializing others and thereby setting the white norm for democratic collectivity. The invisibility of a racial category defined by whiteness was ironically the desire of the *demos*. Whiteness came to stand in for the collective ideal of the people. The natural rights of the ruling *demos*, it would seem, were the only portion of the body politic presupposed to have the correct type of body, a white body. To this end, upper-class white Americans became the only people who had the "right" to foster and become the enlightened subjects of stories of "American" peoplehood. As Étienne Balibar points out in his recent work on democracy, the discursive dynamics of this "double-faced construction" of the people—the *ethnos/demos* split—is essential in our understanding of the democratic making of people, public spheres, borders, liberalsm, and the dichotomy between racial and political subjects. Without it, one cannot fully ascertain how this dual construction of the "people" has created an internal logic of exclusion that lies buried within the politics of people-making in democratic culture. The double-faced constitution of the people results in a tension between a universal notion of the people that make up the majority of the population, and whose ideals define the rhetorical parameters of democracy, and a racialized and invisible people whose particular interests are in the minority and relegated to the private.[22]

Charles Taylor's recent look at democratic inclusion and exclusion in the United States reveals a similar dichotomy in democratic culture. Turning theories of democracy on their head, he argues that democracy is inclusive because it is founded on the representation of a common people—the *demos*—but, paradoxically, this is also the reason that democracy leans toward exclusion.[23] Exclusion, he argues, is a by-product of the need in self-governing societies for a high degree of collective cohesion. Despite the multicultural heterogeneity of the United States, the democratic state that has emerged ironically desires a common identity to maintain its union and works to incorporate all subjects under the universal ideal of "the people." This begs the question of whether the race/democracy and *ethnos/demos* contradiction can ever be disentangled. For if the exclusion of the collective *ethnos* is a founding dynamic of democratic peoplehood, is democracy's relationship to racial otherness bound to reinscribe hegemony as long as the liberal state must incorporate minority individuals? The stories of Mexican peoplehood in this book represent and, at times, contest this contradictory logic of democratic incorporation.

Despite these points about America's racial democracy, Ramírez's critique of the United States does not conclude by arguing that democracy should be abolished as a political system. Rather, he believes that the United States has not lived up to the true ideals of freedom, rights, and civil society. The state, he concludes, does not fairly represent Mexicans; they are greasers incapable of normalizing themselves according to the ideals presupposed by the white American *demos*. Ironically, Ramírez argues for more democracy and fair representation, and he believes the United States should uphold its liberal promise of equal protection under the Treaty of Guadalupe Hidalgo of 1848. Ramírez is representative of a number of Mexican cultural workers in this study who create stories of peoplehood in order to show both U.S. democracy's hegemonic founding and its libratory potential for Mexican America. In effect, they look to democracy as a constitutive element in their story of peoplehood in order to remake it for a better collective Mexican existence in the United States. In this way, Mexicans are drawn to the possibilities of structurally and affectively transforming the founding notions of democracy into an expressive and empowering collective self-fashioning form of political, racial, and gendered representation.

Take, for example, Alonso S. Pereles, a founding member of an early civil rights organization, the Order of the Sons of America. His story of Mexican peoplehood, "The Evolution of Mexican Americans," first presented to a Mexican public in 1923, argues:

> We Mexicans should take more of an interest in our government. Ours is a republican government, and in the words of the great president Lincoln, "a government of the people, by the people and for the people." . . . No one person in whose veins flow blood from another race that makes up this nation has the right—even if he does have the audacity—to will us that we are not "one hundred percent Americans."
>
> As I have already said, based on ethnicity, history and geography, nobody—except for the pure blooded Indian—has more right than we, the descendents of Hidalgo and Cuauhtémoc, to call themselves one hundred percent American. (Quoted in Kanellos 155)

Reinscribing foundational elements of democratic peoplehood, Pereles emphatically concludes that since Mexicans in the United States are "the descendants of the Mexican revolutionary Hidalgo and Aztec emperor Cuauhtémoc," then the United States should bestow on them the rights of democracy, facilitating their evolution as one of the "people" to whom, Pereles argues, President Lincoln refers in his works (quoted in Kanellos 156). What I find so interesting here is that Pereles recovers the historical ancestors and history of the Mexican people in order to meld them to the symbolically universal democratic language of Lincoln. His work, therefore, reveals the complex political and cultural negotiations that Mexicans struggled with in creating stories of peoplehood that paradoxically merged the *ethnos* history of the Mexican people, what Perales referred to as "mestizaje," with the universal ideal and norms of a white *demos* (quoted in Kanellos 156). This reconstitution of democratic peoplehood, he hopes, will end the racial inequality that Mexicans have endured for decades. In the end, Perales argues that Mexicans must all learn about their new political system, democracy, for it is the "evolutionary" means to their future equality and justice as a collective. According to Perales, the collectivity presupposed on Enlightenment ideals and norms can ironically work for Mexicans. Despite the contradictions it creates for Mexicans in the United States, his story of peoplehood is nevertheless radically different from those the party of Lincoln espoused; it recognizes the ancestry and *mestizaje* of the Aztecs in order to reimagine the very idea of white democratic peoplehood in the United States.

In this volume, *The Emergence of Mexican America*, I uncover a range of varied cultural forms by and about Mexicans in the United States from 1821 to 1939. Included are representative stories that emerged in liminal moments when debates arose around the meaning of white American peoplehood and subsequently affected the constitution of Mexican peoplehood itself. The book maps the beginnings of U.S. expansion into Mexico and the imperial wake this caused for Mexicans and European Americans in the decades up to 1939. I begin with the early transnational relationship between the United States and Mexico and the emergence of the Mexican nation-state in 1821—a period of profound importance to modern Mexican peoplehood in the United States. I then chart the years surrounding the U.S.-Mexico War of 1846–1848 and the collective racialization of Mexicans; explain the importance of the Reconstruction Era for Mexicans in the 1870s; study territorial consolidation in the southwest at the turn of the century; and end with the New Deal Era, the period when the United States repatriated over one million Mexicans in hopes that they would disappear from the democratic landscape.

By focusing on the early foundations of Mexican American peoplehood in the public spheres during these liminal moments, I hope to paint a more complicated portrait of today's NAFTA (North American Free Trade Agreement) era and what some are calling the "browning of America."[24] I do not examine moments from the nineteenth century to the early twentieth century in order to argue that the twentieth century is in binary opposition to the nineteenth;[25] in fact, it may actually be necessary to have certain sorts of preoccupations in the present in order to be able to understand certain aspects of the past. It may actually be advantageous at times not to approach the past with an open mind but to become interested in a particular historical problem because it is deeply tied to the past's present. In this way, although in this book I primarily map the early cultural formations of Mexican America, I look to these founding moments as a way to perhaps better understand the present condition of Mexicans in the United States. Through the study of cultural forms of Mexicans in the U.S. public spheres, in *The Emergence of Mexican America* I tell an untold story of the relationship between U.S. democratic and racial culture, one in which Mexicans question Yankee justice adjured upon them by appropriating or overturning democratic ideals and recovering space and lands in their stories of peoplehood in the U.S. public spheres.[26]

The public sphere, therefore, holds a particularly important location in my own story of the early emergence of the Mexican peoplehood. In his influential book *The Structural Transformation of the Public Sphere,* Jürgen Habermas explores what the category of "public" meant to Western bourgeois society and how its meanings and material operation were transformed in the centuries after its constitution (Calhoun, *Habermas and the Public Sphere* 5). In this historical study, Habermas sketches the eighteenth-century emergence of a zone of rational discourse in association with print, mediating between the monarchial state and the "lifeworlds" of society. He contends that over the course of the nineteenth and twentieth centuries, the various forms of capitalist mass media steadily undermined the autonomy of the public sphere.

Reconsidering the demise of this space in *Between Facts and Norms* and in *The Inclusion of the Other,* Habermas's public sphere is central in his latest philosophical works on democracy and culture's formative relation to the state. The public sphere, in Habermas's theories, remains as a zone between the law-making powers of the state (the sphere of public authority) and the essentially private pursuit of happiness by ordinary people. It is a space that allows for a more nuanced study of how power constitutes the subject and how citizen-subjects in fact become aware of their collectivity. Moreover, Habermas's work allows us to better understand the reciprocity between cultural forms and politics and how stories of peoplehood affect the meaning of "the public," in turn affecting modern notions of peoplehood, citizenship, and democracy itself. The relationship between stories of peoplehood and the state is fundamental to citizen-subjectivity and how individuals (either cultural workers or readers of culture) imagine their collectivity in a democracy and their places within it. As such, the public sphere becomes the space where stories of peoplehood emerge and through their circulation becomes the space in which individuals learn about their own democratic collectivity and, in fact, emerge as an imagined but nevertheless tangible collective.

Stories of peoplehood in the public spheres, therefore, have the potential not only to thematically represent democracy but also, as public discourse, to influence democratic norms that constitute individuals as subjects of a given people. They are an important element in the creation of a democracy, an organizing principle of democratic associative relations (*Transformation* 49; *Facts and Norms* 365). In this way, stories of peoplehood and democracy are developmentally linked and contingent on one another (Warner, *Letters of the Republic* 172). In this book, then, I posit a different relationship between cultural forms, land expansion, race, and democracy. In order to apprehend and analyze democracy, I argue that we must read it as an organizing political system that is foundational to the formation of a given people's "social imaginary" and thus study a historical range of cultural representations, racial dynamics, and material conditions that define democracy's contours in the public spheres.[27] In the end, I am proposing that the contradictions that develop between democracy, race, and the universal concept of "the people" are contingent on and develop from the ways in which a given group represents its interests through their cultural production.

Since the initial expansion of the U.S. public spheres during the 1830s, Mexicans in the United States who represent various political, gendered, and sexual locations have been actively engaged in questioning the tenets of peoplehood and, in doing so, have actively participated in questions of American statecraft. Through the cultural workers of this study, this book asks: What are the racial limits of democracy? How did America's Manifest Destiny affect its rise as a democratic nation? What are the geographic limits and possibilities of democratic inclusion and collectivity? How do enclosures of the land affect racial and political ontology and epistemology? What role does capitalism's accumulation of land have in the making of democratic subjects? What are the cultural rights of Mexicans in America, and how do they attain public inclusion and recognition in a land that sees race through a black/white veil? How do Mexicans come together as a political group within a land dominated by white Americans? What contradictions develop when Mexicans in the United States engage the Enlightenment ideals of democratic inclusion and peoplehood?

In the chapters that follow, I focus on varied cultural forms that exemplify moments when Mexicans in the United States engage the democratic public sphere, moments when the political landscape can no longer maintain its monocultural ideals of racial exclusion but are expanded by their competing stories of peoplehood in the public spheres. Certainly, in mapping one hundred years, I could not have included all of the founding moments and complexities of what I am calling stories of Mexican peoplehood. I do, however, read varied forms in order to render a fuller and more complicated picture of the stories of Mexican peoplehood that emerged in democratic culture. In doing so, I take as my focus a number of stories about Mexican peoplehood created by and about Mexicans: murals, art, travel writing, novels, film, short stories, poetry, music, history, theater, documentaries, magazines, economic tracts, political speeches and manifestos, legal cases, treaties, maps, advertisements, academic scholarship, and ethnographic studies.

In addition to focusing on Mexican stories of peoplehood that reveal the heterogeneity of the early formation of Mexican America, I also read Anglo-American stories of peoplehood that are concerned with the presence of Mexicans in the United States. In *The Emergence of Mexican America*, then, I am equally interested in the effects Mexicans have had on Anglo-Americans' social imaginary and their own understanding as themselves as *the* majority people in the United States. Central to my premise in this book, however, is that Anglo-Americans were not the only racial culture to constitute the political and geographic limits, as well as the possibilities, of early Mexican American peoplehood. Although Anglo-Americans played a part in the racial constitution of the political people now ethnically defined as "Hispanic," the first Mexicans to engage the public spheres in the United States reinvented their racial and political ontology and therefore refashioned the contours of Mexican peoplehood. I treat a range of texts created by Mexican and Anglo-Americans who locate their peoplehood according to different and at times antithetical regional, political, gendered, class, and racial ideologies. In many instances, I attempt to look at the struggles over the meaning of peoplehood, not only between Mexicans and Anglos but also between Mexicans themselves, showing that the rhetoric surrounding the meaning of Mexican peoplehood and their inclusion develops through disagreement, not consensus or homogeneous group politics.[28]

The varying meanings of Mexican peoplehood, however, emerge with and against the universal ideals and norms of U.S. democratic inclusion.

Let us not forget that Mexicans in the United States have always been racialized as political and cultural others. As a racial people in the United States, Mexicans have been lynched; have lived under the legislative laws of Jim Crow; have been classified as mongrels without natural rights and thereby deemed semicivilized, second-class citizens; have been represented as mestizos and greasers in the literary public spheres; and have been classified at times as ethnic and at other times as white. The complicated racialization of Mexicans lies at the heart of the political contradiction of Mexican peoplehood and the reason that it is impossible to locate a singular collective Mexican unconscious. I intend, rather, to study the poetics of Mexican peoplehood and the desires that certain cultural workers had when creating stories that helped facilitate a social imaginary for its given Mexican and Anglo public. To that end, this book is not a sociological study concerned with the formation of U.S. Mexican collectivity (if a scholar could ever do such a thing) but, rather, a study of representative stories that attempt to imagine political peoplehood in the U.S. public spheres, even if that collectivity is heterogeneous in Mexican America.

This being said, although I realize the complexity of locating a national and racial people, I use the phrase "Mexicans in the United States" to encompass the cultural workers of this study. This best allows me to address the complex geographic, political, and racial factors that led to the dynamic self-fashioning of modern Mexican peoplehood in the United States. One of the early cultural workers in the book was originally a Creole under Spanish colonial rule, then a Mexican, and later a Texan, but because he died before the Treaty of Guadalupe Hidalgo of 1848, he was never officially constituted as a "Mexican American." Even after the treaty, Mexicans were anything but "American," and many defined themselves according to regional variations, such as Tejano, Nuevomexicano, and Californio, or as *gente de razón* (people with reason). The political and racial term "Mexican American" was not used until the 1930s, during the consolidation of LULAC (the League of United Latin American Citizens), which I explore in chapter 5. Despite the varying self-fashioning terms and definitions used to encompass the Mexican population in the United States, the Mexicans of this study struggled with the very meaning of their peoplehood in order to counter the geopolitical ideologies that led to Juan Seguín writing in his 1858 memoirs that Mexicans were constituted as "foreigners in their native land" (102–122).

Chapter 1, "Don Zavala Goes to Washington: Translating U.S. Democracy," focuses on an incredibly important though entirely overlooked cultural leader, Lorenzo de Zavala (1788–1836). An influential Mexican intellectual and Texas's first vice president, a writer and ardent supporter of the democratization of Mexico, as well as the Anglo colonization of Texas, Zavala was instrumental in both the writing of the first Mexican constitution in 1824 and the constitution of the Texas Republic in the 1830s. I examine this complicated figure's engagement with the Enlightenment's political and cultural ideals of peoplehood through his travel narrative, *Viage de los Estados Unidos del Norte América (Journey to the United States of America)* (1834), and locate this work with and against his contemporaries who were also participant observers of American democracy, including Alexis de Tocqueville. Zavala stands as one of the first important mediating figures of U.S.-Mexican democratic cultural relations and reveals much about the early expansionist ideologies that would affect U.S.-Mexico relations and Mexican American peoplehood in the United States for the next century.

Chapter 2, "Inscribing Terra Incognita: The 'Mexican Question' in U.S. Print Culture," turns its gaze to Anglo-America and maps the emergence of the "Mexican Question" in public culture from the mid-nineteenth-century Manifest Destiny era to the turn of the twentieth century, a liminal period that marks the foundational transcontinental beginnings of American modernity and the racialization of Mexicans. I explore the moment when landscape, democracy, and the racialization of Mexicans became important in the U.S. public spheres. Tracing the relationship between territoriality and rights from the founding moment of American republican culture, I argue that this dynamic crystallizes with the emergence of American magazine and print culture, the expansionist ideology of Manifest Destiny, and the Mexican Question. Focusing on the Mexican Question in print culture reveals that this inquiry and the geopolitical logic of Manifest Destiny are developmentally linked and contingent on each other. In the end, I argue that the Anglo-American stories of Mexican peoplehood that first emerged in the national public spheres in the mid–nineteenth century would have a profound effect on the constitution of Mexican peoplehood and the stories they wrote in the United States for over a century.

Chapter 3, "Embodying Manifest Destiny: María Amparo Ruiz de Burton and the Color of Mexican Womanhood," recovers the first Mexican American woman to write English-language novels in the literary public spheres, María Amparo Ruiz de Burton. Her story of Mexican womanhood has given us a very important perspective into how Mexican women's bodies became associated with colonial conquest, universal rights discourses, and land expansionism. This chapter expands upon the last by locating her political novel, *Who Would Have Thought It?*, within the masculinist geographic knowledge and the expansionist rhetoric that gave rise to the "Mexican Question," as well as the contemporary inquiry into women's, African, and Native American peoplehood during the Reconstruction Era. This chapter argues that Ruiz's story of Mexican womanhood extends the first-wave feminist (and Ruiz contemporary) Victoria Woodhull's own understanding of the "new woman" and the republican norm of the public and private. Reading her works with and against the racial and gendered legal rhetoric of the Reconstruction Era, I argue that Ruiz recovers Mexican women's bodies through her novel in order to challenge U.S. representations of Mexican women that were so central to America's patriarchal social imaginary.

Chapter 4, "Claiming *Los Bilitos*: Miguel Antonio Otero and the Fight for New Mexican Manhood," focuses on the first and only Mexican territorial governor of New Mexico (1897–1905), Miguel Antonio Otero (1856–1944), in order to study the tensions between U.S. territorial politics and the racial and masculine ideals that informed New Mexican peoplehood. Otero was a prolific writer, cartographer, and statesman, whose story of New Mexican manhood, *The Real Billy the Kid* (1939) was the first English-language biography written by a Mexican in the United States. The book renders a more complete portrait of the relationship between late-nineteenth- and early-twentieth-century territorial land politics, New Mexican manhood, and democratic inclusion. A political foe of the imperialist Theodore Roosevelt and a friend of the expansionist William McKinley, Otero was instrumental in New Mexico's quest for statehood and in Nuevomexicano citizens' role in America's transnational interventions in Cuba during the Spanish-American War. Otero's narrative resurrection of the dead outlaw Billy the Kid as a hero of *la gente de nueveomexico* reveals much about his own public role as a filibuster for New Mexico's statehood and the masculine norms that affected U.S. territorial politics.

Chapter 5, " 'Con su pluma en su mano': Américo Paredes and the Poetics of 'Mexican American' Peoplehood," explores Paredes' inquest into the stories of political organization that Mexicans and Anglos told during a tense period of geopolitical consolidation, the neocolonial period when Mexican radicalism gave way to the new liberal politics of the 1930s. Paredes' "Mexican Question"—What political route should Mexicans take in their collective struggles?—was paramount to his cultural work, and his inquiry reveals much about our present understandings of "brown radicalism" and Mexican liberal collectivity. Paredes' cultural work in the 1930s attempted to come to terms with the contradictory formation of Mexican peoplehood and the debates over its meaning in the United States. He explored and made visible the paradoxical logic of Mexican peoplehood, exploring the failed poetics of Mexican belonging and collectivity. The irony in his works is that, despite the fact that Paredes himself would be considered a leader of the Mexican people and most of his cultural production focused on Mexican peoplehood and collectivity, he was pessimistic about the logic of people-making itself.

The conclusion, "Recovering *La memoria*: Locating the Recent Past" ends where the first chapter begins, the contemporary moment, and signals the liminal possibilities of a transformation of the U.S.'s democratic understanding of itself as a universally white body politic. I end by locating the murals of Judy Baca and other stories of Mexican peoplehood within the historical amnesia of both conservative and neoliberal stories of peoplehood in the NAFTA-era public spheres. I question what this demographic change means for a historically white *demos* whose lands are increasingly becoming brown. Through these chapters I hope to examine important moments in the long history of Mexicans struggling over the discursive meaning of their peoplehood, stories that represent the founding contours of Mexican America.

1

Don Zavala Goes to Washington
Translating U.S. Democracy

Two things have caused me to write of this journey. The first is that I have believed that nothing can give more useful lessons in politics to my fellow citizens than the knowledge of the manners, customs, habits, and government of the United States, whose institutions they have so serviley copied. Secondly, since I offered in my Historical Essay to publish my memoirs, it is now time that I begin, although it may be in incoherent bits and pieces as circumstances permit.

Lorenzo de Zavala, Prologue to *Viage de los Estados Unidos del Norte América*, 1834; English translation in *Journey to the United States of America*, 2005

In 1830, the Mexican exile Lorenzo de Zavala made a historic journey to the United States. A product of this journey is an important, although little known, travel narrative, *Viage de los Estados Unidos del Norte América* (*Journey to the United States of America*), a meticulously written narrative about U.S. democratic cultures and institutions. Zavala's narrative stands as a major document of early Mexican letters in the United States, as well as one of the first theoretical and ethnographic examinations of democracy as a political and cultural institution. Thus, Zavala's book challenges the widespread acceptance by American scholars that Alexis de Tocqueville's *Democracy in America* (1835) is the first book to take United States democracy as a focus of political and cultural study.[1] With the inclusion of Zavala's narrative into the series called Recovering the U.S. Hispanic Literary Heritage Project, Zavala's story of democratic peoplehood will no doubt, in time, be read as one of the founding political texts of U.S. and Mexican democratic culture. As such, he should be placed alongside such political thinkers as Jefferson, Prieto, Hidalgo, Madison, Mill, and Tocqueville.

Equally important is that Zavala wrote his narrative to represent and participate in a story that he hoped would help in the creation of a liberal national identity for the Mexican people. Published in limited numbers in Paris in 1834 and posthumously for the first time in Mexico on the eve of the U.S.-Mexico War in 1846,[2] Zavala's book stands as one of the first texts to investigate the early relationship between not only the constitutions of Mexico and the United States but also of the two peoples themselves. Standing as a cultural mediator between the two, Zavala was fostering comprehension of the foundations of Mexican and American democratic peoplehood during the years that led up to the U.S.-Mexico War of 1846–1848. Indeed, Zavala's text renders a complicated portrait of U.S.-Mexico relations and the colonial contact between the two nation-states that began in 1821–1824—the monumental period when the colonized people of Mexico broke away from Spanish despotism and created a national, democratic constitution under the United States' imperial gaze at Mexican lands to the west.

Zavala's narrative, therefore, extends our modern understanding that narratives of Chicano peoplehood begin with the conquest of 1846 and the U.S.-Mexico War.[3] As Carl Gutiérrez-Jones argues, Chicano historians assert that Mexican American communities grew out of the signing of the Treaty of Guadalupe Hidalgo in 1848, which ended President James Polk's aggressive expansion into Mexico.[4] Juan Gómez-Quiñones argues that this document and this year would mark the liminal moment when the racialization of Mexicans that occurred in the language of the treaty would lead to a distinct minority collective consciousness.[5] Gómez-Quiñones' and Gutiérrez-Jones's arguments lead me to explore the cultural forms in the public sphere that historically led to the racialization of the Mexican people. However, I think we also need to consider the seeds of imperialism that led to the war, the U.S.-Mexico War, and the collective self-understanding of Mexicans as a racialized and bifurcated minority people in the United States. According to historian Emma Pérez, although the Treaty of Guadalupe Hidalgo in 1848 is an extremely important marker for understanding the racial and political constitution of Mexican American peoplehood, the reliance on 1848 as a liminal marker for the sole emergence of Chicano identity inevitably conflates the Mexican and U.S. period between the years 1821–1836 and does not consider the historical significance of this period and how these fifteen years set the stage for the U.S.-Mexico War, the Treaty of Guadalupe Hidalgo, and Mexican American political subjectivity (E. Pérez 8).

It was during these years that Mexico emerged as a nation by breaking away from more than three hundred years of Spanish colonial rule, wrote a democratic constitution modeled on the liberal and federalist traditions of the Enlightenment, and began to feel the effects of the expansionist U.S. policies of the Monroe Doctrine that the United States guised as democratic protectionism. This colonial and imperialist background in U.S.-Mexico relations was the foundation for the politically constituted Mexican Americans who, Gómez-Quiñones argues, emerged in 1848. Gilbert González and Raúl Fernández point out that we need to historicize the period prior to 1848 in order to account for the complicated and contradictory manner in which Mexicans in the United States imagined their political, racial, and economic identity (González and Fernández 1–23). The Monroe Doctrine's neocolonial rhetoric and the contemporaneous constitution of the nation of Mexico, written in 1824, had a great influence on how Mexican Americans and Chicanos would later imagine their social imaginary and democratic collectivity, as well as on how Anglo-Americans would racialize Mexicans and Mexican Americans.[6] Zavala's *Journey* stands as a representative cultural text of this early and dynamic period in American and Mexican histories and renders a more complete and complicated portrait of the contradictory but interconnected making of the Mexican national, the United States Anglo-American, and the bifurcated people who are now defined as "Mexican Americans."

As one of the principal architects of the Mexican Constitution of 1824, Zavala argued that the U.S. Constitution and its liberal principles could be translated to the people of Mexico, who had just emerged from Spanish colonialism. In part, then, Zavala's *Journey* is a panegyric look at U.S. democracy, a utopian primer of liberal democratic mores. Indeed, as the epigraph to this chapter indicates, Zavala's interest lies in both the government and manners of the United States precisely because he feels they serve as representative examples of democracy. Through a travel narrative that reads like an ethnography of democratic mores and governance, he attempts to render a detailed portrait of the United States for a newly constituted Mexican people, one that he feels has not yet fully fostered the manners, norms, and ideals to sustain a democratic political system. For the liberal Zavala, U.S. democracy and its norms and ideals are the cornerstone of individual Enlightenment, political autonomy, and cultural organization.

And yet, an adverb in this opening paragraph of the *Journey* deeply contradicts the panegyric aspects of his travels, for he emphatically writes in a qualifying end clause that the Mexican people have "servilely" copied the democratic institutions of the United States. That Zavala conjures a word that connotes the "spirit of slavery" to describe the relationship that the newly formed democratic nation has with the United States undoubtedly reveals Zavala's own complicated understanding of U.S.-Mexican political and cultural relations in the early nineteenth century. As we know, slavery was a system of extreme personal and collective domination in which a slave had no relationship that achieved legal or political rights or recognition other than with the master. In other words, slavery was an institution that prevented the emergence of autonomous and liberal political peoplehood precisely because the representation of the people, the *demos*, was the normalized white colonial master. As I discuss in the following pages, Zavala's reference to "the spirit of slavery" to describe U.S.-Mexico relations serves as the narrative's political leitmotif and speaks to the contradictory rhetoric that emerged in the wake of the Monroe Doctrine of 1823, a document that awakened the United States' own "spirit of slavery" toward Mexico.

From the above quote we can infer two interrelated yet contradictory logics that inform Zavala's travel narrative: on the one hand, it is a call for the making and establishing of a collective Mexican peoplehood that develops from his utopian representations of the mores and liberal governance of U.S. democracy; on the other hand, he qualifies his story by insinuating that Mexicans should not form their peoplehood with the "spirit of slaves," as imitative subjects who have become dependent on U.S. institutions. In this, Zavala's *Journey* reveals a contradiction that develops from both a desire to erase the legacy of Spanish colonialism and a desire to build a liberal Mexican state ironically based on an emerging American empire that coveted Mexico's lands.

It is this contradiction concerning the modeling of U.S. democracy—Zavala's translating of its norms and liberal ideals in his travel narrative for both the democratic constitution and colonial emancipation of Mexican peoplehood—that I take as the departing point for my own journey into the related colonial and democratic contradictions of Mexican and U.S. people-making that develops in the pages of the *Journey*. Buried within the representational subtext of his travel narrative of U.S. democracy lies the contradictory logic that presupposes the Enlightenment's universal, colonial, and racial legacy that has underwritten Mexican national and then, after the Treaty of Guadalupe Hidalgo, Mexican American people-making.

Zavala's journey to translate the manners, norms, and ideas of U.S. democracy for Mexican Enlightenment presents us with a way to reexamine what Mary Louis Pratt refers to as the "transcultural" logic of travel narratives. For Pratt, travel narratives enact an ethnographic function of "transculturalization," which is the process whereby subordinate or marginal groups select and invent materials transmitted to them by a dominant or metropolitan culture (1–11). Transculturalization occurs within the narrative and historical space of colonial encounters, a public space in which people who are geographically and politically separate come into contact with each other and establish ongoing relations, usually under conditions of coercion, racialization, radical inequality, and intractable conflict. Transculturalization is what occurs in the contact zone, or "colonial frontier of the Southwest," for it is in this space where political peoples constitute one another, although this subjectification is usually asymmetrical (Pratt 6). My contention is that we need to look at the narrative act of transculturalization not simply as a by-product of nationalism but, rather, as the core cultural logic of democracy. For it is through acts of transculturalization that democratic knowledge and peoplehood emerge. However, because this occurs through asymmetrical and colonial relations, the emergence creates a democratic ideal of peoplehood that is based on colonial presuppositions and radical inequality. Understanding democracy as a political system that emerges from colonial relations, as well as from legislative and political doctrines, lets us understand that the democratization of people develops through a process in which the metropolitan center of colonial power bestows "enlightenment" and political norms on another colonized country.

This idea of transculturalization renders for us a very complicated and succinct portrait of the cultural and political function of Zavala's travel narrative in his attempts to forge a Mexican nation. According to political philosopher Rogers Smith's recent look at the foundational role that narrative plays in the emergence of a political collectivity, "stories of peoplehood" are narratives that constitute a given group as a political and organized body, an autonomous collective democratic people (*Stories of Peoplehood* 8–9). In effect, Smith is trying to locate the embedded constitutive stories (cultural forms) that enable the social imaginary, which are cultural ways of creating and understanding peoplehood, to become collective entities themselves, mediating collective life. In Zavala's story of peoplehood, the idea of a "national people" is a paradigm of the modern social imaginary. As Dilip Parameshwar Gaonkar and Benjamin Lee argue, a nation's distinctive features include its representation as "we"; its transparency between individual and collectivity; its agential subjectivity, in which a people acts in time; its unfolding in progressive history; and its posited environment of mutuality with other national peoples (5).

Zavala's story of peoplehood is complicated in that its presupposes a complex transnational matrix of democracy and colonialism—informed by the legacy of imperial Spain, the emerging nation of Mexico, and, most immediately, the United States' expansionist gaze toward Mexico. What further complicates Zavala's narrative is that it is written in a complex period of Mexican and American nation-building, a period when the emergence of both nations is interrelated. In the 1830s, Mexico and the United States were both in the early foundations of their respective nations and struggling to find a collective political identity. Mexico was a newly formed nation that within a decade had gained its independence from Spain and created a democratic constitution. The United States in 1834 had been a democratic nation for only forty-six years, after the states had ratified the Constitution in 1788. However, the process of nation-building for the United States was by no means complete. In fact, it was only in the 1830s that the United States would begin to promote its "Manifest Destiny" as a nation with stories of peoplehood that would help (re)define its national borders; its expansionist rhetoric, in fact, justified and motivated the conquest and colonization of Mexican and Native American lands.

Within this complex matrix of nation-building, Zavala first attempts to create a national "we" in "We the people of Mexico," only to find himself thereafter living in exile in Paris and then Texas, trying to come to terms with his own transnational search for peoplehood. Zavala's *Journey* is a story of peoplehood that attempts to resolve the contradictions of creating a national people that emerged from Spanish colonialism only to find Mexico in an asymmetric relationship with a Jacksonian America forging its own story of peoplehood by expanding into Mexico's borders and Texas. Zavala's *Journey* illustrates his contradictory desire for the creation of Mexican and then Texan peoplehood in the wake of imperialism and his own contradictory colonial social imaginary.

The Spectacle of Lorenzo de Zavala

One of the most revealing instances of Zavala's own social imaginary and his motivations to look at the spectacle of U.S. democracy is the following quote:

> I was leaving the anarchy of Mexico where I had seen myself so often exposed to being the victim of parties. . . . Oh Niagara! With my eyes fixed upon your swift currents, they seemed to indicate that I was completely engrossed in the grandiose spectacle, I was seeing in you the most melancholy representation of our disastrous revolutions. I was reading in the succession of your waves the generations that hasten on to eternity, and in the cataracts that proceed to your abyss the strength of some men that impels others to succeed them in their places. (*Journey* 57)

Leaving the unrest of a newly formed Mexican nation, Zavala ponders the spectacle of Niagara Falls and sees Mexico's "disastrous revolution" and his own inability to succeed as a liberal statesman in the country he ironically helped to free from the despotism of imperial Spain. Zavala's personal reminiscence of Mexico while looking at the natural spectacle of the United States is paradigmatic of his own journey toward Mexican selfhood in his travels. Indeed, as he notes, Zavala wrote his travel narrative, in part, as a personal memoir, the autobiographical self-fashioning of a Mexican political statesman. It is worth detailing the autobiographical self he creates in this collective story of Mexican peoplehood, for both are constructed through the journey and descriptions of the mores and governance of the United States.

Zavala's travel narrative presents us with a bifurcated spectator whose experiences in the United States are "transferred" to the newly constituted Mexican self that has emerged from imperial Spain, thus converting the journey to a mode of both individual and collective introspection. Here we have, in part, a narrative where the inner and outer historical worlds collide from the legacy of Spanish colonialism. This collision is complicated by Zavala's national and cultural subjectivity as part of the still unsolidified collectivity of Mexico and the outer United States world he observes in his travels. Zavala's complicated "self-interrogation" finds its impetus through what Pratt refers to as the intersubjective logic of travel narratives, which are mediated through the colonial worlds the subject is viewing. For Pratt, these "autoethnograhic expressions" are instances in which colonized subjects undertake to represent themselves in ways that engage with the colonizer's own terms (7, 9, 102). In the case of Zavala, his *Journey* can be read as an autoethnographic story of peoplehood that responds to or engages in dialogue with the U.S. metropolitan political institution of democracy.

Nevertheless, Pratt's notion of autoethnography does not neatly fit the political and cultural figure of Lorenzo de Zavala. Although I began this section by pointing out that Zavala is trying to come to terms with the "spirit of slavery" that underpins Mexico's relations with the United States, I am not willing to label Zavala a colonial subject *of* the United States, at least not in his own eyes or in a strict postcolonial sense. Indeed, before he began to self-fashion himself as a Mexican politico in the United States, under Spanish colonial rule, he was a Creole. As Ralph Bauer argues in *The Cultural Geography of Colonial American Literatures*, Creoles occupied an "ambiguous" political space, neither colonized nor colonizers but, rather, colonials who often stood apart from the geopolitical interests of the Spanish imperial metropolis (15–23). What the complicated figure of Zavala represents is an ambivalent Mexican self-fashioning that develops first under the rule of imperial Spain as a Creole, a subjectivity that would affect the writing of his *Journey*.

When Zavala was born in Yucatan in 1788, Mexico (New Spain) was under Spanish rule, and the Gachupines—the immigrant Spaniards, who were the representatives of the crown in New Spain, were in political control. Under Spanish rule, only the elite Spanish-born immigrants were able to hold any significant political office. The remainder of the population of New Spain was composed of Creoles like Zavala, who was a third-generation Yucatecan. Under Spanish colonial rule, the Gachupines controlled the economy, education, and the Roman Catholic Church. Although Zavala attended school, the Spanish colonial ideologies discriminated against Creoles, and inequality affected their ascendance in the political and religious hierarchy. Creoles like Zavala, however, desired to improve their conditions. Having no political ties to Spain, the Creoles considered New Spain their homeland and saw the people inhabiting the provinces as their compatriots. The Spanish monarchy and the Gachupines considered Creoles subjects of the crown whom they exploited and racialized for political control and for the crown's economic gain. Moreover, Creoles like Zavala did not share the conviction that the Gachupines should remain as the sole representatives of a Mexican people who were struggling for their own autonomy from Spain; they were people who found themselves creating a social imaginary tied to Mexican lands rather than to Spain. In this way, the Creole collective self-concepts that emerged in New Spain threatened the crown's dominance in the Americas.

The Spaniards viewed the Creoles, who had lived in New Spain for generations, in thoroughly negative terms. Indeed, a number of Spanish natural historians and ethnographers argued that the savagery of the lands affected the character and disposition of the Creoles in the New World. In other words, the Spanish were creating their own imperial stories of peoplehood that imagined the savage environment and the Indians who inhabited the lands as markers for collective Creole racialization (creolization). Creoles were collectively seen as a distinct racial type separate from the people who made up and represented the body of the Spanish King, Ferdinand VII (Bauer 129).

Growing up under the powerful racial ideologies of creolization, Zavala searched for a political philosophy that would help liberate the Creoles and facilitate the transfer of power from the metropolis to colonial New Spain. Spain, for Zavala, was a despotic imperial power, and in the *Journey* he often speaks of Spain as holding a tyrannical yoke over the people and inspiring terror. Zavala thought that only by separating from Spain and placing the control of the government in the hands of the people could the privilege of the clergy and the Gachupines be broken and the conditions of the natives be improved. Zavala would find the impetus for his anticolonial stance at an early age at the seminary in Mérida, where he taught himself French and English and read the important thinkers of the European and American Enlightenment. There, he began his lifelong studies of liberalism and democracy through the writings of Locke, Abbe Reynal, Rousseau, and Jefferson. Although critical of Rousseau's failed influence on France's government and revolution, Zavala found in Rousseau the worth of the liberal self and the idea that government should be based on the democratic consent of the people and should guarantee the rights of the citizen, not hinder them. At the onset of the Mexican independence movement in 1810, Zavala and other liberal thinkers in the Yucatán met weekly to debate the writings of Locke, Voltaire, and Rousseau. The Enlightenment and its political ethos, democracy, fueled the young Zavala's political and self-understanding and served as the basis for his political thought throughout his life. Most important, the Enlightenment provided the basis for Zavala's belief in the universal norms and ideals that underwrote the egalitarian formation of a liberal people and their pivotal role in the creation and maintenance of sovereign nations. Zavala felt that the idea of a free and autonomous people, with individual and collective rights, who were subject to each other,was fundamental to the emergence of a new Mexican state. He spent his life trying to create a state that guaranteed the rights of the people. Zavala's belief in a liberal state was antithetical to the Spanish monarchy and the colonialism that created people as subjects and objects of the crown, rather than enlightened free thinkers with individual rights and autonomy.

Zavala defined himself as a liberal thinker, circulated his ideas about democratic governance, and critiqued Spanish colonialism through the creation of one of the most powerful democratic institutions, the newspaper. In 1813, he was a principal editor for *El aristarco,* which he felt would "for the first time [bring] liberty and equality" to Mexico (Zavala, *Ensayo* 123). He also founded and edited *El redactor meridiano* (The Mérida compiler) and *El filósofo meridiano* (The Mérida philosopher). Zavala believed that newspapers were central to the dissemination of liberal democratic ideals and the perfect discursive medium in which to critique the Spanish crown. For Zavala, newspapers were the cornerstones of democracy. In this way, Zavala was one of the first Mexican cultural workers to create and maintain the public spheres within the Yucatán Spanish colony and Mexico City, for his newspapers were extremely important in influencing and disseminating democratic knowledge and Creole collectivity in various parts of Mexico (Cleaves 5–12). Indeed, on numerous occasions Zavala points out in the *Journey* the direct correlation between newspapers and the "emancipation" of Mexicans from servitude under Spanish colonialism. For Zavala, popular sovereignty, liberalism, and freedom were directly related to the public circulation of thought and criticism. And the newspaper was the form of publicity that could help promote and maintain citizenship (*Ensayo* 88). It is worth noting that Zavala's creation of newspapers and their facilitation of critical public spheres in colonial Mexico reveal that the emergence of "the public sphere" was not isolated to Europe, as Jürgen Habermas has argued in his influential book, *The Structural Transformation of the Public Sphere* (24–41). Moreover, it further reveals that public spheres and stories of peoplehood can emerge within the ideological constrictions of colonialism. Despite the colonial power of Spain, however, from the beginning Zavala was actively writing stories of peoplehood on behalf of the creation and maintenance of Mexican democracy.

Because of his political treatises and indictments of the Spanish crown in his newspapers, Zavala was imprisoned in 1814. He spent three years in the dismal and partly submarine vaults of the old fort San Juan de Ulúa. Despite his incarceration, he was able to smuggle books in, and he continued his work on political philosophy, natural science, history, and geography and trained himself as a medical doctor. It was also here that he initiated a secret Masonic lodge through which to form political alliances. Zavala's time in jail did little to change his political beliefs. After his release in 1817, Zavala continued to publicly criticize the Spanish crown and fight for the independence of Mexico. He joined and took a leading role in numerous political organizations and societies to forge the Mexican independence movement from 1810 to 1821. During these years, Zavala became a principal thinker and revolutionary and was chosen as one of the delegates to draft a statement of demands of the colonies on the Spanish crown. Once Mexican independence arrived with the Plan de Iguala, in 1821, Zavala was elected to the first Mexican Congress as one of its "founding fathers."

As a principal architect of the Mexican constitution, Zavala fought vehemently against a monarchical and centralized government. Convinced that a liberal and federalist state would best serve the Mexican people and would allow for equality among all of its inhabitants, he was one of the few Creoles who championed property rights for the indigenous peoples of Mexico and of mestizo rights in general. He was also one of the chief proponents against slavery and fought vehemently to exclude that institution from the new nation and its constitution (Cleaves 32–69). After participating successfully in the creation of a national constitution, Zavala was made a state representative and later the governor of the state of Mexico. He helped create the first public libraries in Mexico and its national bank, and he helped reform public education for all of Mexico's citizens. He also took measures in alleviating the new nation's national debt.

Despite his foundational work on the Mexican constitution, public education, and the sovereignty of the Mexican people, in the end Zavala would never live in a Mexican democratic republic. Because of the strong centralized factions in Mexico City, which were still influenced by the Spanish crown, the Catholic Church, and the Gachupines, Zavala was labeled a liberal reformer and exiled in 1833, when Santa Anna assumed the presidency through a coup d'état (Cleaves 74). Because of his belief in the Enlightenment and liberalism, Zavala specifically rejected the legacy of Spanish colonialism that the centralists maintained. The centralists praised the reform-minded Bourbon administration of the Spanish colonies before independence and emphasized a strong central government (Camp 23–50). They were also not fully behind liberal reforms and Zavala's idea of the state, for his ideals ran contrary to the postcolonial absolutist government. The centralists favored a strong executive because, they argued, it would follow naturally after centuries of authoritarian colonial rule. They also felt that the Catholic Church should play a major part in government.[7]

Zavala and the liberals, in contrast, wanted a much more definitive separation of church and state. Indeed, Zavala often argues in the *Journey* that religion is antithetical to true democratic peoplehood and that Catholicism, in particular, was the primary obstacle of true democratic reform in Mexico following its independence. In many ways, Zavala's political philosophy was ironically not much different from that of Andrew Jackson, whom he admired and would meet while in the United States. Like Jackson, Zavala found the operations of political and religious authority crippling, not enlivening, the talents of the people. As a critic of a colonial system that stifled the potential of the people, Zavala followed Jackson's republican belief in a diffused government, where the nation emerged and maintained its collectivity through the people themselves.

Zavala's beliefs in a strong and secular democratic state composed of a people bestowed with natural rights under a republican-inspired, federalist government clashed bitterly with the centralist's absolutist ideals of political governance. When General Anastasio Bustamante gained power in late 1829, Zavala's political career as a Mexican liberal leader changed drastically. Zavala begins his *Journey* by writing that the Bustamante regime and a centralist-controlled newspaper had labeled him a traitor, declaring that his liberal ideals had led the nation "to the brink" of self-destruction. Moreover, because of his leadership in a liberal revolt in 1828 against the centralists, started at the Acordada prison and followed by days of riots and looting of Gachupín businesses, as well as by President Manuel Gómez Pedraza going into exile, Zavala became the object of hatred among the conservatives, who would later have the last word on his political leadership (Cleaves 86–87). When in 1830 Zavala's liberal associate, President Vicente Guerrero, was deposed, Zavala came under severe pressure from conservatives and, fearing for life and limb, went into exile forever, a bitterly defeated Mexican liberal who had lost the country that he felt he had built (Sierra 222–225).

Zavala's Utopian America

In 1830, Zavala left Vera Cruz, Mexico, in the schooner the *United States*. Although he left his homeland as a political refugee, Zavala traveled to the United States in hopes that his journey would help forge a democratic Mexico. He wished to create a distinct democratic Mexican peoplehood, one that could emerge from the despotic legacy of colonial Spain and the centralists who had led the nation back to political despotism. By representing the mores and governance of the American people, he believed he could establish a transcendent national model of state and peoplehood patterned after the United States. In doing so, Zavala's travel narrative employs a classical ethnographic element of the objective observer. But Zavala also remains the romantic political historian trying to relate a Mexican story that, to him, as yet had not been fully realized. He does this by employing and representing traditional concepts of the travel narrative itself, one that attempts to create an all-seeing and all-knowing spectator who is guided by the very Mexican people he is trying to serve. As he states in the prologue, the Mexican people are his "Maecenas, and they guide my steps through the United States" (3). Nevertheless, as much as Zavala's "Maecenas" guide his travels, the reader is always aware that Zavala's journey aims to be instructive, "and that the book be read with attention . . . that when you have finished it, you will have changed many of your ideas—not in prejudice to reason, nor even less to morality, nor to religion, whatever it may be, but in favor of them" (5). Addressing his implied Mexican audience, Zavala entices a public to repeat his experiences. What Zavala sees, the Mexican reader will see; what Zavala feels, the Mexican reader will feel—and, in doing so, the reader will become part of the very people he imagines in the narrative.

This act of bringing the public into his travels is unique, although contradictory, because Zavala envisions Mexican peoplehood by gazing on an imperialist country that had already begun to declare its design in the Americas at the expense of lands and peoples that had once been part of New Spain, including Florida and Louisiana—the American Republic was at the very doorstep of Mexico in its advance westward. As the first Mexican travel narrative to explore the United States,[8] Zavala's is in some ways antithetical to traditional European and American travel narratives. Travel writing from its generic inception had historically been used to undertake a nationalistic civilizing project and to project racial otherness. In such traditional narratives, the traveler "represents" terra incognita and the colonized subjects in the land visited to his white European audience in order to create and maintain difference and strangeness between the colonizer and colonized. By depicting and defining the primitive other and his environment, travel writers were able to (re)define their world as politically or culturally civilized and thereby to legitimate a range of political agendas. These stories of peoplehood would underwrite the political and cultural justification for expansion into a given region or country that the traveler defined as uncivilized and primitive. As such, travel writing, which was, in some cases, funded by metropolitan governments, was one of the first discursive institutions of empire-building and served to introduce and reinforce racial and political domination of the "mother country" and the colony.[9]

What makes Zavala's narrative so interesting is that his journey to the United States stands in stark contrast to the imperialist mission that has been traditionally associated with the European and American travel narratives to Mexico that were published after his work.[10] Zavala did not make his U.S. journey to implement an imperialist expansion into the United States. As stated above, Zavala looked to the United States in order to compare and contrast his own government and nation with the "modern" and still emerging nation to the north. Zavala's comparative project of peoplehood hinges on his consideration of the United States as a theoretical space, where he can question and explore the very logic of democracy. In this way, Zavala's journey is rooted in the Greek notion of *theoria*, which in classical political philosophy is associated with modes of seeing, such as journey, travel, spectacle, and observation.[11] Emerging as both political epistemology and cultural ontology, *theoria* is what enabled the production of individual and collective political knowledge through the cultural act of travel. A traveler's imagined journey to another cultural land and the political theory that develops from travel are interrelated. As political philosopher Sheldon Wolin argues, "*theorias* took the form of a story told by a traveler who has recently returned from a voyage" (34, 202–203). In these travels, he—the traveler is usually a "he" because he renders himself as a masculine vessel of the nation—journeys in order to represent the "foreign" space solely for the benefit of his country of origin. What is crucial about the Greek *theorias* is that many of these travel writings employ a story of political utopia. The traveler represents the foreign space as an ideal political community, and the writer attempts to identify the "foreign" people and environment as ideal. To an important degree, tis is different from the colonial presuppositions of later European travel narratives that represent the space of destination as uncivilized. Inevitably, these travel narratives construct the spaces as inferior in order to promulgate their own worldview of civility.

Employing early natural science and ethnographic devices of description, the largely embellished Greek narrative of a foreign space is both fiction and nonfiction, straddling both genres in order to create the perfect political state. As both an ethnographer and political philosopher, the narrator's function is to describe the conditions that make the given utopia possible. This enables the traveler to disseminate knowledge of the foreign country solely for the task of creating a collective peoplehood in the land of the traveler's origin.

An ardent student of the Greek travelers and political philosophers, Zavala imitated and enacted a *theoria* through his journey to the United States, a land where he could represent democracy as a utopian spectacle, one that could serve as a prescription for Mexico's postindependence troubles. It is important to note that Zavala's travel narrative reflects what the Mexican public sphere at the time was displaying about the American republic. Many of the newspapers saw the United States as a political model to which Mexicans should look for guidance.[12] An anonymous letter to *El sol*, for example, wrote that the United States was a stable system of government and harbored "virtuous" people. The letter concludes by noting that the Mexican view of the world had been obscured by Spanish colonialism and that an understanding of the United States would lead the Mexicans out of political ignorance (Brack 18). In addition to published letters, the popular newspaper *Gaceta de México* published hundreds of panegyric articles and editorials on the United States and even published the nationalistic works of Benjamin Franklin. The *Diario de México* went as far as serializing the U. S. Constitution, framing it as a model for Mexico's own democratic peoplehood (Brack 18; Hale 190–195).

Reflecting Mexico's fascination with the United States, Zavala enters the United States to do three things in his journey: to explain the political system and its people, to criticize the political system that he has left behind, and to posit a prescription that can lead the Mexicans to a fully realized democratic peoplehood. Zavala undertakes this task by emplotting a Jacksonian America that is, for the most part, full of democratic possibility. From New Orleans to Washington, D.C., Zavala meticulously describes the United States as a nation whose political institutions have evolved to a model state of progress:

If I were trying to produce a work that was a luxury item with engravings, I would have prepared immediately beautiful plates on which would be pictured steamboats, workmen leveling the land and laying planks of wood and iron to form roads, meadows bathed by streams, cities divided by navigable rivers, cities being born of the earth and dedicating themselves to improving it immediately, rooms filled with children of both sexes learning to read and write, workers and craftsmen with plow or instrument in one hand and the newspaper in the other, six thousand temples of diverse cults in which man raises his vows to the creator in accordance with the dictates of his heart, in short tranquility and abundance bringing happiness to fifteen million people. Such is the idea that I have of the United States of the North and the impressions that I received from New Orleans to Cincinnati. (63)

The above quote is not isolated. In each chapter, Zavala sets out to meticulously describe each U.S. city's history, geography, culture, and political institutions in such a way as to construct an ideal political community. The people of the United States, he finds, have no social or class distinctions, and the laws have been set up, for the most part, under the auspices of equality. He writes: "No law, no custom, no historical record exists in that country whose tendency would be to form an aristocratic class" (114). This stood in direct contrast to the Spanish colonial system that still exerted its hold on Mexico. Under Spanish colonialism, he argues: "There was an absolute separation between the conquerors and the conquered. The former had the wealth, privileges and the pleasure that provided the inclination and the tastes that they engendered" (86). Zavala argues that because of this Spanish colonial legacy, Mexico has legislated "exceptional laws: to perpetuate a privileged aristocracy that is antithetical to Republican ideals" (86).

In the United States, however, the stability of the American people and their institutions are the direct result of the dispersion of material prosperity and the ability for most Americans to hold private property. This, Zavala writes, allows for a democracy in which citizens participate in all matters of state formation. This democratic participation is based on a deliberative model where citizens are able to foster bourgeois identities and form public spheres through debate. Indeed, in the United States Zavala finds the formation of reasoned political spheres in every city, cultivated through the public circulation of legislation and political resolutions found in newspapers and broadsides. Moreover, reasoned discourse among the American people and their representatives has created a utopian political system, where discourse—not wars and revolutions—constitutes the people of the nation.

Zavala's panegyric, of course, was not unprecedented at the time. He was in many ways merely capturing the feeling that Americans themselves proclaimed in the 1830s. Indeed, Americans in the age of Jackson were defining their country and its government as utopian, unique among the nations of the world. Ralph Waldo Emerson represented this well when he wrote in his journals that the perpetuation of American government "will be a matter of deep congratulation to the human race; for the Utopian dreams which visionaries have pursued and sages exploded, will find their God to bestow upon United America" (2:323). As historian Daniel Feller argues, Americans in 1830 placed their faith in the beneficent workings of national self-interest. "In their thinking," he states, "liberty became the key to individual achievement and social advance. In the expansive space of the United States, people might at last reach their true potential" (2:8). The United States' utopian mission found its ultimate expression in the Age of Jackson. Indeed, Daniel Webster prophetically stated to a large audience at Bunker Hill: "Let our age be the age of improvement. . . . Let us develop the resources of our land, call forth its powers, build up its institutions, promote all its great interests, and see whether we also in our day and generation, may not perform something to be remembered" (2:34). The United States' nationalist rhetoric appealed to Zavala's own nationalist desires for Mexico. Moreover, as someone still fighting the political legacy of colonial Spain, Zavala found it appealing that Americans fashioned themselves a people who had released themselves from the shackles of old-world tyranny and oppression and were free to pursue their own happiness.

Emerson anticipated that travelers like Zavala would come to the United States and behold that "the free institutions which prevail here and here alone have attracted to the country the eyes of the world" (2:325). Politician and writer Hugh Swinton Lagré echoed Emerson when he wrote that in the subject of America there lies no "nobler and more interesting of contemplation and discourse, than the causes which lead to the foundation of this mighty empire—than the wonderful and almost incredible history of what it has since done and is already grown to—than the scene of unmingled prosperity and happiness that is opening and spreading all around us—than the prospect as dazzling as it is vast, that lies before us" (quoted in Feller 6). Indeed, Zavala is in some ways representative of a number of travelers who came to the United States in the 1820s and 1830s to represent its ostensible political utopia for their own countries, journeyers who were trying to see America as a unique place in world history. Much like Zavala, John Hector Crève-coeur, Marquis de Lafayette, and Alexis de Tocqueville were all panegyric in their travel narratives of the United States and representative, for the most part, of the utopian rhetoric that flourished in the Age of Jackson. For Crèvecoeur, America was the birthplace of the new American man; James Fenimore Cooper's semifictional travel narrative about General Lafayette, *Notions of the Americans*, noted that Americans are the freest and the happiest in the world. Tocqueville in *Democracy in America* found in the United States what he termed "an absolute democracy." Zavala was not alone is his *theoria* and, like the above-mentioned French travelers, came to prescribe and represent the political culture that emerged in the 1830s.[13]

Zavala also found cultural mores central to the political project that emerged in the United States. Indeed, each of Zavala's chapters frames its discussion with the manners of the Americans. Although geography and history are important to his comprehension of the American people, cultural manners are central to his representation of the utopian political system he identifies as having emerged in the United States. In fact, no more than two pages pass at a time without Zavala discussing the manners of the Americans. He even addresses the most famous of all travel narratives to examine American manners, Fanny Trollope's extremely popular *Domestic Manners of the Americans*. Unlike the acerbic wit of Trollope, however, Zavala's examination of American manners is much more guarded and inevitably reinforces his panegyric look at America. In *Journey* Zavala goes as far as critiquing Trollope, taking exception with the "excessive" sarcasm of her look at American manners and noting that she did not fully understand the Americans (34–35). To Zavala manners in America were as refined as those of Trollope's own home country:

> For a Mexican who has never left his country, or has not done so for a long time, the first impression as he arrives at any point in the Untied States or England is that of seeing all classes of people dressed. . . . What a pleasant spectacle to the eye of the beholder is that of a society that announces by its appearance of decorum and decency the industry, the comforts and even the morality of a people! On the contrary how unpleasant is the aspect of nudity and lack of cleanliness and what a sad

idea a nation gives of the state of its civilization and of its morality when such people inhabit it. (42)

For Zavala, manners are the cornerstone of the democratic progress of a nation, and they lead to the emergence of nationhood.

Zavala's focus on manners as integral to the constitution of people-hood anticipates Pierre Bourdieu's understanding of the political significance of manners (96–99). To Bourdieu, manners define a given individual's political worldview and help bring that subject to an understanding of his social imaginary, what Bourdieu calls the "habitus." In other words, an individual's body actions initiate him/her into a particular political and classed collective. For Zavala, manners are the cornerstone of the democratic self and the people he is trying to foster; they are, in Zavala's narrative, the "origins" of the political (*Journey* 164). American manners are central to the logic of his *theoria* because he is trying to represent for the Mexicans the gestures that constitute the body politic. Through certain embodied actions, he is trying to render a portrait of the universal democratic body, one that he argues Mexicans should imitate.

Mexico and the Contradictions of Imitation

Zavala's employment of the Greek *theoria* to frame his story of people-hood, however, sets up many contradictions that neither the narrative nor Zavala himself ever truly resolved in his own lifetime. This, in part, is due to the fact that on the one hand he represents the United States as a liberal utopia so that, as he states in the introduction, Mexicans can emulate and create a liberal state. Yet, on the other hand, when he follows the *theoria*'s logic of locating the faults of his own country of origin and its inability to foster liberal ideals, he tends to reinscribe the racial stereotypes of Mexico and Mexicans that fueled the expansionist rhetoric of the 1830s. Ironically, at the very moment that he was setting up the United States as a model of democratic mores and governance, the United States was solidifying its expansionist policies toward Mexico. As Reginald Horsman argues, it was in the 1830s that American expansionism took hold, and Americans felt they should conquer and control the continent (187). Written during this expansionist fervor, Zavala's *theoria* ironically sets up some rather striking contrasts between the two countries that at times repeats the expansionist discourse of the 1830s. For example, Zavala relates in his narrative that the Mexican people have not cultivated the individual or the collective democratic body (1–4). Zavala goes as far as castigating and racializing the Mexican body when he states:

> The Mexican is easy-going, lazy, intolerant, generous almost to prodigality, vain, belligerent, superstitious, ignorant, and an enemy of all restraint. The North American works, the Mexican has a good time; the first spends less than he has, the second even that which he does not have; the former carries out the most arduous enterprises to their conclusion, the latter abandons them in the early stages; the one lives in the house, decorates it, preserves it against the inclement weather; the other spends his time in the street, flees from his home, and in a land where there are no seasons he worries little about a place to rest. (4)

In many ways this quote, which begins Zavala's narrative, falls prey to the stereotyping that has mediated modern relations between the United States and Mexico. At the very time that Zavala was castigating the manners of Mexicans in his narrative, Americans were already seeing Mexico as politically and racially inferior. In the U.S. public sphere, Mexicans were viewed as "little children who need to be educated and learn proper economic behavior" (Wairda vi). Mexico was seen as "developing" toward the U.S. model—presumably liberal, democratic, pluralist, and oriented toward free enterprise. Indeed, one of the first English-language analyses in the United States to examine Mexican politics and to perpetuate this attitude appeared in a long article, anonymously published in the *Democratic Review* in 1830, entitled "Politics in Mexico," which discussed Zavala's role in Mexican politics at length; the writer further considers Mexico's political history only to conclude that the country must emulate the United States in order to catch up with America's level of development as a political, cultural, and economic power.

The question arises, then, as to whether Zavala was consciously reinscribing U.S. expansionist discourse in his *theoria*. Indeed, Zavala spends much of the book trying to address his critics and anticipating that his countrymen would yell: "How awful! See how that unworthy Mexican belittles and exposes us to the view of civilized peoples" (*Journey* 4). Zavala asks the reader not to take his critiques in a negative manner, for the Mexican people guide his pen and he travels for the betterment of

Mexico. One could argue, therefore, that he is merely imitating the logic of Greek *theorias*, which often spent time critiquing their country of origin. The critique, as mentioned, was aimed at helping their country and leading it to political collectivity. Moreover, unlike nineteenth-century biological and ethnographic determinists who underpinned the racial characterization of Mexican people and their democratic potential, Zavala locates the reason for Mexico's political chaos in the legacy of Spanish colonialism (45). Throughout the journey, he goes to great lengths to point out the effects that Spanish colonialism has had on Mexico's political and cultural dispositions and its emergence as a democratic nation (164). Zavala's focus on the effects of Spanish colonialism as the root cause of Mexico's national character stands in stark contrast to white America's racial stereotyping of Mexicans that had much deeper roots, not only in the expansionist doctrines but also in the Spanish Black Legend, the *Leyenda Negra* (Horsman 34; Bauer 131).

Despite Zavala's structuring his narrative as a utopian *theoria,* he nevertheless offers stark contrasts between the United States and Mexico, contrasts that inevitably render Mexico as the more enlightened country. For example, Zavala is extremely critical of the hypocrisy of the United States in professing Enlightened ideals while maintaining a slavocracy. As a statesman who fought for the abolition of slavery in an independent Mexico, Zavala finds that when he travels from Mexico, "to the states which permit slavery in our sister republic, the philosopher cannot fail to feel the contrast that is noted between the two countries, nor fail to experience a pleasant memory for those who have abolished this degrading traffic and caused to disappear among us the vestiges of so humiliating a condition to the human race" (26).

He further states in his narrative that slavery "is not very natural in a country where they profess the principles of the widest liberty. Nothing, however, can overcome the concern that exists with respect to this particular subject" (27). More critical of U.S. slavery than any other author of a travel narrative at this time, Zavala goes on to ask questions that would haunt the United States for centuries: "How does one remedy that embarrassing situation of free colored people in the center of society?" "Will the day come when they [slaves] will be incorporated into the state and form an integral part of the community?" (111). In the end, slavery to Zavala is "degrading" (26) and "antiliberal" (28) precisely because it does not respect the individual liberties of all the subjects of the state. In other words, slavery is antiliberal precisely because the master/slave dialectic is antithetical to the logic of the liberal state. The government, which should be unobtrusive, should ensure freedoms of the people, not restrict them.

Zavala's opening point, that Mexicans imitate the United States servilely, or in the spirit of slavery, thus becomes clearer now that he has expressed his exact sentiments about that practice. If, according to Zavala, slavery is the ultimate antiliberal act, then Mexico's "blind" imitation of the United States cannot foster a Mexican liberal state; it would merely replicate the master/slave dialectic. If Mexico were to imitate the United States completely, then it would in effect become a restricted liberal state that never fully achieved its autonomy and liberty. This antiliberal logic of imitating the United States is fundamental to Zavala's story of peoplehood. And Zavala returns to this point of imitation and the emergence of an autonomous liberal state in his conclusion. In many respects, the conclusion is the most theoretical of all his chapters; it is here that he delves deeply into the logic of democracy and what this form of political organization means for Mexico and its future.

In the coda to his treatise, Zavala instructs the Mexican people to avoid reproducing a strict copy of U.S. democracy, but asks them, rather, to become inspired by the United States in order to create their own representative version, one rendered with Mexico's aesthetics of democratic peoplehood:

> There is no more a seductive example for a nation that does not enjoy complete liberty than that of a neighbor where are found in all public acts, in all writings, lessons and practices, an unlimited liberty, and in which instead of the disastrous cataclysms that have overwhelmed some peoples in their anarchical revolutions, or in their bloody despotic systems, one sees the spectacle of the peaceful joys of the numerous segments of the human race, lifted up by the simultaneous energy of its popular intelligence to an eminently free and happy social rank. Could the legislators of the Mexican people resist so strong an influence when they have in their hands the arranging of the destinies of their constituents? (210)

Referring to painting and the language of aesthetics to define the political relationship between Mexico and the United States, Zavala theorizes that Mexicans must become their own autonomous political artists. In the last sentences, he wants the Mexican people to adopt a theory that he has described in his travels—the *ideal* of democracy and a liberal state:

> The model is sublime, but not to be imitated. Those who set themselves to copy a painting of Raphael or of Michael Angelo at times succeed in imitating some of the shadows, some of the characteristics that bring them somewhere within range of the original. However, they never manage to equal those sublime concepts. Original artists do not copy or imitate others, they invent, they create upon the models of nature, and they study her secrets and divine mysteries. (210)

Zavala's comparison of the aesthetic and the political anticipates the political philosopher F. R. Ankersmit's (121) idea that aesthetic representation is the cornerstone of "political reality." For Ankersmit, it is through aesthetics that we come to understand the representational logic of the body politic, and it is through aesthetic representation that the people realize their collectivity as a nation. What makes Zavala so much more nuanced than Ankersmit, however, is that Zavala himself creates an aesthetic story of representation, the travel narrative, as a model for the creation of peoplehood. Yet within this narrative, Zavala calls attention to the mimetic fallacies of peoplehood as a strategy to reveal to Mexican "Maecenas" the fact that "stories of peoplehood" are presentational tools that guide but do not wholly define the sovereignty of a people. One must question whether Zavala's self-reflexive moment in the narrative about the representational value of "stories of peoplehood" is made visible precisely because it serves Mexicans' own realization of their autonomy. In the end, it is not that Zavala wants Mexicans to mimic the United States and to become Americans; rather, his narrative is an aesthetic representation that renders for them a portrait of becoming an autonomous national people who can emerge from the legacy of Spanish colonialism.

Texas Colonization: The Seed of Manifest Destiny

While still in Paris, Zavala turned his eyes to Texas, where he hoped a liberal utopia could arise based on ideas from the Enlightenment. Texas would serve as an alternative geopolitical space, located culturally and politically between Mexico and the United States. Zavala believed that liberalism would stand as the mediating form of political and cultural organization in such a way that a liberal Texas state could usher the heterogeneity of different individuals into a collective people. He further believed that Texas would be the space and the Texans the people to mediate culture and politics between Mexico and the United States. It would become a region forged through universal individual rights that would inevitably support a democratic collectivity. In other words, the diverse peoples who colonized Texas would come together and form a heterogeneous people, the Texans, through a collective belief in a democratic state that ensured individual rights:

> Once the way was opened to [Texas] colonization, as it should have been, under a system of free government, it was necessary that a new generation should appear within a few years and populate a part of the Mexican republic, and consequently that this new generation should be entirely heterogeneous with respect to the other provinces or states of the country. Fifteen or twenty thousand foreigners distributed over the vast area of Mexico, Oaxaca, Vera Cruz, etc., scattered among the former inhabitants cannot cause any sudden change in their ways, manners, and customs. Rather, they adopt the tendencies, manners, language, religion, politics, and even the vices of the multitude that surrounds them. An Englishmen will be a Mexican in Mexico City, and a Mexican an Englishman in London. (*Journey* 96)

However, in the end, I suggest, his faith in liberalism led to a miscalculation of the antiliberal expansionist policies of the United States.

Zavala had first supported the colonization of Texas in the 1820s while he was writing the Mexican constitution. Zavala believed that rapid population growth in Texas was vital to Mexico's survival as a newly formed nation. In many ways, he followed the liberal Argentine thinker, Juan Bautista Alberdi, who argued that "to govern is to populate" (Weber 158). In 1824, Zavala was one of the framers of the Texas Colonization Law that authorized the Mexican congress to devise programs to populate Texas with "foreign inhabitants." The law guaranteed land, security, and exemption from taxes for four years to foreign settlers and imposed few restrictions. However, for Americans to own land, they had to become Mexican citizens. They also would own their land under the auspice of an *empresario*, an immigrant agent of Mexico. Zavala also owned a large tract of land that he had inherited for his service in the Mexican government in the 1820s. By 1830, however, more than seven thousand Americans had settled in Texas, outnumbering Mexicans in the region by more than four thousand (Weber 166). In 1830, three days before Zavala went into exile, Mexico ended settlement in Texas by foreigners, fearing that Texas was becoming far too populated with Americans. Pablo Obregón, Mexico's minister to Washington, had argued earlier that Americans would only become Mexican citizens in name and their loyalty would still lie with the United States (Weber 158–169). One of the strongest opponents of Texas colonization, Lucas Alemán, prophetically declared that "where others send invading armies, [North Americans] send their colonists" (Weber 168).

Since the presidency of John Quincy Adams in the 1820s, the United States had looked to Texas as an important target for eventual expansion westward. As a principal author of the Monroe Doctrine, Adams believed that "the whole continent of North America appears to be destined by Divine Providence to be peopled by one nation, speaking one language, professing one general system of religious and political principles, and accustomed to one general tenor of social usages and customs" (quoted in Stephanson 59). Andrew Jackson echoed this sentiment as he hoped to annex Texas and "secure the U.S. borders and add to the nation's riches." Numerous other statesmen and politicians had expressed interest in the annexation of Texas (Stephanson 42–49). Even Tocqueville observed that "the vast provinces extending beyond the frontiers of the Union towards Mexico are still destitute of inhabitants" (156). White Americans, he continued, "will take possession of the soil and establish social institutions" (160).

If Zavala did know about the United States' intentions for Texas, he carefully masked it within his works. He did, however, refer to Mexico's fate at the end of his *Journey* with a rather prophetic observation about United States' expansion into the Mexican territories: "The American system will obtain a complete bloody victory" (213). One year after he wrote this sentence, Zavala arrived in Texas in hopes of establishing a liberal republic. Texas at that time was primarily under the leadership of the American Stephen F. Austin, who was already organizing an Anglo-American independence movement from that country. Dismayed at the political situation in Mexico, Zavala quickly supported the Texans' pursuit of autonomy from Mexico. He subsequently participated in writing another constitution, this time for Texas. Soon thereafter he served as governor of Texas and later as the republic's first vice president. Once again, Zavala was involved in shaping a people. This time, however, he would do so as a Texan. Despite Zavala's work for Texas, some scholars argue that his personal letters reveal that he hoped Mexico would remain engaged in Texas' political and cultural emergence (Cleaves 145). Indeed, Zavala argued that Spanish should be the official language of Texas and, in fact, he translated the constitution and saw that it was issued in both English and Spanish. For his commitment to a prosperous and liberal Mexico, however, many Texas politicians did not trust Zavala, fearing that he was simply using his position in Texas in order to return to Mexico with power. For his part, Zavala also grew tired of Anglo-Texans' political pursuits, and he resigned as vice president of Texas only one month after he took office. Nevertheless, nothing suggests that Zavala ever intended to return to Mexico; in fact, he died on Texas soil in 1836.

Zavala did not live long enough to see the U.S.-Mexico War or feel the racialization and later proletaritization of the Mexicans who lived in the United States. His colleague Juan Seguín summed it up well two years after Zavala's death, when he wrote that he and the other Texas-Mexican people had become "foreigners in their native land" (98). This would have applied to Zavala also, but in many ways he was never fully a native of any land. Born under the Spanish crown in New Spain, briefly a citizen of an independent Mexico, later a political refugee in Europe and the United States, and again briefly a citizen of the Republic of Texas, Zavala was ironically a man without a people. Perhaps this explains his desperate, insistent intent on creating a peoplehood, first for Mexico and then for Texas.

Zavala's *Journey* was finally reprinted posthumously in Mexico on the eve of the U.S.-Mexico war in 1846. By then, Mexico had branded Zavala a traitor for his role in establishing the Texas Republic (Cleaves 139–141). In the end, Zavala's participation in the founding of the Texas Republic would paradoxically help to facilitate the U.S.-Mexico War and the "bloody victory." Indeed, Zavala was hardly a traitor of the Mexican people, and he was not a blind devotee of U.S. liberalism. Rather, the complexity of Zavala and his *Journey* lies in the contradictions resulting from the dual legacy of Spanish colonialism and American imperialism, a legacy that continues to influence the development of Mexican people-hood in the United States.

2

Constituting Terra Incognita

The "Mexican Question"
in U.S. Print Culture

Of all strange corners of our strange West, this is the strangest; and
it is a chosen and beloved abiding place of the strangest and least
comprehensible of all those who make up our national character.
. . . In the burning noontide comes a slow gray burro, meek and pa-
tient; his head drooped, his eyes mere glinting peepholes in his out-
ward shagginess,—every line, curve, and movement full of unobtrusive dignity. And this sedate aspect eminently befits his estate, for he
is no ordinary beast; he is bearer of the presiding genius of the
desert,—the mestizo, the Greaser, half-blood offspring of the marriage of antiquity and modernity. Time cannot take from him the
unmistakable impress of old Spain. But his Spanish appearance is
not his dominant characteristic. His skin has been sunbrowned for
centuries; his nose and cheeks are broad; his lips are thick; his
brows are heavy, his sheltering eyes soft, passionate, inscrutable.
King in his own natural right, master of a blessed content, he is the
strange progeny of parents who waged warfare against each other,
and all but perished in the strife. . . . Anomalous as he is, he is one
of the few distinct types in our national life whose origin is fully
known to us. . . .
    As all this goes to make manly character, the Greaser is a mere
fragment of a man in stature. According to the artistic dictum,
which pronounces the curve and the line of beauty, the Greaser
should assuredly be beautiful, for his make-up is superlatively rich
in curves. His pudgy head and face bear an obtrusive lot of curling
lines, which wriggle sinuously down the neck and shoulders, until
they are lost in the portentous curve of his waistband. For he is fat.
Rich or poor, idler or loafer, he never runs to leanness. The women
are like the men. Perhaps you have heard or read of beautiful mestizo maidens? Traveler's tales! Save in the pictures of susceptible ro-
manticists, I have never seen a beautiful Greaser girl.
                    —William Lighton, "The Greaser," 1899

51

Imagine, if you will, that it is August 28, 1899 in New York, and it is a bit warmer than usual in the growing industrial city. Because of the hot, humid day, Mr. Drake decides not to take the new trolley system. Too many people, he recalls, so he decides to walk home from his job on Wall Street. He has been working with the Wall Street banking firm, Smith and Barney, for more than thirty years and was recently made a full partner of their commercial real-estate division, putting him in charge of their expansion into the west. Walking home will also allow him to continue his monthly ritual, a quick stop at Ransom's Drugstore to buy the Atlantic. Although he reads other literary and cultural magazines, he is particularly fond of the Atlantic and has read the magazine since its first issue.

Mr. Drake lives in a rather elegant apartment by Central Park. He is a bachelor, which is part of the reason why he took on his firm's economic expansion into the west; he will have to move to New Mexico in three months.

It all began with his trip to the World's Fair in 1893. He heard a historian, Frederick Jackson Turner, declare that the frontier was closed and economic expansion was entering into its final stage in the once Mexican lands. Indeed, Turner's speech gave him the idea to expand Smith and Barney's banking firm into the frontier. He vividly remembers looking over the map of the United States with his boss, Mr. Holcomb: "It is public domain," he told his boss; "someone will have to control the land titles."

And yet, despite the riches that await him in the southwest, he no longer is sure if he is ready to leave his New York world of high society, with its Friday night operas and late-night excursions to local restaurants. He would even miss the trolley, he thinks. His family has lived in New York for four generations, and he will be the first to leave.

Maintaining his long-standing reading ritual, Mr. Drake sits in his parlor and opens the pages of the Atlantic. He usually reads the magazine from cover to cover, but this month will be different. Last month's issue noted that it would have a special story on the Mexican people of the southwest, a story called "The Greaser." Skimming past the literature sections, the advertisements, and the etiquette section, he turns to page 989, "The Greaser." He softly says the word to himself several times, trying to capture its meaning.

He had heard of greasers before; indeed, the Atlantic frequently used this term. He recalls an article by Teddy Roosevelt and numerous travel narratives that vividly described the Mexican people of the southwest. Even recently he read an Atlantic article called "Americanisms," which defined the "proper" way to classify Mexicans of the southwest: "greasers," noted the magazine's etymologist, John Sotten.[1]

The article "The Greaser" was but a symptom of what had been commonly called the "Mexican Question," which was, perhaps unknown to Mr. Drake, the American effort to define and classify the Mexican people of the United States. When he was a boy he had learned about Mexicans in the magazines that his father read. The Democratic Review, Vanity Fair, and Scribner's, to name a few, wrote numerous articles that dealt with the Mexican Question during and after what the magazines termed the "Mexican War."

He fondly remembers the nights his father would read to his entire family. Read and debated aloud, these articles educated him into thinking that Mexicans were everything he wasn't, that Mexico's Republic was America's republican antithesis. Mexico, he learned, was a premodern, uncivilized land of mongrels who deserved the American conquest in 1848. America's conquest of Mexico, he had read, was a Christian act that would help Mexico and its people become civilized for democracy. The Mexican people are lazy and Catholic. The American people are hard workers and Protestant. Mexicans have darker skin, and their features are unrefined. He is white, and he has blond hair and blue eyes; he is a civilized gentleman. Mr. Drake is not sure if he has made the right decision to go live among the greasers, a race of people so very different from his own. "The Greaser," he said to himself a little louder than before.

This month, then, the article on the greaser would be very different to him; it would evoke a personal experience. No longer a race on the other side of the expanding republic, Mexicans would soon be part of Mr. Drake's private and public life. He would soon be living among them.

As he read the article, Mr. Drake grew uneasy. Although alone in his parlor and more than three thousand miles from a half-civilized "greasy" Mexican body—a "man with large lips and a broad nose"—he begins to feel as if this other race is entering his private space. How would he deal with these people, a "race" the article notes, that is "the strangest and least comprehensible of all those who make up our national character." "Stranger than the Indian, than the African," he ponders.

He continues to read, realizing that they are everywhere in the southwest, hiding like snakes in the rocks, the article notes, and even occasionally walking in public areas like the street. They will even touch the food they serve him. His boss told him that he would have to deal with some of the rich greasers, but, as the article proclaims, they, too, are a mongrel and lazy class. How would he look this other race in the face and actually do business? He had never actually seen one before, only in magazine pictures and exhibits at the museum. This time, however, the power of the descriptive language of the magazine article horrified him. "The Greaser," he said to himself again.

In the past, it had been so much easier to read about the Mexican Question from his parlor. He knew that they were far away, and that their lands had made the nation complete, but it had been easier to define them from a distance. Now he, as well as the rest of the eastern United States, realizes that the Mexicans are both far and near. After reading about the greaser, Mr. Drake realizes that he will never be the same; this trip will change him forever, and the vivid description of the article begins his metamorphosis. "The United States will never be the same. Why did we go to war with Mexico?" He kept asking the question over and over.

At what moment in U.S. history did questions about Mexican peoplehood emerge in the national public spheres? In this chapter I suggest that they began with the invention of the inquest that became known as the "Mexican Question." The Mexican Question was a European American inquiry into the very constitution of Mexican peoplehood that found its rhetorical dimensions within the perimeters of democratic expansion and racialization of the Mexican peoples who lived in the "frontier." As such, stories of peoplehood that evoked the Mexican Question found their rhetorical focus on the geography of the southwest. As my fictional story of Mr. Drake attempts to capture,[2] for Mexican and Anglo contact, the Mexican Question found its roots in the period of expansion into the western and southwestern lands of Mexicans and Native Americans, the period when both the promise of terra incognita and the savage other emerged in the consciousness of the American public. This is the specter that haunted Mr. Drake and the eastern public culture he was a part of in the nineteenth century, for it is in the place of otherness where they saw themselves and the ontological origins of their political subjectivity as a civilized American people, as a member of the *demos*.

The discursive origins of the Mexican Question found its place of dissemination in representations in American print culture, and the epigraph that opens this chapter begins to reveal the democratic and racial constellations that it mapped. Published in the prestigious *Atlantic*, William

Lighton's "The Greaser," demonstrates the nineteenth-century public sphere that reflected America's expansive period as a key moment of inquest into the founding Enlightenment questions concerning democratic statecraft, race, geography, and Mexican political peoplehood itself. According to Lighton's "The Greaser," it would be in "the strangest corners of the west" where Americans would question the "natural rights" of the greaser, who is "a mere fragment of a man in stature." We begin to see that questioning the natural rights of Mexicans and the rights that Anglos have to their lands foreshadowed the contradictions that otherness and terra incognita present to America's enlightened inquest into transcontinental dominance.

Echoing Rousseau and Hobbes, Lighton's "The Greaser" locates the "mestizo" Mexican within the strange frontier territory in order to posit him as the prepolitical "savage man," the antithesis of the civilized political subject known as the American man (Clifford 39–40).[3] What the article sets up for middle-class Mr. Drake and the eastern American public, therefore, is a question concerning not only the racial and geographic constitution of the Mexican greaser but also a question concerning Mexicans' innate ability to emerge from the landscape as a political people with natural rights. Moreover, in his embodied description of the political and geographic location of the greaser, Lighton is asking fundamental questions about democratic statecraft and the ontological and racial constitution of American peoplehood. Is a dark-colored mestizo, a person who is not physically the same as white Americans, capable of attaining natural rights? If so, can Anglos justify claiming the lands of the west? As such, whoever is bestowed with natural rights and whoever can obtain them marks the rhetorical dimensions of Anglo-American territorial expansion and leads to the creation of the "Mexican Question."

The greaser stands as the ambivalent figure of political subjectivity with rights precisely, as Lighton suggests, because he is an amalgamation of both the European Spanish and Indian races, a mestizo. Lighton's "Greaser" is simultaneously the "King of his own natural right," and thus bestowed with certain rights, freedoms, powers, and obligations, and a mestizo, whose racial character and geographic ignorance locates him as a semicivilized political being, a savage man without "reason" (Clifford 39–40). This allows Lighton to posit the greaser as Rousseau's savage, a prepolitical person who inhabits the undefined terra incognita against which the American Enlightened imagination of the east would define civilization. This, in turn, allows the American citizen to reaffirm his ontological status as *the natural* political people of U.S. democratic culture and Mexicans as the *ethnos* other.

Lighton's "Greaser," along with the hundreds of similar essays about the rights and status of Mexicans in the United States, may have found its discursive impetus in the strangeness of frontier place, but the explosion of American print culture facilitated the circulation of stories of Mexican peoplehood concerning the Mexican Question, which began in U.S. literary magazines in the 1840s, the years when both Manifest Destiny took hold of American democracy and, not coincidentally, mass cultural forms emerged. It is important to remember that magazines were the first and only medium of widespread public communication. During the period of territorial expansion, there were no radio or film industries, no official national newspapers, and no regular medium of information and entertainment that reached a national audience except for magazines. The "house magazines," such as *Scribner's, Century, Harper's,* and *Atlantic,* which were the preferred literary and cultural magazines of the middle class on the east coast, sold over 250,000 copies each. The sales records, however, do not include the thousands of copies that were shared and read in coffeehouses, libraries, and drugstores (Schneirov 5). As Matthew Schneirov argues, the house magazines served as the cultural models for the late-nineteenth-century popular magazines that sold nearly one million copies (21). Not only vehicles of advertising and consumer culture, then, magazines, both elite and popular, provided a dynamic discourse that affected the constitution of peoplehood; they were the most powerful institution of the growing national literary public sphere (23). Reading magazines was a way that the nation debated its most salient issues; magazines were pivotal in America's democratic self-fashioning.[4] What is also so important about magazines and print culture is that their emergence coincides with the geographic expansion of the United States. Indeed, in the years that Americ defined its geographic boundaries from the Atlantic to the Pacific, print culture also expanded its geographic and literary space, fostering a print revolution informed by American imperialism.

What happens when you consider the cultural power of this modern form with the fact that magazines published thousands of stories of peoplehood about "Indians," "Negroes," "Chinese," and "greasers"? If, as scholars have suggested, magazines exerted such a profound influence on modernity, mass public culture, American subjectivity, and democracy, what can we learn from the pages of these magazines that were filled with stereotypical images of the other races that lived, immigrated, or were "incorporated" into American lands? For in just the elite literary magazines alone—*Scribner's, Century, Harper's, Atlantic,* and others—there were more than two thousand articles that dealt with Indians, Negroes, Chinese, and Mexicans.[5] Our concern here, of course, is the "Mexican Question," for it originated within the covers of magazines, and in the years that followed its introduction to the American public in 1845, over 750 articles dealt with the subject. It should be noted, however, that the Mexican Question was not only debated in American magazines. Shelley Streeby's *American Sensations*, a study of empire-building and the U.S.-Mexico War through dime novels, demonstrates that many print forms were complicit in America's geopolitical understanding of itself (3–28). Although I locate American magazine culture within the larger emergence of print culture that Streeby finds in her study, I focus primarily on American magazines because it is here where the geopolitical designs of the Mexican Question would emerge in the public spheres. Moreover, because American magazines mass published such varied forms as sensational literature, political speeches by politicians, presidential speeches, short stories, ethnographic tracts, serialized romance stories, novels, and works on history and art, they are a very special cultural form in their own right. As such, they were representative of the dynmics of American print culture itself and were one of the most important forms that circulated the first stories of Mexican peoplehood by Anglos. The national questions of the Mexican in these magazines, which began in the years leading up to the U.S.-Mexico War, would not only help promote America's imperialist expansion into the southwest but would set the geopolitical foundations of Mexican incorporation.[6]

Because nearly 750 articles dealt with the Mexican Question in just the middle-class eastern magazines, I focus here on the Mexican Question in two sections, which represent interdependent parts of this national inquiry. I map this question by discussing representative examples that reveal the geopolitical logic of this inquest in pre- and post-1848 and how it affected Mexican peoplehood in the United States. The first section, "Terra Incognita: Locating the Space of the Mexican Question," focuses on the first articulations of the Mexican Question and the rhetoric of Manifest Destiny in order to establish the geographic, racial, and democratic logic that underpinned its early emergence in public culture. The second section, "A View from the Parlor: Incorporating Eastern Modernity against a Pre-modern Southwest," explores how postannexation representations of the recently acquired Mexican lands, now America's "public domain" after the U.S.-Mexico War, became intertwined with questions concerning the border, contact, regionalism, industrialization, and modernity.

Terra Incognita: Locating the Space of the Mexican Question

In the spring of 1845, John O'Sullivan, editor and founder of the *Democratic Review*, sat down to write two essays that would reveal much about the territorial and racial dimensions of democracy: "Annexation" and "The Mexican Question." In "Annexation," he coined what has become perhaps one of the foundational geopolitical phrases of U.S. history, "Manifest Destiny." For O'Sullivan, Manifest Destiny gave the United States the "right" to "overspread and to possess the whole of our continent which Providence has given us for the development of the great experiment of liberty and federated self-government entrusted to us" (234). O'Sullivan's coupling of expansion and democratic rights, of course, was not isolated to 1845.

Since the Northwest Ordinance of 1787, Americans melded natural rights discourse with land expansionism. Indeed, since its founding moment, U.S. democracy was a spatial endeavor, created from the openness and vastness of the U.S. continent. No other than the American democratic observer I discussed in the last chapter, Alexis de Tocqueville, would confirm that the vastness of America's geography gave the nation the means to achieve a lasting democracy. The U.S.'s democratic imaginary had a territorial dimension that found its roots from the rhetoric established through both liberal and republican discourses of the Enlightenment. This blend of political thought, in fact, informed the American constitution itself, for the open space of the west became the conceptual terrain for the U.S. republic's democratic social imaginary.

O'Sullivan's phrase "Manifest Destiny" was timely because it not only captured the historical implications of coupling geographic expansionism with the "development of millions of democratic peoples" (235). It also discursively marked a moment when "frontier" land would become a material reality for the U.S. masses. This was the period when the lands west of the Mississippi became part of the United States, and not merely understood as an abstract marker for democracy's expansive potential.[7] It is important to remember that the period when O'Sullivan coined the phrase Manifest Destiny in the 1840s, the United States was undergoing unprecedented territorial growth. By the end of this period, the United States had grown by 70 percent and was a transcontinental democracy, a nation whose boundaries went "from sea to shining sea." In this period, America realized its Manifest Destiny by annexing, conquering, and stealing lands of the west with the mission of promoting democracy. In many ways, the years surrounding O'Sullivan's creation of the phrases "Manifest Destiny" and the "Mexican Question" were defining modern moments in American geopolitics, a liminal period that would test the foundations of democracy and its territorial roots, for at the same time that the United States' geographical boundaries expanded, the nation questioned its new democratic mission of expansion. Two interrelated and fundamental questions took hold of American public culture: What "rights" did the United States have in acquiring Mexican lands? And could the norms and ideals of democracy such as rights of the people extend to these recently incorporated lands?[8]

O'Sullivan's essay "The Mexican Question," written within months of his coining of the term "Manifest Destiny," dealt with both of these issues. The Mexican Question revealed both the rights-based language that fueled America's expansion and the anxiety that racial others and their lands created for U.S. democratic culture. For O'Sullivan, "The Mexican Question" was primarily an inquest concerning the United States' "natural rights" to expand west, and asking what people—the Mexicans or the Americans—had the right to these lands (22). To this end, much as in "Annexation," in "The Mexican Question" O'Sullivan argued that Mexican lands enabled the free development of the American people. Important to his inquest was his exploration as to how the United States could reconcile how "natural rights" gave the United States the democratic justification to occupy Mexico's sovereign lands. His question was complicated by the fact that Mexicans were a distinct people who had created their own democratic government. In order for O'Sullivan to resolve the question of Mexico's sovereignty over their lands, he felt that the United States had to find that democracy could naturally extend to the western territories, for it was the providential natural right of the American people. Not surprisingly, O'Sullivan ultimately argued that the American people held the natural right to the lands. But what is interesting are the political maneuvers that he made in his essays to answer his own Mexican Question.

O'Sullivan merged a Lockean notion of individual natural rights with the rhetoric of Manifest Destiny and bestowed the sovereign nation and its collective people with the same natural rights as the individual in "nature." It is important to remember that natural rights are those that God bestows on individuals at birth; in secularized Lockean republicanism, natural rights are those that a person is born with in the state of nature. These "naturally" entail the right to life, liberty, and the pursuit of happiness. O'Sullivan then followed Jeffersonian Enlightenment rhetoric that argued that rights were "naturally" rooted in the soil of the providential United States and thus were foundational to the development of peoplehood. Much like Jefferson, O'Sullivan considered the natural landscape to be the source of the democratic ideal of rights. O'Sullivan's coupling of individual rights and Manifest Destiny were finally dependent on the argument that Mexicans were not capable of "imagining" the concept of natural rights and peoplehood in the first place (23).

O'Sullivan was not alone in this argument, for it appears in a number of essays in his publication, the *Democratic Review*. Perhaps the most striking that would discuss the racial implications of the "Mexican Question" was "Mexico," written by the American expansionist and ardent supporter of republican ideologies, Caleb Cushing. In this essay, Cushing begins by establishing that the Mexican Question is one that affects "the just estimation of our [America's] own rights" and concludes that the United States has the right to lands because of the remarkable racial differences between the two countries. The U.S. population of whites consists of over "six-sevenths of the whole population," while Mexico constitutes only "one-seventh" (434). For Cushing, "race is the key to much that seems obscure in the history of a nation and its ability to foster a free and representative democracy" (435). Since Mexico is mostly Indian and half-breeds, Cushing argues, Americans will look in "vain" for an "enlightened population."

Many articles in O'Sullivan's *Democratic Review* revealed that Mexico remained firmly within the geopolitical imagination of the United States. But it was O'Sullivan's essays ("Annexation" and "The Mexican Question") that established the inquest concerning Mexico's sovereignty for generations. Moreover, because of O'Sullivan's reign over the *Democratic Review,* the Mexican nation would become crucial to the construction of the American national imagination in the nineteenth century and well into our own century. Moreover, the construction of Mexico in the public sphere shaped the U.S.'s conception of the U.S. borderlands, culture, and southwestern territories. In fact, the inquest that began in the *Democratic Review* spilled into the middle-class magazines.

The *Atlantic*, for example, published many articles that explored the geopolitical relationship that the United States and its citizens would have with Mexico and Mexicans. Many of the magazine articles constructed a pre-modern nation that was unable to prosper as a unified republic that Zavala so desired. In an 1860 article in *Atlantic*, entitled "Mexico," the unnamed author argues that the "question" for the U.S. public is why Mexico, which, like America, "possesses the greatest natural advantages," fails to reach its potential as a nation and is the "failure of the century" (53). This, he argues, "is the very question we [Americans] seek to answer." Creating a crude geographic history, the author's hypothesis is that the "true foundations of all national fortunes are the character of its people" (57). A great nation, he argues, is one that can use its natural resources. This can only be achieved through hard work by people who are devoid of "half-breeds." Therefore, Mexico is doomed to failure as a true republican nation because of its racial makeup and its inability to work the land into a valuable capitalist resource. America, in contrast, has tapped into its natural resources and controlled its geography such that it has become a great republican nation, one that will conquer Mexico because white men are hard-working, Protestant citizens. According to this article, capitalism is implicitly the driving ethos of American nationalism. In this way, the article constructs an American national ethos against a semifeudal, preindustrial Mexican nation that does not live up to its geographic "capitalist" potential, for Mexicans are not an industrious race who can turn their natural resources into capital.

I cannot underscore enough that "The Mexican Question" that emerged in O'Sullivan's *Democratic Review* set the rhetorical foundations for American and Mexican relations in the decades to come. First, it revealed how the United States came to terms with the expansion of a continent through an expanded notion of "natural rights" discourses and racial imperatives over another democratic nation with sovereignty (Stephanson 43). Second, for O'Sullivan's and the nation's immediate manifest designs, the Mexican Question fueled the justification for a "rightful," "just" war against Mexico. Indeed, one year after O'Sullivan wrote "The Mexican Question" and "Annexation," the United States declared war against Mexico and began its "rightful expansion" into the west through force (O'Sullivan, "Annexation" 32). In the end, rights-based arguments of expansion gave the U.S. people the moral justification to limit the freedoms of Mexico and the people of the west.

The U.S.-Mexico War solidified the spatial, racial, and democratic foundations of the Mexican Question in the United States. The war created geographic boundaries that expanded America's empire by more than a third and promoted racial stereotypes of Mexicans that affected Mexican and Anglo relations for generations. Moreover, the U.S.-Mexico War was the United States' first war on foreign soil and was arguably one of the most important landmarks in the development of American democracy and peoplehood (Montejano 38). For the young nation trying to define itself, the war helped promote republican ideals domestically, as well as demonstrated to a growing global economy that America's was a republic of destiny, one able to win a war with a foreign power.

As cultural historian Robert Johannsen argues, the Mexican War also played an important part in the breakdown of American parochialism: "It marked America's first intimate exposure to a life and culture that differed significantly from anything in the American experience. . . . The American people . . . would never be the same" (12). As a consequence, however, the war and the Treaty of Guadalupe Hidalgo that ended it in 1848 would greatly challenge the rhetoric of the American public sphere and the political and racial identity of white Americans.

The military campaign against Mexico quickly cast the Mexican people as foreign and exotic in the public imagination. Occurring during a backdrop of American technological innovations, including the beginnings of widely circulated newspapers, magazines, and dime novels, the war touched more American lives than any other event in America's history up to that moment. The perception of Mexicans in the American imagination, however, was not flattering. The literary public spheres represented Mexicans as people with "exotic and foreign manners," a "darker phenotype," and speaking an inferior language. These and other stereotypes inevitably constituted Mexicans as racially inferior in the minds of Anglo-Americans. Such a racial outlook inevitably helped promote the war effort. Indeed, for the United States to gain support within the American public, the American government and the larger public used a number of propaganda techniques to cast negative stereotypes of Mexicans as a people in America's social imagination. Like the racial stereotypes that Lighton's "Greaser" exhibited, the public sphere was concerned with defining a racial people according to specific embodied characteristics. In other words, body type became the defining contour of Mexican peoplehood.

Let us not forget that the public during the Antebellum and Recon-struction periods endorsed a eugenics approach to embodied identity and advanced a theory that characteristics of the natural body determined a people's political "essence" (Dyer 32). A widely publicized 1848 study undertaken by a Cincinnati phrenologist found that the Mexican people "were destitute of Comparison, Causality, Constructiveness, Ideality, and Benevolence, while they possessed in abundance Combativeness, De-structiveness, Secretiveness, and Acquisitiveness," and "Mexicans' thick skulls" revealed that they were very coarse and more animal than intel-lectual (*Niles National Register* 68). Neil Foley argues that these "race scientists" influenced American's popular thinking on issues ranging from Mexican immigration and interracial marriage to citizenship well into the mid-twentieth century (5).

The racialization of Mexican people coincided with the publication of more than 350 articles that dealt exclusively with the U.S.-Mexico War, and there were over twenty-five hundred references to it. The articles were mostly nonfiction histories, travel narratives, biographies, political treatises, and narrative accounts of battle. Most of the early articles about the war were concerned with questioning why the United States went to war with Mexico and what this act meant for the American people. Many of the middle-class magazine articles also tried to separate fact from fic-tion and felt that it was their duty as intellectual magazines to educate the public about the war. In the *United States Magazine*, for example, in an article called "The Mexican War: Its Origins and Conduct," the writer begins by arguing that it is a response to the "public attention" and is meant to take into "consideration the war as a national measure of pub-lic justice"(291). The writer then argues that "these are questions that be-long to history, which other nations will regard with interest and in that view they will be treated" (292). Realizing that the war was an important aspect of America's new national character, the writer meticulously sketches a history of a corrupt Mexican republic. He states that the United States was merely protecting its interests from a hostile govern-ment. The piece then relates that only by Mexico's embracing an American-style government will it be able to rise to its "potential." The U.S.-Mexico War, he concludes, will inevitably "help the people of Mex-ico, not hurt them" (292).

Like this article, many of the magazine articles showed an awareness of the national significance of the war for the United States.[9] What mag-azine culture helped perpetuate in the public sphere, however, was a benevolent U.S. history that depicted America as a moral, not an imperialist, nation that was civilizing an unjust Mexican nation.[10] Article after article cast Mexico as an inferior nation whose racial people and civilization were barbaric and not capable of natural rights. In the anonymous article, "The Occupation of Mexico," for example, the author argues that "the curse of Mexico" is the absence of "a commercial principal." Only America, who is "the great conservator of peace and internal tranquility," can bring democracy to this backward people (385). Only through a benevolent U.S. occupation of Mexico will it become a great and independent nation and a prosperous people. Implicitly, then, a benevolent occupation of Mexico will also lead America to become a great and independent nation.

In effect, early magazines helped erase an imperialist history of the U.S.-Mexico War through a democratic language that elided colonial ideology. During the nineteenth century, America was still constructing what Benedict Anderson defines as an "imagined community." This imagined community, however, was based as much on ideals and norms of democracy as it was on America's geographic imagination and the imperialism that informed its emergence. As such, a just and democratic republic of people could not construct a democratic *demos* on an imperialist ideology of expansion. Americans had to believe that their war was not one of aggression but one to extend democracy. Creating an imagined and "mythic" history of the war in the public sphere was a powerful discourse that helped the American people continue its rhetoric of natural rights to expand across the continent (Slotkin 191). If the war was just and America was a just nation of people, then Manifest Destiny was God's gift to this benevolent nation, as O'Sullivan reasoned years prior.

With "peace" in sight, however, the rights-based presuppositions of the Mexican Question once again emerged in the United States. Now, however, the question shifted from the war with Mexico to questions about the Treaty of Guadalupe Hidalgo that would end the war and, in theory, grant Mexicans in the United States the same rights as Anglo-Americans. If America acted as a benevolent and just nation during the war and rightfully expanded into foreign lands, how do they write an enlightened and just treaty? How would they define the rights and status of Mexicans in the United States, especially considering the imperialist project of the war itself? And, most important, could Americans incorporate Mexicans, which meant endowing them with the same rights as whites in the United States? In an article written two weeks before the signing of the Treaty of Guadalupe Hidalgo, "The War: The New Issue," the writer, who only uses the initials D.D.B., details the treaty. He explains how America's empire will grow tremendously, 1,500,000 square miles, and that the United States will even pay Mexico—with its "Gotho-spanish race"—for its lands (114). The writer then goes on to argue that America is just in its actions, for most nations are not so generous with their treaties and never pay for lands they have "won in a just war" (115). In another article, "Peace—and What Next?," the unnamed author questions how United States/Mexico relations, land issues, and the Mexican people in the new territories will affect the nation. Written one month before the final ratification of the treaty in May of 1848, the article begins by stating that the war with Mexico will go down in history in a rather special way. Other nations, he argues, "may hereafter pursue the career of conquest with the same Christian principles" that America has undertaken (295). America's war and the treaty, he argues, should be models for othr nations to follow.

The concerns over the possible signing of a treaty with Mexico were not limited to the middle-class magazine public, however. Charles Averill's 1847 dime novel, *The Mexican Ranchero or the Maid of the Chapparal: A Romance of the Mexican War*, would be the first fictional document to deal with the treaty and relate to a working-class public how "peace" was a resolute answer to the war.[11] I do not want to delve too deeply into this fascinating story, but it is important to point out the role that the treaty had in a dime novel published a year before the United States ratified the treaty. In this romance narrative about a cross-dressing woman hero who fights frontier monsters and Anglos for the honor of Mexico, no other than the American diplomat Nicholas Trist (who was "delegate of peace" in Mexico and the real historical architect behind the 1848 treaty) serves as the narrative's moral and democratic consciousness. Throughout the narrative, he is the voice of reason and reminds the characters and therefore, the implied readers, of the importance in the United States of creating a peaceful and reconciliatory end to a war that is spoiling what he refers to as the "romantic lands of Mexico" (Averill 43). For most of the novel, Trist's pleas for peace are in vain, for the Mexican and Anglo characters see no reason for peace; they would rather die in battle, fighting a "bloody warfare" against one another. By the last page of the novel, however, all of the characters come to understand Trist's desire for a peaceful resolution to the war. The story ends with the narrator explaining to the implied eastern readership the importance of peace, as he states: "The war is well nigh self-exhausted; Peace with its smiling face is treading close upon the bloody footsteps of the grim old King of Carnage—and rare now can be the opportunities which can call for the uplifting of the dreaded sword of Mexico's Lion" (Averill 100).

As Shelley Streeby argues in *American Sensations*, this romantic and peaceful ending is due in part to the fact that the national race questions are resolved between Mexicans and Anglos, and by the end of the story, most of the characters form one people through their romantic unions. The dime novel's imagined resolution to the war conflict created for the readers was, in the end, slanted toward Anglo-American advantages for peace. Indeed, as I discuss in the following pages, Mexican race questions were anything but resolvable in the American public. Moreover, the peaceful end to the war was not romantic for Mexicans. The signing of the Treaty of Guadalupe Hidalgo, which rendered a "peaceful resolution to the war," was, according to Chicano historian Juan Gómez-Quiñones, one of the harshest treaties ever signed in modern history (212).

The signing of the Treaty of Guadalupe Hidalgo on February 2, 1848, also marked a significant moment in the rights-based inquest into the Mexican Question. For this is the first document to deal with both the question of U.S. democracy's capacity to expand into the west and to establish, in natural rights theory, the newly constituted political subject known as the "Mexican American." The Treaty of Guadalupe Hidalgo is the first document to address the civil rights of Mexicans as an incorporated U.S. people (Gómez-Quiñones 213). Articles 8 and 9 of the treaty granted Mexicans the legal right to be included in the body politic as "American citizens" at the same time that it geographically defined Mexican lands, borders, territories, and property rights[12] (Figure 4). In theory, the treaty became the first document that constituted Mexicans as American people endowed with the natural rights of Americans and the once - Mexican lands as U.S. public domain.

Under the provisions of the treaty, Mexicans in the United States were afforded the right to enter the public as citizens and as property owners, while still maintaining their private traditions as Mexicans who were Spanish-speaking Catholics. However, as Martha Menchaca and Deena González have argued, the treaty only gave a semblance of democratic inclusion, natural rights, and land rights.[13] Mexican Americans' mixed race background, Menchaca argues, historically placed them in an ambiguous racial and legal position in the public sphere (245). In effect, their private racial body collided with the universal imperatives of the democratic pub-

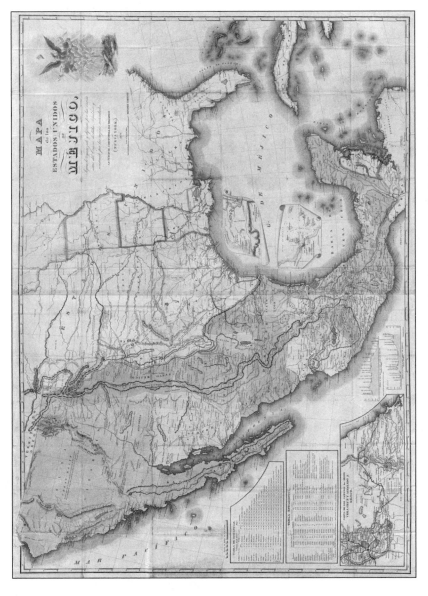

Figure 4. J. Disturnell's Map: Mapa de los Estados Unidos de Mejico attached to the first Treaty of Guadalupe Hidalgo, 1847–1848

lic and the abstract notions of natural rights. At varying times in U.S. history, the nation's legal, political, and literary spheres constituted Mexicans as white, mixed blood, and racially other. This would drastically affect their rights for over a century. In the end, the treaty did not truly guarantee any civil or property rights for Mexicans. Indeed, because of various state ratifications of the treaty, the Land Act of 1851, and the Gadsden Purchase, Mexican Americans found that the treaty did not guarantee any rights for them as an American people at all.

The U.S.- Mexico War and the treaty that followed set a contradictory precedent of democratic inclusion that would haunt both Anglo-Americans and Mexican Americans from the ending of the war well through the twenty-first century. Gómez-Quiñones makes this point when he argues that the treaty would stand as a foundational civil rights document that would affect not only how Anglos constitute Mexican Americans as a people in public culture, but also how Mexicans represent themselves as private and public subjects of an American nation that first promised an "egalitarian" and "benevolent" solution to the war. Moreover, as Norma Alarcón astutely theorizes, the war and the treaty that followed "dichotomized" Mexicans in the United States as a split people, "Mexican/American." According to the contradictory people-making language of the treaty, the Mexicans' designation in the United States constituted them as both a stranger and a member of the United States, and, as such, Mexican people in the United States have had to fight for their inclusion in the courts and in the literary and political public spheres as a dichotomized political subject.[14]

In the social imaginary of the Anglo-American population in the United States, the Treaty of Guadalupe Hidalgo established a civil, racial, and geographic definition of Mexican peoplehood that would help Anglo incorporation of lands across the continent. No other than Karl Marx's comrade Friedrich Engels captured the people-making importance of the treaty for American capitalist enterprise when he questioned:

> How did it happen that over Texas a war broke out between these two
> republics, which, according to moral theory, ought to have been "frater-
> nally united" and "federated," and that, owing to "geographical, com-
> mercial and strategic necessities," the "sovereign will" of the American
> people, supported by the bravery of the American volunteers, shifted the
> boundaries drawn by nature some hundreds of miles further south? Or
> is it perhaps unfortunate that splendid California has been taken away

from the lazy Mexicans, who could not do anything with it? That the energetic Yankees by rapid exploitation of the Californian gold mines will increase the means of circulation, in a few years will concentrate a dense population and extensive trade at the most suitable places on the coast of the pacific Ocean, create large cities, open up communications by steamship, construct railways from New York to San Francisco, for the first time really open the Pacific Ocean to civilization, and the third time really open the Pacific to a new direction? The "independence" of a few Spanish Californians and Texans may suffer because of it, in some places "justice" and other moral principals may be violated; but what does that matter compared to such facts as world-historic significance. (Engels, *Democratic Pan-Slavism* 1849)

For Engels and Marx, the modern implications of a Communist revolution outweighed the geopolitical expansion of the war and the legal rhetoric of the aforementioned treaty that would "violate" the rights and status of Mexicans as a people. I further elaborate on Marx's positions on Mexican rights in my discussion of Emma Tenayuca in chapter 5, but I want to point out now that Marx and Engels were able to justify their arguments because, according to Engels, Mexican people were "lazy." In 1854, even Marx argued that Mexicans were "degenerate," and thus, in the end, they "rejoice in the conquest of Mexico," for Mexicans can learn from the "tutelage of the American people."

Not all Americans were completely sure if the Mexican people were capable of tutelage, however. Although echoing the racial sentiments of Marx and Engels, Senator John C. Calhoun made a statement to Congress that was later printed in the *Congressional Record*; he stated that Mexicans represented "a motley amalgamation of impure races, not [even] as good as Cherokees and Choctaws" (17). He continued to ask the American public if they could "incorporate a people so dissimilar in every respect—so little qualified for free and popular government—without certain destruction to our political institutions. We do not want the people of Mexico, either as citizens or subjects" (17). Calhoun's comments about Mexicans found their impetus in his anxieties about the U.S. ability to "democratically" control the western territories and the newly constituted Mexicans who lived on U.S. lands after the war. Discussing the limits and possibilities of American democracy in the same year as Engels, in 1849, Senator Calhoun asked if the "constitution extended to the territories or does it not extend to them" (341). Calhoun's question reveals how the territorial growth of the United States after the signing of the treaty and the Gadsden Purchase of 1853 would supplant foundational questions about the capacity of democracy and its ability to deal with the new lands that they had forcefully acquired. Much like O'Sullivan in "The Mexican Question," in the end, Calhoun felt that democracy could deal with the new landscapes and the Mexicans, for the racial mission of the United States enabled him to declare that expansion and democracy were not contradictory; they were complementary (34).

As Calhoun and Engels show, the racial and political status of U.S. Mexicans after the war and the geographic space they inhabit—both the southwest territories and the United States' geographic location to Mexico—raised important questions that created anxiety about U.S. democratic sovereignty. These questions remained an important topic in magazine culture. One of the most interesting and widely publicized magazines to address the post-treaty Mexican Question was an 1878 *Scribner's* series on the U.S.-Mexico War, "Recallings from a Public Life II: Texas and the Peace of Guadalupe Hidalgo." Written by an ex–public statesman Robert Dale Owen (not to be confused with Robert Owens, Robert Dale's father), the article historically traces the American conquest of Mexico and argues that the war and the treaty that followed are the most important aspects of our national character. He goes on to tell the American people that we are fortunate we did not acquire all of Mexico. For now that the lands are "public domain," he ponders, what shall we do with Mexicans? Our new lands and the Mexican people, he continues, are the questions of the day. He concludes by noting that it would have been more of a "national calamity" if the United States had acquired any more of Mexican lands and its "parti-colored population" (878). How the national anxiety over the newly constituted "Mexican American" became interrelated with America's inquiry into Mexico, its borders, landscapes, and cultures of contact within the newly acquired "public domain" is the focus of the next section.

A View from the Parlor: Incorporating Eastern Modernity within a Pre-Modern Southwest

Under the provisions of the Treaty of Guadalupe Hidalgo, two cartographic commissions, one Mexican and the other American, were assigned to map the border between the United States and Mexico.[15] This

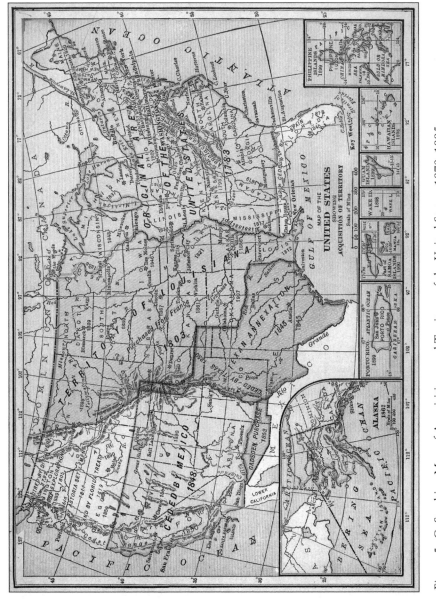

Figure 5. G. Stocking Map of Acquisitions and Territory of the United States, 1870–1885

task was not easy, for this border would not only define the geographic and national boundaries of the republic known as the United States and Mexico; it would also delineate the political subjects known as Mexican and American. Indeed, it took nearly ten years and many maps to finally define the borders as we know them today (Figure 5). Defining the cartographic boundaries between the United States and Mexico was also a defining moment that marks what Étienne Balibar refers to as the "overdetermined" nature of a border's history. The border between the United States and Mexico, then, should be seen as both a real geographic space and as an "institution" that constitutes lived experiences, political subjectivity, differentiated social, class and racial subject positions.[16] In this way, the border marks one of the most complicated elements of Mexican peoplehood in the United States.

It should come as no surprise that representations of the Mexican/U.S. border entered the American public imagination instantly after the U.S.-Mexico War; print culture characterized it as a mysterious, violent place of contact. Magazine articles such as James Pilcher's "Outlawry on the Mexican Border" (Scribner's 1891) and "The Depredations on the Rio-Grande" (Appleton's 1873) helped found a mythic construction of the border as geographic space where American and Mexican people violently collided. As such, the borderlands region between the United States and Mexico was then as well as now perhaps the most challenging geographic space for the magazines to incorporate into the American body politic. One representative magazine article that began to relate the "overdetermined" temporal logic of the U.S./Mexico borderlands that has received much attention from Chicano scholars José Limón and José David Saldívar is John G. Bourke's "The American Congo," published in Scribner's Magazine in 1894. Although they read Bourke's ethnographic representations of the Mexican borderlands differently, taken together, their arguments are important for my own discussion of the overdetermined site of the U.S.-Mexico border and its discursive affects on Mexican peoplehood. Limón's Dancing with the Devil is the first to recover Bourke as a complicated historical figure, who was dealing with his own ethnic ambivalence (24–32). Arguing that Bourke's "American Congo" promoted American expansionism, Saldívar's Border Matters, in contrast, argues that Chicanos from Américo Paredes and John Rechy to Helena María Viramontes have had to undo the plethora of imperializing discourse that Bourke's "American Congo" promoted (166). I suggest that Bourke's "American Congo" is pervasive in the nineteenth and late-twentieth-century public spheres precisely because of its complex presentation of the border that gave rise to the Mexican Question. "American Congo" also begins to show the paradoxes of the border and its critical position in the understanding of not only the geopolitical foundations of U.S. democracy but also how Mexicans later would try to redefine the border's geopolitical designs, which will be more fully addressed in chapter 5.

With more than a dozen full-text pictures of the border region, Bourke's work creates a "synoptical sketch for the readers of *Scribner's*, both of the territory under consideration and the manners, customs and superstitions of the Mexicans to be found within its limits" (Saldívar, *Border Matters* 598). Comparing the border races and the Rio Grande to the African races and the Nile of the "Dark Continent," Bourke meticulously describes the space for his eastern audience as a pre-modern land where a unique culture has developed, one that was born out of conflict and that attempts to maintain a culture separate from the "modern" United States. Bourke argues:

> If we enter into the homes of these people and mingle with them, it soon becomes evident that wehave encountered a most interesting study of ethnology and anthropology; they constitute a distinct class, resisting all attempts at amalgamation. There are to this rule, as to all rules, notable exceptions, and there are on the river some few representatives of the higher stage of evolution; but in general terms, the Rio Grande Mexican resists today, as he has always resisted, the encroachments of the Gringo and the domination of his own Mexico. (606)

Speaking for the Mexican people of the border, Bourke becomes the interpreter of Mexican culture for an eastern public, visually capturing the Mexican's essence through many detailed woodcuts. Although Bourke employs an ethnographic relativism and argues that the people of the border are like any other culture, he inevitably constructs an evolutionary discourse that argues that the Mexicans are America's pre-modern and uncivilized others. The article goes as far as implicitly arguing that their pre-modern and uncivilized behavior is innate. As the preceding quote indicates, higher evolution of a species means a race is civil and modern. And since civilization is equated with the modern United States and a democratic and capitalist first world, then "amalgamation" of the Mexican people into the white republic would be a step toward the civilizing process. Bourke's narrative concludes by arguing that only certain Mexicans are capable of assimilating and notes that Mexican indigenes are incapable of assimilating into white society.

As such, Bourke is not constructing *all* of the Mexican people of the border as pre-modern and uncivilized. As Limón argues, Bourke does find a higher order of Mexican people in the borderlands region: the elite Mexicans (*Dancing with the Devil* 32). Indeed, Bourke even goes as far as to compare this Mexican class to white Europeans: "the Saxons and the Danish" (594). And like the Saxon and Danish lack of effect on the Celts of Ireland, this refined, well-bred Mexican class exerts very little cultural influence "upon the indigenes around them" (594). Bourke's essay is one of the first "ethno-geographic" magazine narratives to acknowledge an elite Mexican people (*gente de razón*) that is distinct from the working-class Mexicans, what he defines as the "indigenes." As I show in the chapters that follow, the distinction that Bourke describes between the racial and uncivilized "indigenes" and the assimilable and refined elites became a pervasive Anglo and elite Mexican inquiry into the characteristics and definitions of Mexican peoplehood after the treaty. To be a civilized person meant that one was a member of the white body politic. And since Anglos had earlier defined the Indians of the frontier as not civilized, and thus not citizens, much of the same rhetoric was shifted to the newly constituted Mexican American population (Slotkin 15–22).

In the end, Bourke's desire to "amalgamate" certain Mexicans on the border with the national body politic reveals that he is trying to set the terms for Mexican incorporation after the war. To this end, Bourke's essay is interesting because he exposes foundational questions that emerged from Mexican and Anglo contact. Bourke's essay implies the question: Can we incorporate the Mexican people into the nation? This ambivalent inquiry, I suggest, continues to affect the politics of Mexican inclusion in the United States (Limón, *Dancing with the Devil* 31–37). Gómez-Quiñones astutely points out that the period after the signing of the Treaty of Guadalupe Hidalgo, when the United States defined its borders and made the once-Mexican lands public domain, marks one of the most important periods of Anglo and Mexican relations. It is important to remember that before and especially after the treaty, Mexican people persisted in maintaining their communities in the face of territorial redistribution. In this way, contact between Mexicans and Anglos in the borderlands delineated as "public domain" became increasingly important to the eastern reading public that Bourke's essay helped define. The question concerning the incorporation of Mexicans was at the heart of the bi-cultural dynamics of the Mexican Question.

The inquiry into the rights and status of Mexicans in the geographic space now called the United States presupposed an intercultural inquest into how Anglos would relate to the newly constituted "Mexican American" during and after Anglo-American consolidation. Indeed, after the treaty was signed, hundreds of regionalist and ethno-geographic essays in eastern magazines went to lengths to define the ethno-landscapes of contact and to describe Mexican and Anglo relations in the west to an eastern public. Perhaps the most interesting of these narratives is that by the American writer Stephen Crane, who captured the intercultural dynamics of the Mexican Question well in 1897 when he wrote a short "regionalist" story for *Century Magazine* entitled "A Man and Some Others." Crane is one of the first "fictional" writers to address the cultural politics of "amalgamation" that Bourke interrogates in his own work.

It bears on this argument to relate that before Crane wrote his Mexican stories, no less a figure than Theodore Roosevelt wrote to Crane with a rather interesting request: "Some day I want you to write another story of the frontiersman and the Mexican Greaser in which the frontiersman shall come out on top; it is more normal that way!" (Wertheim and Sorrentino 201). Published in *Century Magazine* in 1897, one year after Roosevelt wrote this letter, Crane's "A Man and Some Others" responds to Roosevelt's "manifest" request to endorse white masculinity at the expense of the Mexican other. For Crane it is the "laws of fate" in the landscape of the west that (de)construct the embodied identity of his protagonist and inevitably render his white body as a cultural signifier of U.S. western imperialism (603). In the end, Crane's work extends both Roosevelt's request and his own narrative *How the West Was Won*, which rendered the southwest as romantically white and male.

Written after he spent many months in Mexico and the southwest, Crane's "A Man and Some Others," for example, inscribes naturalism onto the frontiers of the southwest to subvert the western romance genre that was popular within the U.S. literary spheres. Many of these stories in magazine culture of the time created a myth of the frontier through their characterization of a brave and resourceful Anglo-American protagonist, taming the west for settlers and, in turn, allegorically perpetuating the expansion of the United States (Slotkin 135–137). Crane, however, uses naturalism to deconstruct the romantic mythos of the rugged individual and explores how the whiteness of the protagonist is constructed and ultimately determined by a colonial encounter between a man and some (Mexican) others on the Mexican/American frontier. In the end, it is a story of peoplehood that explores the role that Mexican otherness has in the formation of white, male people-making. (See Figure 6.)

Set in an unspecified southwestern region, "A Man and Some Others," like many other romantic westerns, begins with a lone cowboy. The plot develops when a Mexican vaquero confronts the Anglo cowboy and asks him to leave his land or he will kill him. From the outset, however, Crane subverts the western romance genre Roosevelt desired him to write. Indeed, Crane's story inevitably exposes the racial dynamics between Mexicans and Anglos that developed in Greater Mexico after the Treaty of Guadalupe Hidalgo. Crane's title, for example, first reveals to the reader the racial dynamic Crane is trying to expose—"a man," presumably a white man, and some others, undoubtedly Mexican "others." And as the first pages divulge, the man, Bill, is indeed a great American cowboy, "an aristocrat, one who possessed unlimited credit in the saloons" and the power to physically lynch a man (605). Adopting the western formula, Crane confronts this great western hero with his moral and racial opposite, the "mystic and sinister" Mexican other (603). The Mexican, like most naturalist brutes, has no name in the story; he is an unknown force, a silent "Other who defines humanity by negation" (Howard 80).

Through this confrontation with death that results when the Anglo outsider meets the Mexican, Crane creates a characteristic that June Howard defines as the "antinomies of naturalism." Crane's narrative exposes how the white embodied identity of the protagonist, Bill, depends on this racial antinomy between himself and the brutal Mexican other, his less-civilized, less-human negation. In this way, Crane's formal dichotomy between "a man and some others" represents the "real" racial antinomy between Mexicans and Anglo-Americans on the (colonial) frontier after the Treaty of Guadalupe. It is a trope that makes the very whiteness of Bill's body visible, thereby revealing how Bill's white manhood depends on the silent, Mexican other's brown racial body. But in a rather ironic conclusion, the reader learns that to be the white, heroic cowboy that Roosevelt requests is not necessarily desirable, for Bill's body has become all too visible in the Mexican territories.

Though given the choice by the Mexicans to peacefully leave their land, Bill decides to stay, and the Mexican other inevitably kills him. Crane intimates throughout the story that though offered the choice to

Figure 6. Frederic Remington's drawing for Stephen Crane's short story, published on the first page of "A Man and Some Others," *Century* magazine

leave peacefully, Bill fails to understand and respect the unknown racial other who confronts him (Robertson 246). Bill's failure, then, lies in thinking that he is the western hero Roosevelt desires, for his pride impairs his ability to realize that the Mexicans outnumber him and that it is not his land. And the laws that Bill espouses in the first pages that he feels protect him under the Treaty of Guadalupe Hidalgo are not Mexican laws (Crane, "A Man and Some Others" 603). Furthermore, his failure lies in not realizing that his whiteness and the privilege that it affords him in the saloons of Wyoming—a more civilized and white space—is merely a construction based on Anglo-American, not Mexican, Manifest Destinies created in heroic romantic myths of a passive Native American or Mexican culture. What the reader and Bill learn, then, is that the southwest and America's "public domain" is not an unreal tale of romance; it is a brutally real site of social conflict. Moreover, through this conclusion, the western lands known as public domain are not depicted as a mythic space for the Anglo-American protagonist to tame in the name of Anglo democracy; rather, the lands that were once Mexican are conflictual and contestatory spaces where cultures disagree, not consent, over political and geographic emplacement.

Crane's contradictory story of Mexican peoplehood is ironic in that it is one of the first and very few examples wherein white Americans in magazine culture begin to publish stories that interrogate the intercultural role that Mexicans have in the formation of white peoplehood.[17] In many ways, Crane set the discursive space in the literary public spheres for the first Mexican American writer of magazine stories, Maria Christina Mena, who garnered success in the literary public spheres through equally complicated fictional stories of Mexican peoplehood. I end this chapter, therefore, with a brief look at this important, though overlooked, Mexican cultural worker who began to remap the contours of Mexican peoplehood within the very magazines that had historically racialized Mexicans in the United States. In this way, María Cristina Mena's story of Mexican peoplehood extends the rhetoric of the Mexican Question and, to some degree, challenges Crane's masculine interpretations of Mexican-Anglo relations.[18] Despite Mena's prolific career as a magazine short-story writer, it was only recently that the U.S. Hispanic Literary Heritage Project recovered her works. Mena was born in Mexico City in 1893. She came from an elite Mexican family who sent her to study in the United States when she was fourteen. She began writing short stories when she was twenty and published over thirteen articles in such magazines as *Century* and *American*. Labeled in these magazines as the "foremost interpreter of Mexican life" (Mena 137), Mena had quite a presence in the U.S. literary public spheres and even had a professional relationship with D. H. Lawrence.

One of the most interesting of her stories is "The Gold Vanity Set," published in *American Magazine* in 1913 (Mena 1–11). This story is important because it reveals how both Anglos and elite Mexicans struggled to define the Mexican "indigenous" peoplehood that Bourke spent so much time detailing in the U.S. public spheres. The story is set in Mexico and focuses on the Mexican woman Petra's encounter with a white woman traveler who has come to study the Mexican people. In many ways, the story is similar to the exotic travel narratives written in the magazines by Anglos; however, in this story the Mexican woman, not the Anglo traveler, is the central protagonist.

Chicano critics have argued that Mena's "folk" representation of Mexican people in this and other stories is contradictory, inevitably perpetuating Anglo racist stereotypes to the eastern public about Mexicans.

Chuck Tatum argues, for example, that "[Mena's] talents are undermined by her tendency to create obsequious Mexican characters who fit comfortably within the American reader's expectations" in the nineteenth century (132). I end with Mena because her folk stories of Anglo and Mexican contact should not be seen as statically racist or "quaint," as Raymond Paredes argues, but, rather, demonstrate the contradictory manner in which Mexicans engaged the Mexican Question through their stories of peoplehood (Paredes 37). The first page of "The Gold Vanity Set" reveals a Mexican's own struggle in defining and setting the terms of Mexican peoplehood in a literary public sphere that delineated the stereotypical boundaries for Mexicans in the United States:

> She grew tall and slender, as strong as a wire, with a small head and extremely delicate features, and her skin was the color of new leather. Her eyes were wonderful, even in a land of wonderful eyes. They were large and mysterious, heavily shaped with lashes which had a trick of quivering nervously, half lowered in an evasive, fixed, sidelong look when anyone spoke to her. The irises were amber colored, but always looked darker. Her voice was like a ghost, dying away at the ends of sentences in fear, yet with all of its tenderness holding a hint of barbaric roughness. The dissimulation lurking in that low voice and those melting eyes was characteristic of a race among whom the frankness of the Spaniard is criticized as unpolished. (Mena 1).

The opening description of Petra's body describes the complexity of Mena's negotiation of the Mexican Question. For the implied Anglo-American public, this vivid description of Petra's Indian body echoes the ethnographic sketches that created physical caricatures and endorsed a racial hierarchy's of whites over Mexicans. In this way, this quote is a prime example of Raymond Paredes' and Tatum's arguments against Mena's "exotic" fictional representations of Mexican folk culture. To them, "The Gold Vanity Set" merely perpetuates the magazine culture's racist definition of the Mexicans as primitive folk. This, however, is not the complete reading of the passage or the story. Let us not forget that Petra is "tall and slender," and Mena depicts her as a beautiful woman. This physical description is very different from the magazine characterizations of indigenous Mexican women, which, as you may recall, characterized them as "dark, short and fat" (Lighton 987).

Moreover, in "The Gold Vanity Set," the indigenous are able to take control of their exoticized bodies from both Mexican elites and Anglos. This is revealed in two pivotal scenes. First, it appears when an Anglo woman and a Mexican Don attempt to capture Petra's corporeal essence by taking her picture.[19] Petra refuses both of them and thus does not become an exotic object, so popular in the turn-of-the-century public spheres. Indeed, in the very same magazines that Mena was writing her stories, photographic exhibitions of Mexicans became very popular.

Equally intriguing is Petra's appropriation of the Anglo woman's gold vanity set through her wrapping it in a cornhusk. Rather than using its make-up contents to "civilize" her Mexican body, she offers it on an altar to the Virgin de Guadalupe. Perhaps to the eastern Anglo reader who is accustomed to these exotic stories, this and the other scene create a quaint or even derogatory view of Mexican folk life, for it reveals that Petra is naive about modern, civilized white women's manners. There is more to this scene, however, for it also reveals that she does not buy into white manners of womanhood. Her refusal to have her picture taken or to use the gold vanity set is a symbolic refusal of not only the gendered ideals and norms of white womanhood but also, symbolically, the U.S. materialistic and economic exploitation of Mexican people. Petra is able to maintain a life that is independent from U.S. capitalism and the gendered manners that attempt but fail to define their Mexican womanhood. In the end, the Mexicans of Mena's stories emerge as a distinct people who define the contours of their peoplehood with and against the United States.

To this end, one cannot simply state that Mena's "folk stories" were either derogatory or liberating for Mexican culture. Much like Petra, who struggles with the meaning of Mexican peoplehood in the wake of U.S. imperialism, Mena was constantly negotiating between a discourse of the Mexican Question that incorporates and limits Mexican peoplehood for racist and imperialist uses in the literary public sphere and another aspect of the Mexican Question which was a celebration of an authentic Mexican Indian culture (like Bourke, for example) that is able to (re)present a mestizo collectivity to the American public. "The Gold Vanity Set" is important because it captures Mena's paradoxical location as a "representative" Mexican woman in an Anglo literary public sphere who comes to represent the dialectic between an authentic Mexican woman writing about Mexican people for the modern, industrial United States with its Anglocentric perceptions of Mexican people in the first place. Like Mena, the cultural workers in the following chapters, and to some degree Zavala in the previous, all had to negotiate the constituting rhetoric of the Mexican Question in their own constitutive stories of Mexican peoplehood.

The Anglo-American Mexican Question mapped in this chapter, which fostered a racial inquiry that affected their political subjectivity in the United States, deeply affected the Mexican cultural workers of this study because the Anglo inquest failed to address the complexities and heterogeneity of Mexican peoplehood. As such, it comes as no surprise that the negotiation and contestation of the Anglo-American Mexican Question led Mexicans in the United States to create different and at times competing stories of Mexican collectivity. What they had in common, however, was the desire to recover their own stories of peoplehood that would answer the inquest into the Anglo-American "Mexican Question" on their own terms and thus allow them to emerge as "a [distinct] Mexican people united through their struggles" (Pereles 45).

3

Embodying Manifest Destiny
María Amparo Ruiz de Burton and the Color of Mexican Womanhood

Thinking of this, the mind is lead to the thought that—with some exceptions, of course—a nation can, with good government, avoid the majority of those misfortunes which we now call *"unavoidable human sorrows."* If we were to trace our troubles to their veritable source, we would often reach, more or less directrly, their origin in [*our lawgivers*]. Not only the dwellers of the frontiers, not only the victims of lawsuits, not only—but I am no political philosopher. I am wandering away from my humble path. We must go back to the readers of the manuscript, and accompany them in their sad task.
Amparo Burton de Ruiz, *Who Would Have Thought It?*, 201.

While living in New England in 1869, María Amparo Ruiz de Burton, the first Mexican in the United States to write an English-language novel, wrote a revealing letter to the once–California Governor Mariano Guadalupe Vallejo. Both intellectuals and leaders of Mexican California's *gente de razon* (people with reason), Ruiz[1] and Vallejo wrote to each other throughout their lifetime and had a close relationship. While Ruiz lived in New England, she wrote more than fifty letters that thematically dealt with politics, history, and her experiences in the eastern states of the republic. The letter she wrote to Vallejo in 1869 is of particular importance because she discussed the racial and gendered aspects of her body that she believed had excluded her from full access to the democratic public spheres. She begins with a rather interesting lament: "Ah, if I were a man. What a sorry thing a woman is!"[2] Providence, she claimed, should make up for having made her a woman, "ugly and poor."

She continues to write that she "no longer has any enthusiasm for this continent [United States]." "What for?" she asks; "neither my race nor my sex will gain anything from it." Therefore, she will no longer consider U.S. republicanism and its theories.[3] She continues by stating that just "hearing" the U.S.'s republican hypocritical ideology of Manifest Destiny "makes my blood boil." "Where are my twelve acres of land?," she concludes. I suggest that Ruiz's critique of republicanism, both Mexican and U.S., reveals that she is participating in a long line of protofeminist thinkers who explored the sexual politics of the gendered body and its significance in people-making.

Ruiz's implicit desire to shed her body is not because she is anti-woman; rather, she understands that her gender prevented her from entering the public spheres as a fully equal person with the ability to fight for individual and collective Mexican rights. She realizes that Mexican racial and, especially for her, gendered ideologies have their limits in a U.S. republic that views Mexican women as objects of conquest. Her letter implicitly reveals that the nineteenth-century republican body politic is based on the representation of a white, masculine *demos*, a Hobbesian body politic where only "the artificial [white] man" who is "naturally" capable of reason is able to enter and represent the people of a given republic (Hobbes, *Leviathan* 81–82). Realizing that her race and gender have done nothing for her in the United States, she concludes that she must give up on all republican theories. Republicanism, she infers, constructs a public and private divide that dislocates both racialized and gendered bodies from U.S. republican ideals of peoplehood. Her body holds what Susan Bordo refers to as an "unbearable weight" within a republic that her class position as *gente de razon* cannot negotiate (23).

Born in Baja California in 1832, María Amparo Ruiz de Burton came from the landed Mexican classes. In 1849, one year after the signing of the Treaty of Guadalupe Hidalgo, she married Colonel Henry S. Burton, who was sent to Baja California to quell a Mexican uprising. After their marriage, Ruiz went with Col. Burton to the northeast, where she began her literary career as a novelist. The northeast affected her tremendously, and in 1869 she began writing *Who Would Have Thought It?*, a novel that captures her experiences of New England well. Ruiz's letter to Vallejo, written the same year she was writing her novel, is consonant with this chapter's leitmotif: locating the representational politics of the racialized and sexualized Mexican woman's body at the core of nineteenth-century republican peoplehood. As Hobbes, Locke, Jefferson, and the founding fathers constituted it, republican ideology and the public and private spheres that it depended on created a democracy that excluded women and people of color from fully participating as full members of the *demos* (Mohanram 81). Like Mary Wollstonecraft, Ruiz could not accept the powerful strand of political thinking that subsumed the interests of women under the universal individual—that is, the male American citizen. This chapter considers this republican ideology against Ruiz's corporeal representations of the Mexican Question in the formation of Reconstruction Era peoplehood.

When Ruiz argues that she has given up on republicanism, and indicts its Anglo "apostles," she does so because republican theory has constituted her Mexican racial and gendered body in the realm of the private. As a Mexican and a woman,[4] her body is both racially marked and sexualized in the public sphere by Anglos, thus she could not enjoy the privilege of becoming an abstracted and disembodied person of the masculine body politic that the U.S. republic has constructed. Unlike her lifelong interlocutor, Mariano Guadalupe Vallejo, a Mexican man, and unlike Lorenzo de Zavala of chapter 2—Amparo Ruiz was a double minority in the republican body politic after the Treaty of Guadalupe Hidalgo. Though both have racial bodies, her "sex," as she argued, had a powerful double meaning, for it denotes her gender and her sexuality, which she finds is just as circumscribed as race in the republican version of peoplehood.[5]

The same year that she wrote the above letter to Vallejo, Ruiz wrote another to him, arguing that republicanism is a utopian form of government that will not foster collectivity for Mexicans. She concludes, therefore, that Mexicans on both sides of the border should not embrace the idea of creating a "Republic of Sierra Madre." According to Ruiz, Mexican male politicos have embraced republican democracy to the country's misfortune, and, as such, they have emasculated themselves in the process. One wonders if she is referring to the likes of Zavala. Following Mary Wollstonecraft and her contemporary Victoria Woodhull, I consider Amparo Ruiz's contradictory investigation into the contested politics of Mexican womanhood as central to republicanism and one of the most controversial legislative acts passed during the era, the Fourteenth Amendment.

Indeed, it is important to point out that Woodhull's public lecture on Constitutional equality and the Fourteenth Amendment followed Ruiz's private concerns about the contested racial politics of womanhood, as Woodhull states:

> A race is composed of two sexes. If you speak of a race you include both sexes. . . . The same line of reasoning applies to the word color, although some assume to say that color in this amendment means black, as white is no color. But how should any know what specific color is referred to in this amendment? One might say that it is intended to mean a copper color; another a mulatto color and still another that of Spanish. (158)

Taken together, Victoria Woodhull's public address and Amparo Ruiz's private correspondences reveal the centrality of the body, gender, and race in Reconstruction Era notions of womanhood and the masculine ideal and norms that structure universal peoplehood. Political philosopher Catherine Holland makes this point when she argues that the body came into direct focus in this period, a moment when the contested place of the racialized and gendered body in the public spheres would forever change how Americans understood their peoplehood. It is important to remember that the Fourteenth Amendment constituted only "male inhabitants of the states for equal protection," and it is the Fifteenth Amendment that introduces the terms "race and color." In effect, after these two amendments, no longer was the body an abstract and universal norm of peoplehood; these two amendments made the body politically visible for the first time in democratic history. According to Holland, the body took up an entirely different meaning in the years of the Reconstruction (123). Once a figure of surpassed and abstract meaning in democratic culture's conception of peoplehood, the materiality of race and the gendered body became a contradictory marker for peoplehood. What political philosophers do not consider, however, is that the Mexican Question informed these debates in the national public sphere.

Woodhull's reference to the "Spanish" race to identify the constitutional complexities of defining the color of "the people" is revealing. When she asks what "color" are the people to whom the amendment is referring, she evokes a Spanish type and the "color" of racial bodies to complicate the amendment's referentiality. Woodhull's question marks the representational crisis that is inherent to the logic of the Mexican Question that I discuss here in chapter 2. Ironically, her question about the representational contradictions of the Amendments reveals the masculine desires for European Americans to define the Spanish and Mexicans in the United States according to an embodied or "colored" notion of peoplehood. To this end, Woodhull's reference to Spanish color is not an accident; she is using the masculine and racial inquests about Mexicans in the United States (whom she refers to as "Spanish") to advance the fight for woman's suffrage.

When Woodhull evoked the Mexican Question, the landmark case of *People v. De La Guerra* [40 Cal. 311, 337 (1870)] was brought to the California Supreme Court and asked the very same question that Woodhull did in her essay. In this case, the State of California argued that De La Guerra was not a white citizen despite the fact that he had claimed that he was a Spanish-American, a Californio landed elite—a *gente de razon*—whose family had lived in the lands of the United States for hundreds of years. A distinguished citizen of Santa Barbara and a delegate of the first Constitutional Convention in California, De La Guerra stated before the court that he was a person of predominantly Spanish, not Mexican, ancestry. As such, the United States should constitute him as a member of the democratic people. The state countered that there was a question concerning his bloodline, arguing that he was a mestizo and therefore a person of color. Ironically, the lawyers for the state of California argued that as a mestizo he did not fall under the Fourteenth Amendment's legislation of protection and citizenship. With De La Guerra, the State of California, in fact, was trying to answer Woodhull's question.

Legal scholar Guadalupe Luna and anthropologist Martha Menchaca astutely argue that during the Reconstruction Era the U.S. public spheres created a harsh racial climate and questions concerning Mexican rights were extremely prevalent. For them, the Treaty of Guadalupe Hidalgo's legal rhetoric had not yet answered the questions of Mexican peoplehood in the United States. This post-1848-treaty period that American historians define as the Reconstruction Era created complex legal questions concerning the rights and status of Mexicans as an included people of the United States (the rhetorical inquest I located in chapter 2 as the Mexican Question). And much like John O'Sullivan's and the other essays concerning the Mexican Question, I want to insist that the national public spheres predicated its rhetoric on the democratic representation of the Mexican body. For him, it was De La Guerra's blood that defined his race and rights. The democratic conditions of equality set in motion after the signing of the Fourteenth and Fifteenth Amendments, then, not only were based on the black body, as historians argue, but also were predicated by the inquiry into what exactly constituted and represented a Mexican body. Were they similar to or different from other people of color in the United States, as Woodhull implicitly asks?

The Body of Who Would Have Thought It?

Amparo Ruiz's private letters about the politics of Mexican womanhood as it relates to the masculine presuppositions of the Mexican Question presents for us a complicated backdrop of her public persona as a writer creating stories of Mexican peoplehood in the U.S. literary public sphere during this post-treaty era. The struggle that Amparo Ruiz dealt with in her desire to write a story of Mexican womanhood for a European American audience presents itself in a review of *Who Would Have Thought It? in* 1872:

> A Native Californian, authoress—a literary incognito lost in an interview—a new sensation for the public, Mrs. Burton is a native Californian; her beauty is of a pure Castilian type, graceful, non-chalant and easy. Judging from her present appearance, her form and features, and the bright glance of her eyes, so well preserved, what she must have been at sweet sixteen—A perusal of the book is sufficient to satisfy the reader that Mrs. Burton has talent, descriptive and narrative power, and a critical though perhaps too cynical habit of observation. (Ruiz, *Conflicts of Interest* 492)

This review is interesting and telling of the representations surrounding Mexican women in the nineteenth-century literary public spheres. On the one hand, the review goes at length to characterize the body of Ruiz and the sexual attraction that her body creates for the male reviewer; only a few lines actually review the content of the book. The review, then, works to make Ruiz's body the focus of her literary achievements, not her mind or aesthetics. There is a desire by the literary public sphere, here represented by the reviewer, to circumscribe her body, to highlight its importance in the creation of a novel. In effect, the reviewer is trying to come to terms with her book and its content through her Mexican body, and in merging them, he is attempting to conquer the sardonic wit of the novel and its critique of U.S. political culture. Certainly, this would not be the first time Ruiz was an object of male fantasy. She was first known in Anglo public culture through the song "The Maid of Monterey," an 1851 ballad about the U.S.-Mexico War. The song represents her as the "senorita" who mended Anglo soldiers on the U.S.-Mexico War battlefield and whose "bright beauty" drove "death's pang away."[6] As a Mexican woman and an object of male desire, Ruiz enters the literary public sphere through her body first.

Of course, the representations of Mexican women's bodies were not new to the nineteenth-century literary public spheres. From dime novels to maps to short stories to poems, Mexican women were the sexual objects of the white American male gaze. As Antonia Casteñeda argues, Californiana and Indian women were objects of the colonization process, representations that marked the "beauty" of conquest.[7] While Ruiz lived, there were countless European American novels and works that represented the relationship between Mexican women's bodies and geopolitics. From dime novels to newspaper articles in which the recurring figures of La Malinche and Califas are rendered, Mexican women's bodies became central to the geopolitical designs of the United States. I highlight two important representations that illuminate the masculinist landscaping of Mexican women's bodies: the Tallis illustrated map of California and Mexico (1851) and John Gast's landscape painting *American Progress* (1872) (Figures 7 and 8).

In the Tallis map of California and Mexico, the marginal emplacement of the naked Mexican woman in the bottom left-hand corner reveals much about the rhetoric of conquest that inscribed Mexican women after the treaty. The cartographic practice of placing symbols on maps was common in the seventeenth, eighteenth, and nineteenth centuries. Instead of Mexican women, however, sea monsters would often encompass the margins. By moving dangerous or potentially resurgent elements to the margins of the map, fear of threats to the virgin land were circumscribed. According to this map, Mexican women were yet another space to occupy, control, and fear. This would ensure that the land remains virgin or empty, a space waiting to be filled or dominated. In effect, clearing space (or mining space) in the west became a tool to establish whiteness and male dominance over Mexican women and men—thereby differentiating eastern expansionists from Mexicans through sexual designs.

Indeed, clearing space for whiteness through controlled representations of womens' bodies is perfectly illustrated in John Gast's *American Progress*. Here a white woman's body becomes the manifestation of Man-

Figure 7. Tallis's map of California, the Southwest, and Mexico, 1851

Figure 8. John Gast's painting *American Progress, or Manifest Destiny*, 1872

ifest Destiny itself, clearing the landscape of foreign bodies. Equally important here is that the relationship that brown Mexican women's bodies held to the land was not the same as white women's bodies. Mexican women, like the land, are that which is conquered or marginalized outside of the landscape; white women in Gast's *American Progress* are what clear the land of ethnic bodies.[8] It is no small coincidence that Ruiz's book *Who Would Have Thought It?* was published the same year that Gast's painting was commissioned and was publicly displayed throughout the eastern United States. In fact, Gast's painting was one of the most popular landscape portraits of the period, and prints were sold throughout the United States. Attached to many land advertisements of the nineteenth century, the painting was meant to entice Anglo-Americans to venture into the west and the lands of California where Amparo Ruiz lived.

Considering the images associated with Mexican women and conquest, it is surprising that Ruiz was able to enter the literary sphere in the first place—as a writer, the reviewer notes, who created a sardonic critique of the United States. This achievement of being the first Mexican novel written in English and published by a very prestigious publishing house, Lippincott, should not go unnoticed in Mexican American literary history. Moreover, it is important to point out that the American literary public spheres had never seen anything like her in the history of American letters. The irony here is that the literary public sphere was perhaps the most inclusive of all publics. It was the only space that women and people of color could create publicity for the advancement of womanhood. It gave Ruiz the ability to question republicanism and reinscribe the Mexican Question through a Mexican perspective. Indeed, it would be in the opening scene of María Amparo Ruiz de Burton's *Who Would Have Thought It?* where we begin to see this embodied logic, as it reveals the novel's central theme: the problems of locating what was in the nineteenth century referred to as the Mexican Question in an Antebellum American culture that based its racial and geographic imaginary primarily on black/white and south/north binaries:[9]

> And finally, impelled by that liking, the doctor betook himself to California, which is full of "*natives.*" And as a just retribution for such perverse liking, the doctor was well-nigh "roasted by the natives," said the old lady. Whereupon, in behalf of truth, I said, "Not by the natives, madam. The people called '*the natives*' are mostly of Spanish descent, and are not cannibals. The wild Indians of the Colorado River were

doubtless the ones who captured the doctor and tried to make a meal of him." "Perhaps so," said the old lady, visibly disappointed. "To me they are all alike,—Indians, Mexicans or Californians,—they are all horrid." (Ruiz, *Who Would Have Thought It?* 11)

That the above quote centers on the eating of white northern bodies— "the roasting" of the New Englander Dr. Norval—by racial others imagined as "cannibals" announces that the ways in which questions concerning the geopolitics of defining the Mexican race in the novel are inextricable from attendant discourses of the human body. Indeed, it is this opening scene that introduces the reader to the protagonist, an orphan named Lola Medina, whose metamorphic body represents the novel's inquest into the Mexican Question's geopolitical and racial discourses.

With *Who Would Have Thought It?* occurring during the backdrop of the Civil War, western expansionism, and industrialization, the plot unfolds when Dr. Norval "saves" Lola from Indian captivity and brings her back to his New England home. Because Lola's Indian captors have dyed her body, her racial and cultural identities in New England are entirely ambiguous. As the story progresses, we learn not only her true identity but that she has inherited gold and diamonds, which her mother acquired while they were in captivity. The remainder of the novel traces her life and focuses on how she becomes a part of New England culture and the Anglo middle class. The trajectory of Lola's assimilation into Anglo-American culture and her "worth" in New England corresponds precisely to the fading of her dyed body; for as it fades, she undergoes numerous changes in racial status, which overlap and effectively generate her simultaneous acquisition of material wealth and cultural capital. Yet, as Lola racially changes, so does the economic position that the Norvals hold in New England culture, metaphorically representing how Anglo-America and the northern United States economically prospered from Mexican lands after the treaty. Lola's metamorphosis presents an alternative reading of America's racial and material culture during Reconstruction. Her embodied metamorphosis complicates the geopolitical binaries associated with the Civil War (black/white, southern/northern) and in turn reveals the extent to which the geographic and racial identities of the inhabitants of Greater Mexico were important to America's capitalist expansion and national identity.[10]

In many ways, then, the plot of *Who Would Have Thought It?* extends Karen Sánchez-Eppler's foundational study of nineteenth-century culture,

Touching Liberty, in which she argues that two discourses of social protest affected the body's political significance during the Reconstruction Era: "the abolitionist concern with claiming personhood for the racially distinct and physically owned slave body, and the feminist concern with claiming personhood for the sexually distinct and domestically circumscribed female body" (1). Sánchez-Eppler, however, does not consider the important role that expansion and Mexicans would have in the United States' political understanding of the body. The content of *Who Would Have Thought It?* extends Sánchez-Eppler's domestic analysis of the politics of the black/white female bodies and suggests that the corporeal location of Mexicans in the United States following the Treaty of Guadalupe Hidalgo of 1848 revealed that the Mexican body was an equally complicated site of both domestic and geopolitical contestation of peoplehood itself.

Blackness of Another Kind

In *Race Changes*, Susan Gubar locates an American cultural trope she defines as "race change," which she argues "is meant to suggest the traversing of race boundaries, racial imitation or impersonation, cross racial mimicry or mutability, white posing as black or black passing as white, pan racial mutability" (5). Though Gubar focuses on African and Anglo-American racial performance, her ideas help us understand how *Who Would Have Thought It?* subverts this binary through the race changes of Lola Medina. What is so intriguing about Lola is that her metamorphic body represents a racial chain of being, one that mutates from African American, to Native American and diseased, to Mexican, and lastly to a white sexualized "Spanish-Mexican" woman. And though the reader slowly learns that Lola's race changes occur because Indians dyed her skin, the Anglo characters in the novel do not fully understand her embodied identity. Much of the novel, then, centers on defining Lola's racial status and what her place should be in the domestic and public spheres. In this way, the varying race changes that occur in the story and the national race questions that they represent complicate Gubar's white/black binary.

The second chapter of *Who Would Have Thought It?*, "The Little Black Girl," begins to reveal some of these complicated race changes that occur in the novel. Returning from an anthropological study of the newly conquered southwestern territories—now defined in New England as America's "public domain"[11]—Dr. Norval finds the novel's central protagonist, the orphaned Lola Medina. Lola, however, enters New England culture as a specimen: "A nigger girl! . . . who was very black" (16). Questioning her racial identity through her body composition, the New England Anglos undergo a crude form of phrenology and begin to study Lola as if she were one of the rocks that Dr. Norval brought back from his trip.

Never giving Lola the ability to speak for herself about her racial identity, Mattie, Mrs. Norval, and Ruth, three New England images of the young and old white republican mother, begin to question what type of "nigger" she is, for she doesn't fit into the category of black they have seen in their abolitionist causes. "Look what magnificent eyes she has, and what red and prettily cut lips," states Mattie. Mrs. Norval continues to question, "How could she have such lips?—Negroe's lips are not like those." Mattie then begins to question, "I do not think she is so black, see the palm of her hand is as white as mine—and a prettier white for it has such a pretty pink shade to it" (18).

Her ambiguous racial body presents the women with a problem of identity, one that begins to affect their own ideas of their whiteness. Mattie observes that Lola's lips are redder and that the underside of her hands are a prettier white than her Anglo hand. Disturbed by the inference that a "nigger specimen" could have prettier features and even a prettier hue of white, Mrs. Norval tells Mattie not to touch the specimen, for she may have a disease that could infect them all. Disease is important and will become a biopolitical discourse throughout the novel, which I will discuss later. What is important to point out in this first scene, however, is that when Lola's body cannot be defined according to one racial "type," the European Americans mark it as an unknown part of a collective. In this way, when Lola's embodied identity comes into question, so does the very ideal of peoplehood in the novel. According to the novel's depiction of New England, the look of the body is what circumscribes an individual person as being part of given people. After her body is depicted as diseased and therefore ambiguous, Ruth, the young daughter of Mrs. Norval, suggests that perhaps Lola was a member of the Indian and African peoples.

This scene reveals much about the phenotypical body's importance in defining peoplehood. Let us not forget that the "look" of another person is the prima facie ground of our knowledge of him or her as a member of a people (O'Neill 23). We take one's appearance at face value, never questioning if the body is deceiving; culture treats appearances of the body as a "racial" reality of peoplehood. (24). Therefore, as John O'Neill astutely argues in *Five Bodies*, we seek out other bodies in society as mirrors of ourselves; we understand what group we are members of, or who we are not, according to other bodies. Democracy stitches the U.S. body politic with members that are similar in color and nature. Indeed, this ideology would help define whiteness in nineteenth-century America (Dyer 8–11). Because of the expansion of U.S. slavery into Mexican and Native American territories, however, newly constituted racial bodies of the frontier began to rupture the body of the body politic. African, Native, and Mexican bodies did not mirror the white body; they were its antithesis.

At this point in the novel, Lola's ambiguous racial body and its more pronounced but still only partial hue of white challenges the embodied collectivity of New Englanders. She appears as African, Indian, Mexican, and diseased in the first two pages alone, yet she also has European features and has a different hue of white when they look carefully. At first sight, Lola's body calls attention to white as a racial category of peoplehood, but it does so by showing that there are different hues of white. In *Who Would Have Thought It?* whiteness becomes a trope of economic and sexual power that not only the bourgeois eastern Anglos debate, for as the novel progresses whiteness becomes a desired universal marker of political and cultural power for both Anglo and newly constituted Mexican people. What constitutes the "white race" and who can claim a white body as a collective people is one of the complicated racial and political questions the novel explores. That a Mexican woman's body, Lola's, is what evokes such a question is important.

Lola's disruption of whiteness and her metamorphic racial body symbolically represent the political questions and historical questions of what the U.S. whites will do with their own racial minorities after the constitution of the Fourteenth and Fifteenth Amendments, Indian extermination, and the U.S.-Mexico War. Indeed, when European Americans first misread Lola as being ascribed to the African American people, they commodify her body much like African slaves. After questioning the position that Lola will have in the family, Mrs. Norval, who is an activist for the abolitionist cause, hypocritically refuses to accept Lola into her household or to educate her as she has her white daughters. She states: "She will work—I'll see to that—and a good worker is sure of a home in New England. Mrs. Hammerhard will want such a girl as this, I hope, to mind the baby, and she will give her some of her cast off clothes and her victuals . . . she can't expect to grow up in idleness and be a burden to us" (23–24). Lola's position as a worker for Anglos and as an enslaved captive will serve as a subplot throughout the pages of *Who Would Have Thought It?* When Lola first enters as a racial object, her body enables the Norvals to advance economically. This plot line metaphorically situates Lola's body as a "stand-in" for the real historical reality of African slavery and the position that African Americans, whose black bodies were commodified, will hold after the Civil War (Reid-Pharr 3–46).

Mrs. Norval does not want Lola, who at this point she assumes is a "little black girl," to have an education; she wants to control her wealth. She does not want to give Lola the ability to reason and hold a similar subject position as other "civilized" New Englanders who are able to enter the public sphere as reasoned and abstracted bourgeois citizens. Based on Lola's body, which Mrs. Norval believes renders her part of the "Negroid race," she feels that she should remain a docile subject within the private sphere. As Mrs. Norval's actions suggest, the body of the black is what defines his or her role as a domestic laborer for the white elites (Sánchez-Eppler 18). This racist sentiment is further demonstrated when Mrs. Norval argues that she must condition Lola to do what is "natural" for black people: they should work and not become idle or, for that matter, citizens.

Mrs. Norval's sentiments about Lola's body represent a racial and economic "unconscious" discourse in the United States. Indeed, the novel calls attention to the United States' democratic hypocrisy by revealing that this is a "free" country that was built on a slavocracy and on the backs of African people. The question of Lola's position in Mrs. Norval's domestic space, then, is a symbolic question regarding what space African people will occupy after the Civil War and during Reconstruction: the private or public spheres? In this way, though I find their overall work excellent, I do not fully agree with Rosaura Sánchez and Beatrice Pita's argument that *Who Would Have Thought It?* does not fully deal with slavery, abolitionism, African Americans, or the Reconstruction Era.[12] As this and later scenes demonstrate, slavery, the south, and blackness are in fact important tropes of *Who Would Have Thought It?* That the novel begins with such African American racial questions is important and will inform the entire novel's relocation of the Mexican Question.

Who Would Have Thought It? strategically represents African Americans with a guarded sympathy, however. It does this by calling attention to the inherent racism that whites have against black-skinned peoples and the problems that the United States believes it has with its African population that was entering the public spheres after Reconstruction—a fact defined as the "Negro Question" (Foner 43–58). In the last page of the novel, for example, Beau, a power-driven politician who is against the corrupt Grant administration, emphatically argues that he "never cared about the color of the skin or about the character of my followers . . . My blood curdles with horror! My brain reels with indignation! I can hardly articulate, but it must be told. He [Grant] has dared to slight a colored gentleman! No less distinguished a citizen of African descent than Mr. Fred Douglass" (Ruiz, *Who Would Have Thought It?* 298).

Unlike other muckraking and roman à clef novels written during Reconstruction—Henry Adams's *Democracy*, for example—*Who Would Have Thought It?* addresses Grant's failure to invite Douglass to the White House and refers to Grant's weak policies in helping African Americans after the Civil War. This concluding scene demonstrates that the (black) politics of peoplehood are present up to the last page. Moreover, *Who Would Have Thought It?*'s use of Douglass and its implicit allusion to the "Negro Question" is important because it reveals yet another complicated subplot in the novel: the historical and cultural interweaving of African Americans, the south, and the Civil War with the Mexican American War and the Mexican Question in the United States.

To further understand the novel's use of Douglass to create a connection between the politics of black and Mexican peoplehood, it is important to historically contextualize Douglass's relationship to the U.S.-Mexico War and the Mexican Question. In *A Negro View of the Mexican War*, Frederick Douglass argues against U.S. expansion into Mexico and entering the U.S.-Mexico War. He felt that the United States was plundering Mexico for lands and was creating a "hypocritical pretense of a regard for peace and that they were partaking in the most barbarous outrages committed upon an unoffending people" (422). He continued to argue that the war with Mexico was an act of wholesale murder.[13]

Although we will never know if Ruiz read Douglass's article, one can speculate that she did, since the article was published widely while she lived in New England. Either way, by addressing Anglo-Americans' problems with African American peoplehood and the blackness that New England ascribed to its constitution, *Who Would Have Thought It?* is able to create a sustained critique of how the United States constructs racial peoplehood in binary terms, white versus black, which, during the

Antebellum period, were created out of the geographic polarities between the domestic south and north and white and black bodies. Hence the novel complicates what many cultural historians have argued: that African Americans made Anglos aware of their own race and whiteness in the public spheres, as well as made them consider the implications of blood and the body in distinguishing racial peoplehood in the United States (Gordon 103–108). Indeed, as the novel continues, Ruiz shows that Mexican peoplehood represents an equally ambivalent location in American public culture.

I am not suggesting that *Who Would Have Thought It?* is an abolitionist text that is primarily interested in the cultural politics of African American peoplehood and the "Negro Question" during Reconstruction. Indeed, elite Mexican American relations with African Americans during the nineteenth century were strained at best. Many landed-class Mexicans in the United States, such as Ruiz, distinguished themselves from southern blacks in order to create their own bailiwick of political power and to maintain land rights in an American culture that privileged whiteness and disdained blackness. And as Neil Foley has argued, how the United States defined Mexicans racially as a people had much to do with Anglo distinctions, not only from the African American black body and blood but also from middle-class Mexicanos' own racial distinctions from blackness (23–37).[14] Debates over the racial constitution of Mexicanos as a people in Ruiz's native California revealed a similar construction. When the California Constitution was being written, for example, the peoplehood status of Mexicans came down to an embodied discourse that classified Mexicans as whites in order to exclude the African races of the south from full participation in California laws (Almaguer 56). In these debates, both elite Mexicans and Anglos had much to gain by defining Mexicans as whites and not black, for it would help normalize their bodies for republican citizenship standards.

Locating *Who Would Have Thought It?* within this complicated conception of peoplehood, then, I suggest that the text uses blackness as a backdrop in order to problematize how this racial construct of peoplehood has affected race consciousness in the United States. The novel's thematic use of blackness, abolitionism, and the Civil War as cultural tropes expose the text's central provocation: Mexican peoplehood. The novel therefore is not an abolitionist text that fights for the equality of U.S. Africans but, rather, is an abolitionist text that fights for the rights and status of what Ruiz would define in her second novel, *The Squatter and the Don*, as "the white slaves of the Southwest," the newly constituted Mexican Americans (234).

It is worth spending some time on *The Squatter and the Don*'s representation of the Treaty of Guadalupe Hidalgo, for this is the first work of fiction to address the treaty, and it is here where we see Ruiz's discussion of Mexicans bound together as a "conquered people." In this 1885 novel, in chapter 2, "The Don's View of the Treaty," Don Mariano Alamar of San Diego (note the similarity to her lifelong interlocutor, Mariano Guadalupe Vallejo), contemplates what the treaty means for Mexicans of the United States, as he states to an Anglo-American character George in the novel:

> The treaty said that our rights would be the same as those enjoyed by all other American citizens. But you see Congress takes very good care not to enact retroactive laws for Americans, laws to take away from American citizens the property which they hold now already, with a recognized legal title. I think that few Americans know or believe to what extent we have been wronged by congressional action. And truly I believe that Congress itself did not anticipate the effect of its laws upon us and how we would have been despoiled, we the conquered people."
> (165)

Ruiz's representation of the treaty served her in two important ways. First, the fictional Don Mariano's comments are telling and reveal the vexed relationship that the real Mariano Guadalupe Vallejo had with U.S. republicanism and its failed promises of equal protection and public sphere access. The treaty also served as an effective political marker to appeal to her white eastern audience's own anxieties about democracy. Creating sympathy and sentiment for the Californio people enabled Ruiz to point out the limitations of republicanism as a form of political organization that fostered equality among the many people in the United States. In fact, in the pages that follow, George Mecheline and the other European Americans in the novel learn that monopoly capitalism is what governs the people in the west, not democratic justice and equal representation. Representation and equality are only afforded to the corporate body constituted by "the many headed hydra" of monopoly capitalism and the railroad, not citizens' bodies. In both books, then, Ruiz asks a fundamental question of statecraft: Is republicanism the correct form of government to deal with a growing capitalist nation and its large, heterogeneous, and geographically diffuse population?

Amparo Ruiz's question concerning U.S. statecraft would not fall on deaf ears. During her writing *Who Would Have Thought It?* in the Reconstruction period and *The Squatter and the Don* in post-Reconstruction, America's political system of democracy was anything but solidified. After the Civil War, many Americans, especially those of the south, questioned whether a representative republican form of government could account for the needs of all of the people. Indeed, as I point out in chapter 2, with the expansion of the United States, Americans questioned whether a representational democracy could deal with such a large nation and its many inhabitants. As Stephen Hartnett argues, democratic expansion created a crisis of peoplehood that follows from building a large capitalist nation where political obligation and allegiances are increasingly confusing and even incomprehensible. Although Ruiz's critique of the failed promises of U.S. statecraft was inevitably so she could fight for the rights and status of the Mexicans who lived in the farthest regions of the United States, in California, she tapped into this national anxiety in her works. In effect, Ruiz pointed out through cultural forms that republicanism could not afford any citizen the guarantee of civil rights and equality because of its inability to truly represent the interests of particular bodies of the body politic.

Indeed, in *Who Would Have Thought It?* Ruiz alludes to this point through the Anglo-American characters, Levinia and Julian Norval. Levinia is an interesting and incredibly complicated figure. She is the only woman in the novel who is afforded the ability to leave the bonds of "republican motherhood" and engage men in the political public spheres. Inquiring about her brother's imprisonment, she questions the statecraft policies that the secretary of War is using for its POWs. Arguing in vain, Levinia finds that the political heads of the state are not interested in granting her the "right" to learn of her brother's fate, for these are not questions for women of the republic. In the end, she comes to learn that "all she had read in printed political speeches delivered just before election times were not true" (154). Women were not afforded the ability to represent themselves as people. Men represented women and the republican state.

To punctuate republicanism's lack of equal representation, Ruiz focuses on the male protagonist and hero of the novel to make her point even stronger to the eastern public. Colonel Julian Norval, the son of Dr.

Norval and the love interest of the main character, Lola, is accused of arguing against President Abraham Lincoln's Emancipation Proclamation and the suspending of habeas corpus. He pleads to Lincoln that he has done no such thing, and he has not been given the right to represent himself in the political public spheres. Rather, the United States has deemed him a pariah and traitor, as he states:

> I have fought, thinking myself a free man fighting for freedom, and I awake from my dream to find that I do not have the privilege granted to thieves and cutthroats. . . . I wish to have my freedom. If the Negroes have it, why shouldn't I? I did not bargain to surrender my freedom to give it to Sambo. If I have served my country with sufficient credit entitled me to any favor from my state, all I ask is justice, and the protection which our free institutions give to everyone under our flag. (241)

Using the black body ("Sambo") as a marker of both freedom and inequality, Julian's plea for justice and his inability to regain his masculinity is meant to highlight the U.S. government's inability to account for all of its citizen's needs. Julian finds himself unrepresented and unable to represent himself in the political public spheres. In the end, the novel argues that Lincoln republicanism has failed not only the women but also even the men of white America.

"Playing Indian"

As the last section argues, *Who Would Have Thought It?*'s focus on African American blackness should be seen as one part of the work's strategy to set up the most compelling racial question in the book, locating the limits and possibilities of the Mexican peoplehood. However, one cannot consider the Mexican Question in the novel without understanding its relationship to the "Indian Question." Although the first metamorphosis of Lola's body helps bring about the novel's exploration of African blackness and its role in defining peoplehood in American culture, the dialectic that occurs when Lola's embodied identity borders on the Native and Mexican American is extremely telling. Once again, to explore the novel's complicated dynamics of peoplehood, we need to return to its first chapters.

After listening to his wife's racist comments about Lola and her position as a worker, Dr. Norval explains that Lola is not African American, despite her "looking" like she is part of that race. He explains that Indians dyed Lola's body, that her blood is of pure "Spanish" descent, and that she comes from an elite family with a rich heritage (24–25). The dye, he argues, will wear off in time. What is presented through Lola's body is a debate about defining race and subjectivity through the visible body or its underlying genetic code, blood. On one narrative level, the novel represents the body as a vital tool in identifying any differences pertaining to peoplehood. And as we have seen, race is crucial in the process of distinguishing differences among people or, in this case, of interpreting Lola's body.

The novel complicates and exposes this discourse of race by bringing forth the element of blood and its role in defining Mexican peoplehood. Dr. Norval, for example, insists that Lola's blood and ancestry give her the ability to enter the Norval house as an equal person and not as a servant. If her body is seen as white, then she has the ability to enter New England culture as an equal. Mr. Norval goes on to argue that when Lola is able to acquire the wealth that her mother left her, she will not be seen as an Indian or a "nigger," for her money will give her the appearance of equality (27). Class, he hopes, will inscribe her racial body as an equal person.

It becomes apparent in the novel, however, that the tension between Lola's blood and her potential economic wealth lies behind a body that "deceives" Anglo perceptions, a body that renders her as racialized. The novel's question, then, is whether blood or the body defines the rights and status of Mexican peoplehood in the United States. Blood, as Michel Foucault suggests in *The History of Sexuality*, may be a historical reality, but what *Who Would Have Thought It?* explores are nineteenth-century scientific discourses that posited blood or the body as defining racial people. In the late nineteenth century, the idea of blood became an important "scientific" discourse that helped define race in America, just as genetics has in the twentieth (Dyer 24).[15] But as has been suggested above, the body, too, was a central discourse in defining racial peoplehood in the nineteenth century. In this way, what constitutes Mexican racial peoplehood, the skin or the blood, becomes central to the Mexican Question. But in this novel the skin is a false (and falsified) signifier; it is surface, "phenomenal" in Kantian terms, while the blood represents depth, the "noumenal."[16]

This issue is particularly seen when Lola's body begins its last meta-morphosis. As this metamorphosis occurs, she begins to develop dark spots. With dark spots, she is no longer "seen" by the New England public as a member of the African people, for the spots phenotypically define her as part of the Pinto Indian tribe. The Pinto Indians, Mr. Hackwell reminds the Norvals, have spots all over their bodies. Hence Lola's body finally has a racial match. And although Lola's "Spanish" blood line and her dyed skin have become public knowledge, the eastern public still assumes that since her body "looks" spotted, she must be a Pinto Indian; and if she isn't, she must be diseased ("Who Would Have Thought It?" 78–80).

The allusion to Pinto Indians is historically important and reveals how the novel "plays Indian" in order to expose the racial distinctions that developed in the nineteenth century between Mexicans and Anglos.[17] For example, an article written in 1853 in the *San Diego Herald*, after the U.S.-Mexico War, describes the racial distinction that occurs between Pinto Indians and Mexicans in the southwest:

> The population of the State of Guerrero is nearly Aztec, and the descendents of the tribes who fought desperately against the Spaniards. The Pintos, i.e. they are covered with blotches upon the skin, blue, white, and chocolate color—that give them an aspect of ferocity, which has been fearfully verified on all occasions—they have no sympathy or feeling in common with any people who boast of Castillian extraction. (2)

Although the article and *Who Would Have Thought It?* demonstrate the ignorance of East European Americans, I suggest that the novel, and implicitly the article, create a racial distinction between Indians and Mexican Californios through Lola "playing Indian." This distinction exists, in part, because landed Mexicans desired such a racial distinction before and after the war with the United States. Indeed, much as the article depicts Pintos and Indians as savages, so too does *Who Would Have Thought It?* maintain this racist discourse. Moreover, the racialization of Indians in the book by both Anglos and Mexicans occurs because of the racial consciousness that was developing among landed Mexican Californios about their own mestizo bloodlines, an imagined notion of peoplehood called the Spanish Fantasy Heritage.

In *Who Would Have Thought It?* the racial distinction between Mexicans and Indians is particularly evident in the novel's use of Indian captivity and the sympathy that the novel evokes through the demise of Lola's captive mother, Doña Medina. As we learn in the novel, Lola's mother, a "civilized" Mexican woman, is held captive by Indians, whom the narrator, the Mexican, and the Anglo characters describe as a "savage" race. And because Doña Medina has become the wife of the Indian chief, the novel implicitly acknowledging that she is his sexual partner, she cannot return with Dr. Norval; her body has been tainted and violated by the savage race. The narrator sardonically concludes that although he/she is "not a political philosopher," this tragedy of Indian captivity and savagery occurred because the Mexican government allows Indian savages to "devastate Mexican lands." Centered on racial notions of Indian savagery enabled Ruiz to make her most devastating critique of Mexican republicanism's inability to represent the interests of Californios living in what were then the northern territories of Mexico.

The racial antagonism toward Native peoples that the novel endorses is not surprising, especially considering that bourgeois Mexican Americans have racialized Indians for centuries. Defining themselves as *gente de razon* and white, landed Mexicans in California had racist views of Indians and constructed a peonage, hacienda economic system that was similar to plantation systems in the American south. Though they did not create a genocidal frontier like Anglos after the war with Mexico, Mexicans were nonetheless racist in their views. This is ironic, however, since elite Mexican Americans of nineteenth-century California were mestizos, half-Indian and half-Spanish, which is why Anglos racially defined Mexicans as "semicivilized" and "mongrels."[18] However, despite the end of the Spanish-Mexican caste system and the ideology of *gente de razon* after the war, the newly constituted Mexican people in the United States conflated their discourses of *gente de razon* with Anglo-American discourses of whiteness to create a story of peoplehood known as Spanish Fantasy Heritage. This imagined ideal of Mexican peoplehood was particularly seen in *People v. De La Guerra*, where in court he argued that he was not Indian or mestizo. Claiming his Spanish white heritage, and not the mestizo Indian identity of his mother, enabled him to ultimately appeal to the Supreme Court and obtain citizenship as a white Mexican. He became a member, though not equal, of the U.S. *demos* by claiming a European Spanish ideal of Mexican peoplehood. For nineteenth-century Mexican Californios, then, Indians became a racial marker of distinction in order to distinguish themselves and thus create a normalized white peoplehood that, they believed, would, in turn, grant them citizenship.

This contradictory story of Mexican peoplehood that endorsed a Spanish Fantasy Heritage would endure for generations and lead to Guadalupe (Platon) Vallejo, the son of Mriano Guadalupe Vallejo, to argue in *Century Magazine* at the turn of the century: "Spanish Americans are a noble people of the United States" (Powell 786).

As we have seen in Ruiz's very complicated story of Mexican peoplehood, new Anglo ideologies of racial classification and whiteness began to center around blood as well as the skin, thereby creating a tension that the novel explores but never resolves in its depiction of Lola's metamorphic body. Under the pressure of this emergent obsession with blood and skin, manifested in the racial images of Mexicans in the Anglo public sphere, landed Californios endorsed a mythical blood line that created a racial distinction from their "true" Native and African ancestry. What *Who Would Have Thought It?* explores through Lola's blood and body, then, is the intersection of elite Mexican American notions of peoplehood and Anglo-American "scientific" ideas of race and whiteness, an intersection created out of competing colonial discourses. What is important to remember, in other words, is that elite Mexicans denied their Indian and African bodies, their "true" heritage as a people, not only because of the mythic Spanish colonial ideology distinguishing *gente de razon* from racial others but equally because of how the conquering Anglos perceived the newly colonized Mexican population who resided in the southwestern lands after the war. How Mexicans created distinctions between themselves and the other races of the Americas reveals the contradictory nature of Mexicans engaging the Mexican Question, which Ruiz's novel captures well through Lola's metamorphic body. In this way, her novel problematizes the black/white racial ideologies structuring the Reconstruction Era only by effectively endorsing a bourgeois conservative Spanish Fantasy Heritage, thus normalizing Mexican peoplehood as whiter and therefore more classed than Native, African, and Anglo-Americans in the public sphere.

This race and class dynamic culminates when Lola explains to Julian—an Anglo-American in whom she develops a romantic interest—that her body should not classify her as an African or Indian, for her blood comes from a wealthy Mexican family and therefore she is "white." To better understand this scene, it is important to quote Lola's entire dialogue, for it is also the part of the novel when Lola is first able to articulate her own identity and when she obtains agency:

I was an object of aversion because my skin was black. And yet I was too proud to tell you that the blackness of my skin would wear off, that it was only stained by Indians to prevent our being rescued. My mother also was made to stain her lovely white skin all black. . . . I wanted to tell you this many times. . . . I didn't care whether I was thought white or black by others, I hated to think that you might suppose I was Indian or black. But I did not want to say anything to you because I thought you might laugh at me, and not believe me. (101)

Julian replies that he knew otherwise, for his father told him that Lola's blood was pure Spanish. Lola, however, is aware of the tensions between skin and blood in New England racial ideology, as she responds to Julian:

But I often heard your mother say things by which I could plainly see she did not believe that I was white. And when the dye began to wear off, and my skin got all spotted, she sent me away, because she thought a had a coetaneous disease, and she said that Mr. Hackwell said that perhaps I belonged to the Pintos and my skin was naturally spotted. (101)

This scene marks the turning point in the novel, for at this midpoint, Lola's final metamorphosis begins and thus her body reveals the interrelated complexities of Mexican and Anglo ideologies of whiteness that the novel explores.[19] After this scene, Lola's "white" blood begins to match her now fully faded white body. And Spanish blood, according to Julian and Lola, affords her the status of other white Europeans, a defining part of the ideology that landed Mexicans endorsed in California. Yet, as we shall see, once the Anglo characters perceive Lola's body and her blood as "white," Lola's (Mexican) white body becomes sexualized and thereby symbolically represents the reconstitution of the Anglo-Mexican Question.

The novel's opening allusion to Mexicans, Californios, and Indians as equally horrid races, then, is in fact the novel's central provocation. Mexicans, Californios, and Indians are not, of course, cultural equivalents, although Anglo-Americans constructed them as such in the public sphere. *Who Would Have Thought It?* offers the Reconstruction Era public a particular education: namely, that Mexican Californios are a distinct people, one that is different from America's other dark races, one that is also Euro-American and, in fact, a "prettier" hue of white. As such, the Mexican people should be politically represented accordingly. As the novel ends, the Anglo characters begin to comprehend Lola's embodied identity and are thus able to understand the central lesson of Californio racial ideology: that Indians and landed Mexicans are not the same. Mattie, for example, who began the novel by comparing Lola to Africans and Indians, asserts: "Talk of Spanish women being dark! Can anything be whiter than Lola's neck and shoulders?" Ruth and Emma respond by confirming that Lola is "a Mexican," and they infer that, as such, she comes from a people that are whiter than their own (232).[20]

Binational Reunions

As a white Mexican woman who is now in control of her body because of its white inscription, Lola is able to romantically unite with Julian, a turn of plot symbolically representing the complex reunion between the Mexican south and Anglo north after the U.S.-Mexico War. As the role of Lola's inheritance suggests, the courtship and concluding romantic betrothal between Lola and Julian reveals that this symbolic union is ultimately interested in resolving the racial discourse surrounding the Mexican Question according to a capitalist relation. Thus the concluding betrothal should be read as a union of two distinct elite "white" bodies, a union that will enable economically landed Mexican women to take control of their raced and sexed bodies through a "proper" or "chosen" heterosexual union with a white, northern man. The romantic ending between Lola and Julian, then, should be seen as a desire for not only racial but also economic uplift through a geographic union between the members of the bourgeois Mexican south and Anglo north. This geopolitical union between landed Mexican and Anglo-Saxon white blood is not a new trope for Ruiz. Her novel *The Squatter and the Don* (1885) also ended with a union between a Mexican American "white" woman and an Anglo male. Nor is this literary trope isolated to Ruiz's novels. Many landed and middle-class Mexican American women writers well into the early twentieth century explored heterosexual relations between Anglo men and Mexican American women through an equally interesting exploration of Greater Mexican/American relations. Jovitá González's *Caballero* also explored race and sexuality in similar unions. Moreover, historians of this period have found that this literary trope reflected historical reality for many landed Mexican American women after the

U.S.-Mexico War.[21] In the wake of the U.S.-Mexico War, Mexican women became trophies much like the land itself, and white men were the heroic conquerors and bearers of civilization. Indeed, let us not forget that Ruiz herself eventually married an Anglo officer.

It is important to point out that the ending of this novel resembles the Reconstruction Era novels that Nina Silber defines as "romance to reunion" (39–46). Silber argues that the reconciliation of north and south following the Civil War depended as much on the social imagination as on the politics of Reconstruction. Therefore, in the years 1865–1900, novels as diverse as Lydia Maria Child's *Romance of the Republic* (1867), John D. Forest's *Miss Ravenal's Conversion from Secession to Loyalty* (1867), and Henry James's *The Bostonians* (1892), to name a few, created southern and northern protagonists that would symbolically unite at the end of the novel, thus resolving the "real" sectional tension that existed between the United States south and north after the Civil War. I suggest that in *Who Would Have Thought It?*, the concluding romance-to-reunion trope extended far beyond the sectional opposition between the domestic south and north. Indeed, the conclusion reveals that Ruiz subverts this popular trope into a binational configuration between the Mexican south and United States north, thus describing the transnational understanding of American culture the opening scene of the novel brings to the foreground. Hence, the trope of romance to reunion, so popular in southern discourses of the Civil War and Reconstruction that had firmly taken hold of U.S. public culture, serve Ruiz as a metaphor for the unresolved, misunderstood, and forgotten conflict between the Mexican south and the American north after the U.S.-Mexico War of 1848. By inserting "Spanish-Mexicans" into the center of Reconstruction Era–embodied politics and literary discourses, Ruiz hoped to introduce the American public to the question that had affected her and fellow Mexicans since the Treaty of Guadalupe of 1848: What place do Mexicans have in the United States?

Although the novel's ending "reunion" attempts to normalize the rights and status of the newly constituted Mexican in the United States with and against the other races in America and endorses a classed and racial uplift, it should not be seen as an act of resistance or blatant assimilation. Rather, for Ruiz, the concluding union was an attempt to demonstrate that the complex national and racial questions that were shaping New England culture during the Reconstruction Era were not solely centered on domestic northern/southern relations or the place that

African Americans would hold in the white northern public spheres after the Fourteenth and Fifteenth Amendments. For Ruiz, the Mexican Question and its binational implications should be an important inquiry as well. Such a geopolitical configuration in the novel also serves as a reminder that the nineteenth-century domestic south was a transnational space, one that overlapped with and helped shape both Anglo-America and Mexico.

Nevertheless, Ruiz's novel was not as successful as Anglo-American romance-to-reunion novels. Indeed, cultural productions that dealt with the Mexican Question were never as successful as novels about the domestic south, African Americans, or Native Americans. And as history and popular culture demonstrates, the Civil War, not the U.S.-Mexico War, has been an important cultural marker for American cultural production and race relations (Young 1–23; Cullen 8–28; Streeby 1–24). This is not surprising, however. Since John L. O'Sullivan's utterance of the Mexican Question in 1845, America has never truly dealt with the Mexican Question, which has remained an ambivalent discourse precisely because it makes visible the imperialist geopolitical designs of American democracy. Perhaps due to their "semicivilized" status in the nineteenth-century public spheres—part Spanish and thus European; part Native American and thus a mongrel race—the Mexican in the United States has shaped American culture through a democratic contradiction that results from the relationship between their designated "racial" status and universal ideals of citizenship. They are in theory U.S. citizens because of the Treaty of Guadalupe Hidalgo of 1848 and yet are racialized as second-class "mongrel" citizens because they are not fully "white" Americans. What is so important about Ruiz's novel, then, is that it offers the first U.S. Mexican response in English to Anglo-American inquiries into the democratic rights and racial status of Mexicans in the United States. Ruiz does this by inserting landed Californios into the rhetoric of U.S. (white) reunification and thus disrupting the corporeal body politic unified by "one flesh."[22] As such, Ruiz creates a compelling and contradictory model for shifting and remembering the terms of our domestic investigations of American nationalism an racial imaginary to a more binational and inclusive understanding of the contested politics of the republican body politic.

In the end, for Ruiz, the Mexican Question was an inquiry into U.S. statecraft. The irony, of course, was that Ruiz herself would declare in the novel that the narrator is "not a political philosopher." This self-effacing act does not truly reveal her contradictory and brilliant analysis of U.S. and Mexican political culture. Changing her political allegiances from monarchism to liberalism and even ironically, at times, to republicanism, Ruiz was the first Mexican women in the United States to engage the public spheres in order to ask what form of statecraft is best for Mexicans in the United States. What I have tried to highlight in this chapter, however, is that the gendered and racial questions that affected the political constitution of the particular body in the body politic during Reconstruction were an important discourse in Ruiz's inquest into political statecraft. That she was never able to fully reconcile this question and that she created contradictory political opinions and observations is not surprising. Indeed, in the nineteenth century, democracy was still a contested term, and the relationship among monarchism, liberalism, and republicanism were also contested in the public spheres (Downes 23–34). Much like Henry Adams's *Democracy* and the hundreds of other novels that came out in the 1870s that focused on U.S. statecraft, *Who Would Have Thought It?* presents us with a complicated inquiry into the nature and logic of how peoples represent and organize themselves as a nation that was expanding through imperialist policies. That a Mexican woman was able to comment on the state of the union despite the fact that the literary and political public spheres represented her as a racial and sexed object is an amazing accomplishment that should have never have taken 130 years to recover and recognize.

4

Claiming *Los Bilitos*

Miguel Antonio Otero and the Fight for New Mexican Manhood

The Kid was disappointed that the mob did not attack the car since
it would have unquestionably resulted in his escape. He was on the
friendliest of terms with the native element of the country; he had
protected and helped them in every possible way. . . . In Santa Fe
we were allowed to visit the Kid in jail, taking him cigarette papers,
tobacco, chewing gum, candy, pies, and nuts. He was very fond of
sweets and asked us to bring him all we could. The Kid's general
appearance was the same as most boys of his age. I was one month
older than Billy. I liked the Kid very much, and long before we even
reached Santa Fe, nothing would have pleased me more than to
have witnessed his escape. He had his share of good qualities and
was very pleasant. He had a reputation for being considerate of the
old, the young and the poor; he was loyal to his friends and above
all, loved his mother devotedly. He was unfortunate in starting life
and became a victim of circumstances. . . . In looking back to my
first meeting with Billy the Kid, my impressions were most favor-
able and I can honestly say that he was "a man more sinned against
than sinning."

Miguel Antonio Otero, *The Real Billy the Kid*

On the morning of December 23, 1880, Miguel Antonio
Otero Jr. met the infamous Billy the Kid. He would recount this meeting
in the concluding chapters of his biography, *The Real Billy the Kid*, revealing his relationship with a "bandit" who had become a hero of the
New Mexican people during the late nineteenth century. As the epigraph
to this chapter reveals, Otero represents Billy the Kid as a gentleman hero,

a man who loved his mother, a protector of the Native New Mexicans, and who, in the end, was "a man more sinned against than sinning" (134).[1]

In Otero's quote we begin to see how his biography constructs Billy the Kid into what Eric Hobsbawm refers to as a "social bandit." For Hobsbawm, the social bandit protects the people from the onslaught of modernity or colonialism; he is a person who avenges the institutional wrongs the people have felt in the wake of political strife caused by colonialism. On the one hand, to the people who hold the political power of the state, the social bandit is an outlaw; he signifies a lawlessness that the state must control and pacify. To the state, the bandit is one who impedes the civilizing and modernizing mission of a given territory for democracy. On the other hand, the social bandit personifies the marginalized people's political and cultural struggles against the encroaching state. The social bandit himself may not be a revolutionary or a political leader, but the people use the social bandit as a symbolic vessel for their own political identities and collectivity as subalterns. In effect, the individual bandit constitutes the social imaginary of a given group, to the point that the individual "blood of the bandit is the people's blood."[2] In Otero's biography, then, I suggest that Billy the Kid becomes the vessel by which New Mexicans understand their collective self-fashioning during the territorial period that would so drastically change their lives forever.

New Mexican's collective self-fashioning was precipitated by a drastic change in New Mexico's territorial politics at the turn of the century. Spurred by the ever-increasing number of Anglo settlers and the displacement of Mexicans' political and economic power in the territory, a Santa Fe newspaper in 1880 reported that Anglo and New Mexican relations had developed into a "conflict of the races," and questions emerged in the public spheres about the racial and political constitution concerning the Mexicans who lived in New Mexico. As I argue in the preceding chapters, at the turn of the last century, public discourses of the Mexican Question construed both elite and working-class New Mexican bodies as Indian and white, hence constituting them in the public sphere as semicivilized. Therefore, their Mexicans mestizo bodies were not worthy of being part of the fraternal brotherhood of the white republic (Nelson 1–18). Indeed, because New Mexico was so populated and politically controlled by elite Mexicans, as well as by working-class "paisanos," the territory was not allowed by Congress to join the union as a state until 1912. The dynamics of New Mexico's race relations, however, were complicated by the counteremergence of a Spanish Fantasy Heritage similar to the one Californios adopted in their stories of political peoplehood (discussed in chapter 3). The racial and political self-fashioning of the Hispano, or Spanish American, that developed in the racial climate of territorial New Mexico in the nineteenth century revealed the contradictions inherent to the Nueveomexicano social imaginary that constituted them as a democratic people.[3]

The years surrounding Billy the Kid's life reveal much about this dramatic change in New Mexican territorial politics, race relations, and the democratic inclusion of New Mexicans. For it is the years surrounding the life of Billy the Kid that Otero would come to define as the "metamorphosis of the democratic West."[4] As the first Mexican American territorial governor of New Mexico, Miguel Antonio Otero was instrumental in the transformation of New Mexico and the west. It is curious, however, that Otero, the first territorial governor, would mark the life of the "bandit" Billy the Kid in his biography and letters as important in understanding the political metamorphosis of New Mexican peoplehood. In this way, he uses his biography of Billy the Kid to explore the very idea of New Mexican peoplehood and the territorial powers that effected its metamorphic constitution at the turn of the century. According to Hobsbawm, the "metamorphic" conditions I explore in this chapter are essential for the emergence of a social bandit like Billy the Kid. The dynamic historical context in which the social bandit emerges allows for the collective resistance of the political power structures that are dramatically changing New Mexico after 1880. In other words, the social bandit is both a product of social change and hegemony and the people's expression of institutional oppression itself. In effect, as the locus of power, Billy the Kid becomes a conduit to study the volatile colonial struggles in territorial New Mexico that occurred over the very definition of democratic peoplehood, one who counted as an included citizen of the national *demos*.

And yet, the western metamorphosis that occurs in the years surrounding the life of Billy the Kid was not only about the collective struggles of the New Mexican people. Otero himself used Billy in his own masculine and political self-fashioning as a New Mexican statesman. In fact, in this recounted meeting, Otero became friends with Billy the Kid. Claiming that they were both boys and but a month apart in age and very friendly, Otero reveals his own personal and masculine connection with a bandit hero of the New Mexican people. Otero's masculine identification with outlaw Billy the Kid is further advanced when one consider that Billy gave Otero a pair of his spurs and a knife for his friendship. Otero cherished these symbolically masculine items of Billy and even displayed them in his office while he was governor of New Mexico. It is even rumored that he wore them on his inauguration day and when he met with Theodore Roosevelt. In many ways, this meeting between Otero, who was from a very old and established Hispano family in New Mexico, and Billy the Kid, a young working-class Irish American, ironically marks a pivotal moment in Otero's own self-fashioning as a representative and masculine political statesman and eventually the first Mexican territorial governor of the New Mexican people from 1896 to 1908.

In the end, for Otero, Billy the Kid became the mediator between his own individual, representative position as elite New Mexican statesman of the people and the collective territorial New Mexican he represented in the east. Otero's participation in the cultural construction of Billy the Kid, then, reveals much about his own masculine desire to foster what he would call "public spirit" as New Mexico's first modern politician. Otero's emergence as a political statesman with public spirit would occur during what many scholars refer to as the "culture of manhood" that affected political narratives concerning U.S. male peoplehood at the turn of the nineteenth century. What Otero represents in his biography is his own distinctive ability to rise within and, indeed, mimic masculine and civilizing white American stories circulated within the "official" literary and political spheres, with the result that Otero's Billy the Kid becomes a story of New Mexican peoplehood that recounts his most public cause: the contradictory inclusion of the New Mexican people as citizens and the geographic space of New Mexico as a member of the body politic.

The Story of Otero

For generations the Oteros had been important political figures in the southwestern and the eastern United States. The first Otero to serve in public office was Don Vicente, Miguel Antonio Otero II's grandfather. He served as judge under the Spanish and Mexican governments before New Mexico became a U.S. territory in 1850. His son Miguel Antonio Otero I (Don Miguel) was a professor of Latin and Greek at Pingree College, Fishkill on the Hudson, for two years (1847–1849). Like his father Don Vicente, he served in public office; three times he was appointed as a delegate of the New Mexico territory to the U.S. Congress (1855, 1857, 1859). President Lincoln offered him an appointment as a minister to Spain; however, he refused because he wanted to retire from public office and dedicate himself to the banking firm of Whiting and Otero. While working as a banker, Don Miguel decided to take a lesser public job and served as secretary of the New Mexico territory.

In 1857, Don Miguel married Mary Josephine Blackwood, a southern white woman raised in Charleston, South Carolina. This intermarriage between a Mexican man and a white woman was extremely rare in the nineteenth century, as marriages between Mexicans and Anglos were usually between Anglo men and Mexican women. The couple raised two boys and two girls; the eldest son, Page Blackwood, was born on January 4, 1858; Miguel Antonio Otero II, on October 17, 1859; Gertrude Vicente in 1865; and Mamie Josephine in 1867. Miguel Antonio Otero was the only member of the family to keep the Mexican "Otero" surname.

Miguel Antonio II's first years were spent traveling with his family throughout the United States. In 1866 Miguel and his brother Page were sent to a boarding school in Topeka, Kansas. As his memoirs attest, this was one of the most unpleasant periods in his life: "The school proved to be a detestable place and its horrors are still fresh in my memory, though nearly seventy years have passed since then. I can only compare my experiences at the frontier boarding school with those which Dickens relates in *Oliver Twist*" (*Autobiographical Trilogy* 1:23).

After his years at the boarding school and his return to the family home in New Mexico, Otero left again to attend college at St. Louis University, where he received a B.A. Thereafter, he received a Master's in classics from Notre Dame. After graduating in 1880, Otero returned to New Mexico and worked as a bookkeeper for his father's company, Otero and Sellar. In 1883, Otero began his long career as a public official; he served as city treasurer of Las Vegas from 1883 to 1884, and from 1889 to 1890 he was a probate clerk of San Miguel County. From 1892 to 1893 he became a national public official and served as Republican Party delegate to the U.S. Congress and received much attention and power in this capacity.

Otero is also one of the first Nuevomexicano politicians to create literary works (publishing in the English language) that recounted his years as a statesman. His first work was a nostalgic autobiography, *My Life on the Frontier, 1864–1882* (1935). He did not finish the other two volumes (*My Life on the Frontier, 1882–1897*; *My Nine Years as Governor of the*

Territory of New Mexico, 1897–1906) of his autobiographical trilogy until 1940. Between the publication of the first and second volumes of his trilogy, Otero became the first Nuevomexicano to write an English-language biography, *The Real Billy the Kid*. The biography was published in 1936, twenty-nine years after his life as a politician; however, the work itself is based on his late-nineteenth-century memoirs. Published by R. R. Wilson in 1936, *The Real Billy the Kid* is divided into three sections.[5] The first is a first-person account of the dynamic period in New Mexican territorial politics, the second consists of ethnographic accounts collected and transcribed by the *raza* of New Mexico, and the third is an autobiographical narrative of his meetings with Billy the Kid in 1880.

As a politician and writer, Otero was keenly aware of his position as interpreter of this volatile period in New Mexican history. His memoir *My Life on the Frontier* captures this when he writes:

> I became persuaded by a few of my closest friends, who argued that I was one of the very few, at that time of living, who had actually taken part in "blazing the way across the plains," and that I owed it to the coming generations to allow them to read first hand my early experiences covering a most interesting period in our country's history, in the early settlement and development of the "New West." (*Autobiographical Trilogy* 1:287–288)

By writing about the creation of the "New West" in his memoirs and biography, Otero hoped that he could relate the "unwritten facts" that Mexicans in New Mexico had yet to publish in the east coast literary public spheres (*Autobiographical Trilogy* 2:3).

Otero began writing parts of his memoirs and his works on Billy the Kid when he had just begun his political career at the national level in 1893. This year is important, for it historically marked the moment when Frederick Jackson Turner gave his famous "frontier thesis" paper at the World Columbian Exposition setting at the American Historical Association's first meeting. The paper, titled "The Significance of the Frontier in American History," was a narrative that captured this period's transition. The frontier experience, he argued, is the defining ethos of American democracy and the American character. After praising America for its imperialist conquest of native lands and peoples, however, he concluded with a rather disturbing lament: "Four centuries from the discovery of America, at the end of a hundred years of life under the Constitution, the frontier has gone, and with its going has closed the first period of American history" (Turner 62).

Though publicly arguing this idea in 1893, Turner's thesis is rooted in a much longer discourse of white masculinity that began with the signing of the Treaty of Guadalupe Hidalgo in 1848, the treaty that ended the U.S.-Mexican War and ceded to the United States millions of acres of Mexican land. At one narrative level, Turner's statements implicitly summarize the imperialist doctrine that America was now in control of the continent from the Atlantic to the Pacific. For Turner to state this boldly meant that Mexican and Native American bodies have now become "part" of the American republic's body politic, but only by means of assimilation, extermination, or dehumanization. Turner's democratic parable would not have been manifested in his historical unconscious without America's imperialist actions against nonwhite bodies during its westward spread across the continent.[6]

Turner's thesis represents an equally pivotal juncture in Anglo-American and Mexican contact because it marks an important change in late-nineteenth-century thought that manifested itself shortly after the U.S.-Mexico War: the realization that America's Manifest Destiny was ending on the continent and that America was entering a period of "limited resource capitalism" (Fisher 6). Moreover, as Mark Seltzer reminds us, the closing of the frontier challenged any conceptualization of the nation's topography as dominated by the white males, which, in turn, led to a heightened discourse of racism and imperialism in the United States (150). Amy Kaplan also astutely notes that, in fact, Jackson's speech helped forge the ideology of white masculinity at the turn of the century. Therefore, what was of particular importance for the definition of Anglo-American masculinity and the grounds for its authority was a white male professional-managerial class annexation of the once Mexican territories, an act presumably ensuring that the southwest would enter the national body politic as a white member.

The political control of New Mexico, then, one of the last territories of the southwest, was a particularly enticing prospect for eastern businessman, as its abundant resources, pastoral beauty, and trade routes would garner millions of dollars. However, because New Mexico was mostly Mexican and Native American in population, as well as being politically controlled by elite Nuevomexicanos, the dynamics for Anglo political and economic control were extremely volatile. Indeed, as Otero recounts in numerous writings, both private and public, in the years before

Turner's statements, the territory of New Mexico was undergoing profound economic and social changes. At stake for elite Nuevomexicanos, as Otero recounted, was to maintain control over the political public spheres during the transitional period from "old" Hispano Nuevomexico to the "new" New Mexico. Gerald Nash makes this point when he writes that Otero was the mediating public figure during this period:

> New Mexico entered the twentieth century in more ways than one. These years saw a blending of the old and new, a meeting of peoples and time periods. The blending of peoples was important, of Native Americans, Hispanics, and the increasing flow of [Anglo] Americans. The Otero era also witnessed a confluence of the old agrarian economy of the nineteenth century with the beginnings of industry and service industries more characteristic of the years after 1900. These years were also a time of amalgamation for political institutions of the Spanish and Mexican periods with those the Americans brought. Presiding over this complex interaction of diverse cultures was Miguel Antonio Otero, the genial territorial governor of New Mexico and long-time political arbiter in the state. In his own person, part Hispanic, part American, he personified the sweeping changes that were affecting New Mexico in the twentieth century. More than most other individuals, he symbolized the old New Mexico with the new. (Nash 4)

Nash's characterization, though astute, does not capture the violence of this amalgamation between Anglo whites and Mexicans. Nash does not consider that after the Northwest Ordinance of 1787 and the Wisconsin Organic Act of 1836, as well as the Treaty of Guadalupe Hidalgo of 1848 and the Gadsden Purchase of 1853, the socioeconomic power that once had been autonomously controlled by Nuevomexicanos would no longer exist in the "new" New Mexico that Nash locates.

During the period that Nash historicizes, New Mexico became a colony ruled by a foreign empire rather than a state of the United States. It is important to remember that the articles to the Treaty of Guadalupe Hidalgo stipulated that it was up to Congress to determine the political participation of Mexican citizens, and Congress controlled the inclusion of New Mexicans by withholding statehood. Despite the fact that New Mexico had become a territory in 1850, they did not obtain statehood status until 1912, remaining one of the last "Mexican" territories. As Juan Perea argues, this sixty-two-year delay is the longest in United States history, with the exception of Puerto Rico (150). In part, this delay was due to the questions that surrounded the democratic inclusion and management of the racial people known as "New Mexicans." Senator Albert Beveridge, the chairman of the Senate Committee on Territories at the turn of the century, echoed the nation's racial ideologies against New Mexicans when he wrote a report the same years Otero was governor, where he argued that the Mexican "race element" in New Mexico was incompatible with statehood and the guarantees of peoplehood (Perea 151). The "proper time" for New Mexican inclusion would come only if New Mexicans learned how to become a "credible portion of American citizenship" (151). Beveridge's comments are suggestive and reveal what Dana Nelson argues about the political constitution of the " fraternity of White men" in U.S. democracy. Indeed, Beveridge's comments reveal the desire for manhood to mandate and manage difference in the name of social and political unity of the American people (Nelson 14). Otero was "disgusted" with the likes of Beveridge and spent his years as governor arguing in his own reports that "the people of New Mexico are capable of self-government and worthy of full citizenship" (*Autobiographical Trilogy* :212–215).

Despite Otero's contestation of Beveridge and his likes, Beveridge's report proved detrimental to Otero's plea for New Mexican statehood. Despite his status as a "Mexican" territorial governor, Otero could not fight the effects that Beveridge's report had on President Roosevelt's decision to keep New Mexico as a colony of the United States (*Autobiographical Trilogy* 3:217). Otero fought Roosevelt about statehood a number of times, but Roosevelt insisted on maintaining the colonial relationship that the United States had with New Mexico. By denying statehood, New Mexico's racialized inhabitants remained politically, socially, and economically subordinated to a distant, ruling metropolitan center (Washington, D.C.) after that same center had by force, defined in American history as Manifest Destiny, conquered and incorporated the region into its growing empire. This, then, allowed for Anglo political and economic spheres to take control of the territory, for they had the full backing of Washington, D.C. And despite some economic and political control within the Nuevomexicano community after the treaty, it was overwhelmingly a period when Anglo-American structures of power subordinated Mexican culture and threatened the older way of life in the southwest (Melendez 11). The southwest amalgamation that Nash locates, then, was more like a conflict of colonial interests in New Mexico between Anglos and Mexicans.

For Otero, what epitomized the racial questions and the metamorphosis of the once Mexican frontier into a territory was the frontier war in Lincoln County. Lincoln County was a small community 150 miles south of Albuquerque in the New Mexican territory annexed through the Gadsden Purchase. Its main reason for existence and development was as a site for trade and barter for the entire territory. Although sparsely populated, Lincoln County was a microcosm of New Mexico: there was a large population of poor Indo-Hispanic farmers and small ranchers who had lived there for generations or had recently migrated south from northern New Mexico after the treaty. There were also a small number of elite Anglo-American and Mexican American landholders who owned the vast majority of the lands. Since the Gadsden Purchase, Anglo settlers in the country had begun to purchase and steal lands throughout the region from the Indo-Hispanic ranchers, farmers, and elite Mexican Americans (Goméz-Quiñones 241–279).

As in many other territories, Anglos from the east were politically and economically controlling New Mexico during the 1870s and 1880s (Montgomery 66). Anglo settlers created and challenged the economic livelihoods of the old Nuevomexicano families who had maintained bailiwicks of political and economic control in Lincoln County and northern New Mexico. However, because the new Anglo settlers created regimes that were backed by powerful Anglo business leaders from the east, as well as the U.S. government, these Anglo "rings" ended up winning and controlling most of the New Mexican lands. The old Nuevomexicano families, despite their political and economic strongholds in the public spheres at the beginning of U.S. domination in New Mexico, became economic rivals of the new settlers from the east. And despite controlling the public spheres after the Treaty of Guadalupe Hidalgo, in time, many Nuevomexicanos, such as the Oteros, lost control of the public spheres.

By 1878, the Murphy, Dolan, and Riley families—the owners of the Murphy-Dolan Store—economically and politically controlled Lincoln County. The power that they achieved was facilitated by the Santa Fe Ring, a political constituency affiliated with the Republican Party in Washington, D.C. The ring had dominated northern New Mexican territories since 1864 and by the 1880s had begun to attack the Oteros' power in the territory in order to take control over and manage the Mexican people. In effect, the Dolan-Murphy faction was made up of Santa Fe Ring delegates who assisted in acquiring lands in the regions that surrounded Lincoln Country. As Mares argues:

> Mainly, they [the Santa Fe Ring] concentrated on amassing huge land holdings through the manipulation of Spanish land grants and the laws regulating the public domain. But wherever money was to be made, especially where facilitated by governmental action, people suspected ring involvement. Cattle, railroads, mining and army and Indian contracts all captured the attention of the ring members. (34–35)

Before the Santa Fe Ring controlled New Mexico's public and economic spheres, the Otero family constituted the major economic and political power base in northern New Mexico. To the Oteros as well as to many other elite Nuevomexicanos of the region, the Santa Fe Ring and the political leaders associated with it were political and economic adversaries.[7] As Otero noted in *The Real Billy the Kid*:

> The all-powerful Santa Fe Ring, political powerhouse of New Mexico and the most lawless machine in that territory's history, became actively interested in the Lincoln County slaughter, lining up solidly behind the Murphy-Dolan Faction. Headed by Attorney Thomas Catron, ruthless overlord of all the southwest racket interests, the Santa Fe Ring numbered among its more notorious members, Samuel B Axwell, Territorial Governor; and J. B. (Billy) Mathews, Clerk of the District Court. The allegiance of the Santa Fe Ring gave the Murphy clan a semblance of legality and lawfulness that only the cold facts belied. (54)

In essence, the Santa Fe Ring was a cartel that promulgated and, in time, maintained the white male imperialist power structures that had been created after the Treaty of Guadalupe Hidalgo.

John H. Tunstall moved to Lincoln from the east and formed an opposing business and a subsequent economic and political power base in the county. The Oteros sided with him politically and economically in hopes of countering the stronghold that the Dolan and Murphy clan and the Santa Fe Ring political leaders had on northern New Mexico. The Oteros were familiar with Tunstall and had done business with him years before at the firm of Otero (Miguel Antonio Otero's father) and Sellar and Company in Colorado. Miguel Antonio Otero Sr. had introduced Tunstall to a landholder and merchant who had befriended the Oteros some years earlier: Alexander McSween (Otero, *Autobiographical Trilogy* 1:41). This meeting eventually led to a partnership between McSween and Tunstall. By siding with and, in part, creating the McSween-Tunstall faction, the Oteros hoped to defeat the Santa Fe Ring and maintain their political and economic position in New Mexico.

Out of this rivalry, the Lincoln County war began in the later part of 1878. The Dolan-Murphy faction, with the support of the Santa Fe Ring, employed numerous hired guns from throughout the United States to help enforce its regime (Mares 26). The Tunstall-McSween faction also formed its own extralegal force, primarily composed of Indo-Hispanic farmers and small ranchers who had lost their lands to the Santa Fe Ring. This Anglo versus Mexican aspect of the territorial war is alluded to in Otero's recounting of the famous McSween Ranch battle in *The Real Billy the Kid*:

> The disturbance was caused by McSween entering the towns from his ranch, Rio del Ruidoso, with thirty-five men led by Don Martin Chávez of Picacho, who had insisted on coming to Lincoln to protect his friends against the Murphy Dolan Riley gang. Peppin and all his deputies ran to cover inside the Murphy store and the hotel, where they entrenched themselves against possible attack. Under cover of night, McSween, Francisco Zamora, Ignacio Gonzales, Vicente Romero, Hijinio Salazar and José Chávez quietly entered the McSween residence without being fired upon by the enemy. (66)

As Otero recalls it, the war was divided between the old Nuevomexicano elites and the Murphy Dolan gang.

A member of this band that Otero and the Tunstall-McSween faction formed was Billy the Kid, or El Bilito, as the other native New Mexican farmers had named him. Fighting alongside Mexicans, Billy the Kid became a hero to the Mexican people throughout the territory. He became a symbol of resistance and freedom for the Mexican population. To the Mexicans, El Bilito was on their side, fighting the Anglo regime that had taken their lands and impoverished their lives since the end of the U.S.-Mexico War. Because of El Bilito's courage, he became a weapon that could help fight against the Santa Fe Ring. With the help of Billy, the Oteros hoped to win the war and regain the political and economic control that they had lost to the ring.

The war continued throughout the 1870s, with both factions losing numerous men. However, because Territorial Governor Samuel B. Axtell and District Court Clerk J. B. Matthews financed the Dolan-Murphy faction, the ring was able to defeat the McSweens and the Oteros by association. The shift in power subsequently led to the murder of Tunstall and McSween, as well as Otero's uncle by a ring gunman. As Otero noted in *The Real Billy the Kid*, the U.S. government had taken sides with Murphy-Dolan and the Santa Fe Ring, which made it impossible for native New Mexicans to win (132).

Realizing that they had lost the war, Miguel Antonio Otero Sr. and Otero's Uncle, Don Manuel Otero, ran on the Independent Democratic ticket in hopes of maintaining political control. Control of democratic votes in the territory would possibly give them the power to dismantle the Republicans and the party's economic base: the Santa Fe Ring. However, this would not be an easy task, since most Democrats of the region had converted to Republicanism after the war, when the Democratic ticket began to be associated with the southern pro-slavery stance and as advocates who were against the Wilmot Proviso.[8] With the advent of more and more Anglo settlers who were Republicans, the entire Otero family had been losing its power within the territorial political public spheres since the early 1870s.[9] To regain the political power they had once achieved before Anglo conquest, the Oteros had to convince the Mexicans and Anglos of New Mexico that voting for the Republicans was the same as voting for the people who had taken the lands and created barbarism in New Mexico. In a campaign speech recounted and translated from Spanish in a local New Mexican paper, titled *Thirty-Four* (1880), an anonymous reporter notes that "Mr. Otero professed that he had nothing against the Republican Party. He only fought the damnable 'ring' which was led by men who fought against the union; and failing that, they had banded together to rob the union and oppress the people" (*Thirty-Four* 1).

Despite the efforts by the Oteros to associate the ring with slavery and sectionalism, most Mexicans and Anglo elites, the only territorial members who had the ability to vote, voted for another elite Mexican, Tranquilo Luna, a republican and supporter of the Santa Fe Ring (*New Mexico Blue Book* 473). This demonstrated that New Mexico's "people" were not entirely factioned between Anglos and Mexicans, as many elites did side with the Santa Fe Ring.

Having almost unlimited power, the Dolan-Murphy faction began to go after all of the supporters of the McSween faction. During the campaigns for the 1881 election, Dolan campaigned for and economically supported the election of Pat Garrett with the unwritten agenda to hunt down, capture, or kill Billy the Kid (Tuska 71). Pat Garrett murdered Billy the Kid in 1881, and Garrett subsequently became a public figure in the nation. For the Oteros, the death of Billy the Kid symbolized the passing of their economic power, and their ability to define the political public spheres. The subsequent loss of these early elections meant that the Otero family would lose many of their ties to Washington, D.C., and subsequently various landholdings, as they would not have the ability to fight in the Supreme Court for their Mexican land grants.

Claiming Billy the Kid

To the nation as a whole, one of the most publicized characters to represent the conflict of the Lincoln County war was New Mexico's most notorious citizen, Billy the Kid. A legend even before he died in 1881, Billy the Kid became a mediated public space in which Anglo-Americans and Nuevomexicanos forged a quest for public power in the new New Mexico, an imperialist endeavor predicated, I want to stress, on competing historical discourses of American manhood. Like the deaths of Joaquín Murrieta in California and Gregorio Cortez in Texas, the death of Billy the Kid, an Irish American named El Bilito in a nineteenth-century corrido, marks an important transition in Anglo-American dominance and colonial contact that I have historically mapped. Implicitly, it is the slaying of the Kid, as well as these other border hero bodies, that enabled Turner to argue that the frontier as a geographic line dividing civilization from savagry was closed a little over a decade later. It also enabled the Santa Fe Ring to consolidate power in New Mexico away from the masculine bailiwick created by the Otero families. In this way, inscribing Billy the Kid in the public spheres as a symbol of barbarism or justice became important for both Anglos and Mexicans, for his image would perpetuate a history of either Anglo-American justice or Mexican barbarity. In effect, the rights and status of New Mexican citizens and the question of Mexicans becoming members of the United States had much to do with how Billy the Kid was cast in the eastern public spheres.

The imperialist discourse that predicated Turner's thesis, therefore, was represented throughout the literary and political public spheres after the Lincoln County war through images of Billy the Kid and was later rewritten with Otero's *The Real Billy the Kid*. In chapter 12 of his historical biography, a work that Otero would write over the course of his life, Otero transcribes the following from Martin Chávez: "We have not put our impressions of him into print. And our silence has been the cause of great injustice to The Kid" (quoted in Otero, *The Real Billy the Kid* 121). Chávez was one of the old Nuevomexicano "natives" who rode with Billy shortly before his death in 1881 and would help the Otero faction in the Lincoln County war. After criticizing the previous works about Billy, Chávez tells Otero that Mexican American impressions of Billy the Kid have been silent in the literary public sphere; they have not been able to participate in America's print culture precisely because they, the Mexicans, lost the Lincoln County war, which was the last stand for many Mexican families.

Chávez's lament is important for a number of reasons, most notably his understanding that the imaginary reference point of American peoplehood is constituted through the medium of print. Chávez reveals and Otero proves through his biography that print enables them the opportunity to rewrite the previous stories of Billy the Kid which have characterized the Kid and, by association, Mexicans in the public imagination as semicivilized citizens. In part, what Otero and, by association, Chávez intend to rewrite is the "official" discourse within the American literary public spheres that has associated Billy the Kid's ruthless behavior with Mexican Americans, especially seen in the new form of mass publicity, which framed the discourse of the Kid in the literary public sphere when Otero was a politician: the dime novel.

The Mexican Question and its association with the Kid to which Otero responded was first witnessed throughout the literary sphere of U.S. industrial popular culture in turn-of-the-century dime novels, and Otero's political foe, Pat Garrett, and the Santa Fe Ring continued this discourse. In his study, *Inventing Billy the Kid*, Stephen Tatum points out that between the years of 1881 and 1906 "dime novels specifically devoted to the Kid's real and imagined exploits were published and sometimes reprinted in New York, Chicago, St. Louis, and Denver by such houses as Beadle and Adams, Street and Smith, Richard Fox (publishers of the National Police Gazette, Frank Tousey, and John W. Morrison" (44). Indeed, articles about Billy the Kid were even published in New York's elite magazines, such as *Harper's* and *Century*.[10]

Most of these dime novels cast Billy the Kid as a barbarian and used racial stereotypes to describe his Mexican surroundings. One of the most popular fiction writers who wrote about the Kid and perpetuated a racist construction of the Mexican Question was Emerson Hough, a friend of Pat Garrett and the Santa Fe Ring. In his dime novels, Hough perpetuated an image of Billy as a devilish savage and associated the Mexican American people of New Mexico with his savagry. Therefore, for Hough, the killing of Billy the Kid symbolized that "the Anglo-Saxon civilization was destined to overrun this half-Spanish civilization" (307; see also Tatum 61–64). Hough and other dime novelists characterized Billy the Kid's body as small, racially marked, effeminate, and devilish, which was, coincidentally, the same rhetoric used to describe Mexican bodies at the turn of the century (Robinson 33–42). This corporeal association was negatively cast throughout the east, for the dime novels about the Kid would sell upward of 150,000. Dime novels constructed metaphors wherein the Kid's bloodthirsty body and devilish character were allied with a "border civilization" controlled by corrupt elite Nuevomexicanos who were trying to "monopolize the public domain" (Tatum 45) (Figure 9).

When considering the discursive power in the pages of these fictional treatments, one must not forget what was at stake for Anglo-Saxon manhood during the pivotal decade before Turner declared the frontier closed and in the control of Anglo-Americans. It is no coincidence that while these dime novels were being mass produced, perpetuating a racist construction of the Mexican Question, white Anglo-Americans were attempting to consolidate the once-Mexican territories of new New Mexico into a replica of the white republic. As I mentioned before, New Mexico was especially desired for a number of reasons: its mineral resources, routes of trade, and pastoral beauty. However, unlike the other territories, New Mexico's population was mostly Mexican and Indian, and families like the Oteros had been political scions for generations before Anglo conquest.

One effective way for white masculinity to appropriate and maintain its power in this frontier period was to perpetuate a racialized rhetoric of the Mexican Question through mass cultural forms, such as the dime novel. As Tatum reminds us, these narratives of the public sphere would symbolically render white masculinity as the "civilizer" and creator of the new formations of democratic public spheres in the west, metaphorically representing the location of white American ideals, which were in danger of extinction from an increasingly multiethnic and industrialized, nonagrarian America.

Figure 9. Emerson Hough's drawing of Billy the Kid, 1890s

The public sphere did not necessarily conspire to control the production of dime novels in order to make Manifest Destiny manifest. Nor, for that matter, did the neocolonial regimes like the Santa Fe Ring constitute the essential dynamics of the American literary sphere. Rather, the pages of these new forms of mass publicity reveal the creation of a public discourse that perpetuated America's desire for the maintenance of an imaginary white body politic. As Habermas argues in *Structural Transformation*, the institutions in the public sphere affect democratic legitimacy and norms and thus influence how cultures fashion their political ideologies. Unlike the elite magazines of the east, the dime novels were an institution that created a rather static, racial construction of the Mexican Question.

Dime novels about the Kid demonstrated that the literary public sphere helped consolidate territorial politics in the public imagination, both in the territory and in the east. It is important that these rather cheap productions of the literary public sphere had a very large working-class and bourgeois readership throughout the United States. As Michael Denning argues, they were powerful tools in the fashioning of cultural and political ideologies (*Mechanic Accents* 3–5, 9–26). Considering the discursive power of these forms, then, these works effectively constructed what Habermas defines as "manipulative publicity." This manipulative publicity both explicitly and implicitly fashioned a racialized discourse that would render bodies of the southwestern Mexicans semicivilized, thereby helping confirm the Manifest Destiny of Anglo-Saxon culture to control New Mexico.

Displaying his own "anxiety of influence," Otero addresses the reading public in the preface to *The Real Billy the Kid*, noting that his biography is pure fact and thereby countering those narratives of "pure fiction [that are] wholly devoid of fact," which have helped construe Mexicans, the Oteros, and the southwestern body politic as uncivilized (6). And yet, despite Otero attesting to the factual representations of his sources and his personally transcribed interview with Billy the Kid, the proof of this meeting supported by Billy the Kid's knife and spurs, historians who have studied this period of frontier have ignored Otero's documentation and primarily focused their research on Pat Garrett and Ash Upson's narrative *The Authentic Life of Billy the Kid*, first published in 1882.

Although criticized by some revisionist historiographers, the Garrett and Upson narrative of Billy the Kid has remained the most read and the most "authentic" in southwestern history. Otero himself noted in the introduction of his own biography that with the exception of Garrett's work, all the other works on Billy the Kid were pure fiction. Despite this acknowledgment of the authenticity of Garrett's narrative, however, the historical image of Billy the Kid presented in Otero's biography contests the one created by Garrett and Upson. As the reader will appreciate, these narratives are two competing and conflicting stories of peoplehood. Indeed, these two competing stories represent two of the most dominant oppositional historical views of New Mexican peoplehood: the Anglo version and the Hispano version.

Historically, Garrett's narrative has rendered him a textual authority and a minor hero in popular American culture because the story of peoplehood that emerges from his biography of Billy the Kid answered an Anglo-American, as well as a personal, need to imagine the heroism of the western narrative, thereby helping invent an American frontier that was monolithically European American in culture and history. Garrett and Upson's story accomplishes this by characterizing Billy the Kid and the New Mexican people as villains who have wronged society and democratic progress in the west; therefore Billy must be stopped for the law to be restored and, more specifically, so that the United States can continue its colonial power in New Mexican territory. Garrett and Upson were also motivated in their use of a villainous, murdering bandit and not a social hero with redeemable qualities. Both Garrett and Upson were heavily involved in the Santa Fe Ring, Garrett as a delegate and Upson (as he declares in the introduction to his narrative) as a supporter of the Dolan-Murphy faction in the Lincoln County war. In addition, Upson was elected postmaster of Lincoln County with the support of the Murphy-Dolan faction. Through their characterization of Billy as a murderous villain, Garrett and Upson further the interests of their employers and political benefactors. With Billy the Kid as a killer and a villain, the Santa Fe Ring could show that the McSween-Tunstall faction was just as corrupt as the killer they hired for their cause. The Santa Fe Ring, then, according to Garrett and Upson's story of peoplehood, becomes a just cause, and winning the war represents the white and male restoration of social order and the taming of the west for Anglo peoples in control of its democratic institutions.

Unlike Garrett and Upson, Otero historicizes his version of this story and casts it as a tragedy (J. Rivera xii–xvii). First, the story is cast as a serious drama whose main protagonist is tragically killed in the conclusion; second, Otero creates a protagonist who is flawed by an external force; third, this flaw eventually leads to his tragic death; fourth, through his death, Billy evokes sympathy and pity and becomes a social symbol for the people. Essential to Otero's tragic story of peoplehood is his reclamation of the historical truth surrounding Billy the Kid's life. Throughout Otero's story of New Mexican peoplehood, then, he presents "factual and truthful" oral narratives of the "native *gente*" that dispute the murderous man that Garrett and Upson describe. In narrative account after narrative account, Otero meticulously refutes Garrett's claims as to the historicity of Billy as a ruthless killer. Otero concludes, as do the numerous "native *gente*" he quotes, that Billy only killed a few men, and those were all in self-defense or justified. Although Otero acknowledges a few of Billy's killings, his narrative is moralizing and ameliorates Billy's transgressions: "Billy was a man who was sinned against, more than sinned" (168). Within Otero's narrative, the oral accounts of Hijinio Salazar and Martin Chávez all depict Billy's actions during the Lincoln County war as honorable and for the *gente*. In essence, by disputing the image of Billy as a murderous villain that was perpetuated in the literary public spheres in the nineteenth century, Otero creates a counterstory of peoplehood that attempts to remedy the colonial legacy that exists in New Mexico. In making Billy the Kid a tragic hero who helped Nuevomexicanos fight against the Santa Fe Ring, Otero symbolically revealed the injustices that the Mexican people of New Mexico had endured after the treaty (134). Otero's bioraphy explains, then, how Billy the Kid's body becomes marked in the Mexican community as distinctly Mexican, as El Bilito, a hero of the "New Mexican *gente*."

Throughout Otero's biography, Otero represents the Santa Fe Ring as the "ruthless overlords" who unjustly created the "Lincoln County slaughter" and negative publicity against the Kid (54). Otero's work attempts to counter the discourse of the dime novels and Garrett by indicting the regime that made the Kid the treacherous killer he was in the American public's popular imagination. He does this, first, by arguing that Billy the Kid's supposed "murders" were all in self-defense and for the Mexican people and, second, by recounting that Billy the Kid was unjustly murdered by Pat Garrett, an agent of the Santa Fe Ring. Billy the Kid, he explains that he "was more sinned against than sinning" (123). Indeed, the Santa Fe Ring is the only villain of Otero's biography, not the infamous Billy the Kid.

By attacking those who sinned against Billy, and who, by association, sinned against the Mexican people, Otero renders the Kid's life as the tragic consequence of territorialism. He metaphorically represents that tragedy that Nuevomexicano culture endured after the Treaty of Guadalupe Hidalgo of 1848. In Otero's narrative, then, Garrett's slaying of Billy the Kid does not represent the civilizing of the region and the symbolic control of the Mexican American uncivilized population and their land. Rather, it tells of the unmanly murder of a hero of the territory, another tragedy of the competing colonial range wars between the Mexicans and the Anglos at the turn of the century, here represented by the Santa Fe Ring.

Miguel Antonio Otero and the Mexican Question

The Real Billy the Kid enables Otero to respond nostalgically to the political and racial questions in New Mexico in two interrelated manners: one, the documentation of his family's early political participation in the metamorphosis of the democratic west; two, the critique the imperialist discourses that had rendered his native constituents' bodies as semicivilized and therefore not capable of controlling their own citizenship rights and statehood.[11] This last point reveals the complicated aspects of Otero's relationship to the Mexican Question during his lifetime. Otero was aware that the Mexican Question was directly connected with New Mexico's quest for statehood. In fact, the racial definition of New Mexicans in the public spheres directly influenced the control of New Mexico, as a state of the union, by either Mexicans or Anglos (see Montgomery 71–82). Therefore, as an elite Nuevomexicano politician with "Native" Mexicans like Chávez as his constituents, his own cultural engagement with the Mexican Question, in part, enabled him to maintain his own economic and political power after U.S. conquest.

And yet, Otero's engagement with the "race issue" in New Mexico is even more complicated when we consider his own political position as a "representative" of all New Mexican Mexicans. Otero would come to terms with his own racial subjectivity after the traumatic years of the Lincoln County war, as was witnessed shortly after his appointment as governor. In 1897, he filed a report that C. E. Nordstrom, a Santa Fe Ring supporter, wrote before Otero's tenure as governor. This report defined the "native *gente*" of New Mexico as "greasers" (not much unlike the characterization I discuss in chapter 3), and the New Mexicans attacked Otero's allegiance to the people of New Mexico. In response, Otero's first action as governor was to give a public speech in Santa Fe in November of 1897:

I have on every occasion stood up for and defended our native people, why should I not? I am a native Mexican myself, and I am proud of the fact. My father was a full blood native Mexican who was elected by the Mexican people three times as their delegate to Congress. . . . My blood relations are Mexican, found in nearly every country in northern and central New Mexico. And being of Mexican parentage myself, I could never be guilty of the crime of casting any stain or reflection on my own or my father's ancestry, or the race to which we belong. Such conduct would be utterly miserable and suicidal, and make me an apostate unworthy of your respect. (*Las Vegas Optic* 1897, 11)

This recently recovered speech reveals that Otero was not the American accommodationist that so many Chicano critics have labeled him.[12] What is so interesting is that in this speech Otero positions himself as part of the Mexican race, for the blood of Mexicans runs in his veins. This is important because this alliance to the Mexican people, who were defined in the public imagination as "greasers," suggests that the elite Nuevomexicano Otero realized that the Mexican Question affected his own embodied subjectivity in territorial New Mexico. The Mexican Question affected Otero in a private and a public manner. He realized that it not only affected his people but also, by association, his position as a representative of Mexicans in the east and in Washington, D.C. This public act of claiming "Mexican" ancestry is particularly unique in that it refutes the widespread fashioning of a New Mexican "Spanish Fantasy Heritage" that historians have located in New Mexico in the 1890s. In this speech Otero fashions himself through the use of the derogatory term "Mexican"—which in New Mexico and the east had become associated with racial otherness no different than the term "greaser." His use of collective designation "Mexican" and the heritage of Mexicanness empower him and his people through an act of code switching. In effect, he uses a word that Anglos have used to racialize Mexicans and deny them statehood precisely to create New Mexican peoplehood.

Within this historical framework, Otero's production of a biography of the social bandit Billy the Kid, which he began writing the same year he would write the above speech, is not so peculiar. For what Otero's and the Anglo versions of Billy the Kid are competing for are two versions of the Mexican Question that would affect the power structures of New Mexico for generations. And, for Otero, he recounts how his own body was rendered in the eastern public spheres as a political representative of greasers that were not ready to become a civilized state of the union. Pat Garrett, Emerson Hough, and the Santa Fe Ring's manipulative publicity of the slaying of Billy the Kid implicitly associates the Oteros as perpetuating an anachronistic, uncivilized Mexican past, as well as the emergence of a civilized Anglo territory. In this way, Otero's (re)claiming of the language of racial repression (the Mexican) is similar to his claiming of the outlaw Billy the Kid; they both empower the New Mexican "native" constituents and position him as their representative and interpreter in the literary and political public spheres.

Let us not forget that, in part, because of the mass-produced dime novels and because of the fiction works of Emerson Hough and Pat Garrett in the public spheres, the political powers associated with the Santa Fe Ring were symbolically associated with the advent of white civilization; for Garrett, the ring's hired gun, would heroically kill the Kid and mark a symbolic conclusion to an anachronistic way of life, a quotidian existence once fashioned by the Mexican American Otero family (Tatum 54). In this way, the Santa Fe Ring, Pat Garrett, and later Theodore Roosevelt (Roosevelt appointed Garrett as postmaster, despite Otero's objections) historically symbolized the taming of the west. Therefore a white—and specifically Anglo-Saxon—masculinity, not Mexican American manhood, becomes synonymous with "true American ideals and democratic freedom" (Tatum 60). The frontier, then, will close with democratic white male control.

In all of these works, Billy the Kid's body itself becomes a public space wherein masculinity and the Mexican Question are fought out in the literary public spheres. By appropriating Billy the Kid, one of the most publicized dime novel characters at the turn of the century, however, Otero not only attempts to rewrite the discourses that had historically construed Nuevomexicanos in the public imagination as semicivilized citizens. He was also able to historicize that important period surrounding Billy the Kid's death. His is a history that renders Nuevomexicanos as civilized men, not the Santa Fe Ring, as the direct civilizers of the new New Mexico at the turn of the last century. In effect, Otero wanted to become the representative New Mexican figure that historian Nash characterizes as the liminal agent of New Mexico's move to modernity as a state of the union.

It was not that Otero disagreed with the "civilizing" of the territory and New Mexican statehood; indeed, statehood was one of Otero's most important projects during his political career. Rather, he objected that both dime novels and Pat Garrett's narrative had helped create a bailiwick for Anglo-Saxon, not Nuevomexicano, manhood in the New Mexican public spheres. At stake for Otero and the Santa Fe Ring was a proper construction of masculinity and the type of body that would best represent the civilizing of the new New Mexico: the elite Mexicans as represented by Otero and the tragic hero Billy the Kid, or the Anglo-Saxon male, written into the public imagination by Hough and Garrett. For both factions, the Kid mediates competing discourses of the Mexican Question's masculine presuppositions, which would drastically affect the civic framework of New Mexico well after the Lincoln County war and the murder of the Kid. Ironically, then, after his death, Billy the Kid's "sacrificial" body and the mythic space it holds in the public spheres enables Otero to link his masculine, Mexican body with the disembodied political figure, one who evokes "public spirit."

The Resurrection of Billy the Kid

Less than a year after the Mexican American governor of New Mexico, Bill Richardson, took office he created a "truth" commission into the life of Billy the Kid: "A lot of questions need to be answered . . . Now if we uncover evidence to suggest that Billy the Kid was not in fact the man that killed two deputies, that yes, he was an outlaw but had some redeemable qualities, I will consider pardoning him" (*ABQ Journal* July 13, 1997). This commission posthumously appointed a lawyer for Billy the Kid and is investigating if Billy was an outlaw or social bandit; if Pat Garrett even killed Billy the Kid; if Billy disappeared into Mexico and fathered Mexican children. In December of 2004, this commission hoped to find some of these answers when they exhumed his body and studied its DNA.

According to an 1881 article from the *Las Vegas Optic*, they will recover nothing, as the author insisted that the body went on tour, becoming a historical spectacle of the western and barbaric past, much like the head of Joaquín Murrieta:

> "Save and defend us from our ghostly enemies."
> Scarcely has the news of the killing of William Bonney, alias McCarthy, but known the wide-world over as "Billy, the Kid," faded from the public mind before we are again to be startled by the second chapter in the bloody romance of his eventful life—the disposal of his body. The

stiff was brought to Las Vegas, arriving here at two o'clock in the morning, and was slipped quietly into the private office of a practical "sawbones," who, by dint of diligent labor and careful watching to prevent detection, boiled and scraped the skin off the "pate" so as to secure the skull. The body, or remains proper, was covered in the dirt in a corral, where it will remain until decomposition shall have robbed the frame of its meat, when the body will be dug up again and the skeleton "fixed up"—hung together by wires and varnished with shellac to make it presentable. (*Las Vegas Optic* 1881, 19)

This *Optic* report is, of course a folk tale, but like all folklore the truth lies somewhere between the historical real and the fantastic. It is only the folk of the lore who can determine its validity and meaning. What is known, however, is that the dead body of Billy the Kid had a lasting effect on New Mexican democratic peoplehood. And if as Russ Castronovo (13–34) argues, death and dead bodies in fact structure the logic of nineteenth-century democracy, then Richardson's recent commission to recover Billy the Kid's body and thereby his legend suggests his body is still affecting New Mexico's democratic polity.

The recent resurrection of Billy the Kid would not only be seen in the political public spheres, however. Chicano poet, novelist, and playwright Rudolfo Anaya wrote a play about Billy the Kid in the late 1990s, and it was performed in New Mexico. The play itself centers around a debate of two characters, an Anglo and a native New Mexican, arguing about who can claim Billy the Kid: Mexicans or Anglos. By the end of the play, it is left up to the audience as to whom Billy the Kid belongs. The moral of the play derives from the inability to recover the historical "truth" surrounding Billy the Kid's life. The play's historical paradox is that the Kid remains a symbol of New Mexicans today precisely because they have not yet come to terms with the territorial past of New Mexico. To this day, Anaya comments about the writing of his play that Billy the Kid remains an important social bandit of the *gente* of New Mexico; he is still seen as a vessel whereby New Mexicans enacted their civil rights as a collective people.[13] That Billy the Kid remains a part of the social imagination of New Mexico in a period when the state remains one of the poorest in the country is perhaps not surprising. In the end, as long as the legacy of colonialism remains in New Mexico, so too will the body of Billy the Kid haunt the social imaginary of its people.

5

"Con su pluma en su mano"

Américo Paredes and the Poetics of "Mexican American" Peoplehood

Con su pluma en su mano	(With His Pen in His Hand)
Con su permiso quiero cantarles	(With your permission I want to sing to you)
Aquí un corrido sin tristeza ni maldad	(Here a ballad without sadness or malice)
Con pluma firme muy fronterizo	(With pen held firmly, very frontierlike)
Sin miedo nos forjo nuevo pensar	(Without fear he forged for us a new way of thinking)
En Brownsville Tejas mil nueve y quince	(In Brownsville, Texas, nineteen hundred fifteen)
Américo Paredes fue a empezar	(Américo Paredes began)
Su vida y los quince años	(His life and at fifteen years)
Sus ojos vieron cosas que hay	(His eyes saw things that have)
Que recontar	(To be recounted)
(Chorus)	
Con su pluma en su mano	(With his pen in his hand)
Corazonde fiel Chicano	(Heart of true Chicano)
Mexico-americano	(Mexican American)
Muchos cuentos fue a cambiar	(Many tales he changed)
Con su pluma en su mano	(With his pen in his hand)
Con paciencia y sin temor	(With patience and without fear)
Escribio muchas verdades	(He wrote many truths)
Y respeto nos gano	(And won respect for us)
Se fue la guerra viajo el mundo	(He went to the war, traveled the world)
Después se continuó a educar	(Later he continued his education)

En Austin Tejas poco nerviosos	(In Austin, Texas, a little nervous)
Se pusieron los de la universidad	(Those at the university became)
Palabras justas bien presentadas	(Words of justice well presented)
Aparecieron y así fue a llegar	(Appeared and that's how he became)
Doctorado y decorado	(Doctorated and decorated)
Que hasta México lo fue a honrar	(That even Mexico was to honor him)
Tantas canciones me ha enseñado	(So many songs he has taught me)
Por ser musico poeta y locutor	(By being muscian, poet, and radio announcer)
Yo gaurdaré siempre un tesoro	(I'll always guard a treasure
Las historias de ese amable profesor	(The stories of that friendly professor)
Un gran maestro no se retira	(A great teacher does't retire)
Y es por eso que aquí les vengo a dar	(And that's why I'm here to bring you)
Este corrido porque yo he sido	(This ballad because I've been)
También alumna de Don Américo	(Also a student of Don Américo)

Tish Hinojosa, 1999

In the summer of 1999, I attended Don Américo Paredes' memorial celebration in Austin, Texas, where Tish Hinojosa sang the above corrido for an audience of nearly one thousand mourners. People had come from all over the country: former students, musicians, artists, poets, Chicano and Anglo community leaders, senators and congressman. Hinojosa wrote this song to pay tribute to the long and distinguished career of Paredes as a writer, musician, ethnographer, teacher, leader, and, in many respects, creator of Chicano studies. Hinojosa's corrido was timely and moving. It not only honored the man who became known to the Chicano community as Don Paredes, but it also captured the poetics of Mexican American peoplehood that Paredes himself would be so interested in exploring during his long and distinguished life.

With a guitar in her hand, Hinojosa sang "Con su pluma en su mano" in the same versification, rhythm, and structure that hundreds of other corridos had been sung for generations. "Con su pluma en su mano" relates the biographical story of Paredes, creating for us a lyrical bildungsroman. Through the corrido, the listener learns of his birth in 1915; his work as a soldier in the Korean war; his work as a broadcaster, poet, musician, and folk singer; and his emergence as a scholar and teacher at the University of Texas. Like the hundreds of corridos that had helped define Mexican peoplehood in years past, Hinojosa's eulogizing corrido worked as a modern story of Mexican peoplehood, poetically making Paredes the leader and embodiment of all of us in that room through the use of a historical form. In this way, the poetic inscription of Paredes through a uniquely Chicano cultural expression whose themes resonate with populist ideals and norms, the corrido, becomes a founding discourse of our (post)modern Mexican American collectivity. The cultural form that had been so important to Mexican collectivity and resistance in the nineteenth and early twentieth centuries continues to affect the Chicanos who were in the room in the summer of 1999.[1]

It is of no small importance that this memorial was taking place when Mexican American peoplehood was drastically changing: Mexicans in Texas were quickly becoming the majority population. At this moment of demographic change, we came to mourn and memorialize Paredes, only to find that the corrido had in some brief instance made us aware of the founding origins of our own Chicano collectivity. As many would attest, Paredes had in one way or another affected every person in the room, and the poetic effect of the corrido reinforced our mutual historic and present connections as Mexicans and Chicanos. José Limón has argued so eloquently in *Mexican Ballads, Chicano Poems* that the corrido has a unique ability to create a complex relationship to the past, which enabled it to connect to the present (65). This temporality of the corrido, however, led to my own present reflection, as I cannot stop thinking about the historical contradictions that "Con su pluma en su mano" creates for all of us in the room. In the end, I find that the corrido molded him into a new "Enlightened" border hero of Mexican (democratic) peoplehood, a man, who "with pen in hand," "forged for us a new way of thinking" and gained respect as a "writer of truth."

Known mostly to the Mexicans who were in the room, Hinojosa's "Con su pluma in su mano" rewrites the popular corrido "With a Pistol in His Hand," a corrido that Paredes himself spent the better period of his life studying. It is important to remember that in his path-breaking study of the corrido, *With His Pistol in His Hand*, Paredes recovered the folk ballad "With a Pistol in His Hand"; in doing so, he brought to life the history, geopolitics, culture, and poetics of the Mexican American people of Texas in the nineteenth and early twentieth centuries. The corrido, his study argues, came to personify a resistant collectivity that emerged from a colonial worldview in Texas (Paredes). The corrido was a populist form in that it poetically captured the heroic stories of the "common" Mexican and thereby created and maintained their collectivity (Limón, *Mexican Ballads, Chicano Poems*; Saldívar, *Chicano Narrative*).

The corrido of Gregorio Cortez relates the geopolitical tensions on the South Texas border that developed when Gregorio Cortez Lira, a ranchhand of Mexican parentage, became involved in a bloody shootout with a white American sheriff. Cortez escaped, "with pistol in hand," and the ballad maps the heroic acts of Cortez in Texas—his escape, the chase, and mostly his radical resistance against the power structures that had begun to take land from Texas Mexicans. The corrido marks a historical record of the geopolitical struggles between Mexicans and Anglos during the turn of the century. Not unlike Billy the Kid, Cortez personifies the hero of the Mexican people in Texas. As such, he also represents the violent border chaos and, most important, a radical tradition of fighting against white oppression with force. In the corrido, Cortez symbolizes a brown radical tradition and a period in history when Mexicans would collectively fight with "a pistol in their hand" to change the Anglo system of law and justice that had oppressed them. The corrido poetically relates what Mexicans had come to believe about U.S. democratic enlightenment: that the guarantees of U.S. citizenship would not address their particular collective needs as a racial people. The corrido, therefore, reinforced what Mexicans in the United States had known since the Treaty of Guadalupe Hidalgo of 1848: democracy and the legislation that defines its contours had failed Mexicans in the United States. The falsely accused, incarcerated, and eventually lynched Cortez personified Mexicans' own disenfranchised existence under democracy, as well as their inability to own land and have a voice in legal spheres. Cortez's individual use of a pistol and violence to challenge an American democratic system that had collectively failed Mexicans represented their own desire for equality through radical action. Cortez and the corrido that they nostalgically sang about him reinscribed their collective resistance and gave them hope inthe poetic ideals of radicalism itself.

Set against the historical and radical origins of the corrido, Hinojosa's substitution of "pen" for "pistol" in her corrido for Paredes creates an ironic though telling story of the changing dynamics of Mexican peoplehood in the United States. By substituting "pen" for "pistol," the very notion of brown radicalism is obfuscated by the democratic ideals signified through the notion of print. No longer the masculine corrido hero symbolizing violence and the radical emancipation of the Mexican people, Hinojosa's corrido symbolically depicts Paredes as a democratic leader, who "with a pen held firmly, very frontierlike," is the educator, the reasoned philosopher, and the doctor. In Hinojosa's corrido, Paredes is firmly working from within the ideals and norms of democracy; he is the gentleman-citizen who personifies print culture as author, writer, and scholar. In the end, he embodies democracy by embodying print and education, for he is a man with pen in hand who taught us a new way of thinking. He is the symbolic "Mexican American."[2]

Through Hinojosa's corrido, then, we cannot ignore that perhaps the Mexicans at the memorial at this turn of the twentieth century have, for the most part, formed a peoplehood in a different manner than the collectivity forged during some of geopolitical struggles at the turn of the nineteenth century. The corrido of Gregorio Cortez personified a radical brown tradition that challenged the very ideals and norms of democracy precisely because democratic norms and ideals had not accounted for Mexican people within the borders of the United States, despite the signing of the Treaty of Guadalupe Hidalgo in 1848. Though the corrido builds on the legacy of brown radicalism, Hinojosa's corrido inevitably creates a poetics of democratic peoplehood that uses the tropes of the Enlightenment to incite the social imaginary of those in the room. I also suggest that Hinojosa's corrido and the liberal substitution it evokes captures the contradictions of Paredes' own examination of Mexican peoplehood in South Texas during the 1930s. Hinojosa's corrido embodies Paredes' struggles with the geopolitical tensions brought about by the dialectic between the radical and imperialist past and the democratic ideals and norms that Mexicans in the United States have had to negotiate since the Treaty of Guadalupe Hidalgo.

This is not to say that Hinojosa's corrido intends to create a bifurcated and assimilated Mexican American who must forget imperialism, radicalism, and our resistance to Anglo networks of power, all of which make up our collective Mexican past in order to locate a democratic future. Rather, the corrido advocates, for better or worse, that Mexican Americans engage democracy as *the* form of political organization and efficacy. Indeed, Hinojosa captures what we have come to understand about modern Mexican American peoplehood since the 1930s: we have come to accept the norms and ideals of democracy as the political form of our collective organization and civil rights within the borders of the United States. No longer are we grasping for pistols in hand as the Sediciosos did in South Texas during the early twentieth century; we are all now holding pens in order to write a new story of Mexican peoplehood, one molded through the language of democracy. In the end, Hinojosa's corrido calls attention to the negotiated circumstances that have formed Mexican peoplehood and the historical contradictions that underpin its present and future development within the borders of the United States.

In this last chapter I explore the idea that Hinojosa's substitution of "pen" for "pistol" has its roots in Paredes' own vexed poetic examination of Mexican peoplehood in the 1930s, a period that drastically changed how modern peoplehood would be understood in the United States. Moreover, I look at this period and Paredes because this liminal moment would mark Paredes' own entrance into the public spheres and print culture, the period when Hinojosa notes he began to take a pen in hand and poetically related the struggles of Mexicans in the United States through his poetry, short stories, and novels. In his works, Paredes explores what form of political organization would best deal with the geopolitical struggles of Texas, the colonial period when radicalism gave way to the new liberal politics of the 1930s. Paredes' "Mexican Question"—What political route should Mexicans take in their collective struggles in the 1930s?—was paramount to his cultural work, and his inquiry reveals much about our present liberal understandings of brown radicalism and Mexican collectivity.

To be sure, Paredes' examination of Mexican political collectivity spoke to the cultural concerns of the 1930s. Within the national public spheres, the very idea of an American collective "people" was widely debated in the Depression years and the New Deal Era. Warren Sussman argues that it is in this key moment when the singular significance of "the people" became the central element in the 1930s political and cultural spheres. After the Depression ruptured the unified ideal of the American people, the New Deal attempted to create hundreds of policies that would enable the constitution of "a people" that had never existed before in America (Sussman 49). From the establishment of Social Security to the

Worker's Progress Alliance, the New Deal gave way to a welfare state that redrew the contours of our modern understanding of "We, the People."

Though the state policies of the New Deal and its agencies would drastically affect the liberal ideals and norms of the people in the 1930s, it was in the arena of culture where the debate about the people took center stage. According to Sussman, "there was one phrase, one sentiment, one special call on the emotions that appeared everywhere in America's popular language, the people" (83). No other than Kenneth Burke captured this well when he wrote that "the symbol I should plead for, as more basic, more of an ideal incentive, than that of the worker, is that of the people" (quoted in Denning, *Cultural Front* 55–56). Echoing Burke, Samuel Siullen wrote in the New Masses "the People . . . are the heroes of our most gratifying books" (quoted in Denning, *Cultural Front* 142–143).[3]

Though there were a number of periods when the constitution of the people was important, as I have argued in this book, the rhetoric of populism that flourished in this era drastically affected the modern liberal understanding of the people we live with today. This populist rhetoric, however, did not include all of "We, the People." Despite the New Deal Era's focus on "the people," many racial, ethnic, sexual, and gendered groups were not included in the populist narratives of the period. Indeed, let us not forget that it is in this period that Jim Crow–like segregation had its grips on the minority peoples of the United States, and the laws guaranteed that only white Americans would have the full rights of citizenship. Segregation and disenfranchisement were the norms for minorities in the 1930s.

In fact, the public and legal spheres created most people of color as not fitting the homogeneous criteria of "the people." This, of course, was an ironic historical period in the racism that pervaded the United States, which was antithetical to the liberal ideals espoused by white Americans who attempted, but failed, to forge a populist message in the 1930s. We must not forget, then, that the official populist rhetoric of the New Deal presupposed a liberal notion of a white, not universal, *demos*. As such, the people of the 1930s were, to quote Michael Denning, "the white plain people" who worked hard and maintained white bourgeois ideals (*Cultural Front* 126.) To ensure this protection, all Americans must adhere to the liberal ideals and relegate their racial, gendered, or sexual identity to the private. As such, the populist rhetoric of the 1930s was not so radical after all: it fostered a normalized ideal of the people that affectively maintained a segregated notion of the American people.

During the national rhetoric surrounding peoplehood, the 1930s also ironically marked an important period in the emergence of a new modern understanding of Mexican democratic peoplehood. Indeed, it is of no small importance that this would be the period when the term "Mexican American" became a self-defining term for Mexicans in the United States and would give rise to a new political consciousness that was presupposed in the populist rhetoric of LULAC (League of Latin American Citizens).[4] This rising populist consciousness of the Mexican *ethnos*, however, was greatly affected by the legacy of Manifest Destiny, as seen through the divisive repatriation acts against Mexicans in the United States. It is in this period when nearly 500,000 Mexican people were sent back to Mexico because white Americans felt Mexicans did not fit into the national characterization defined by middle-class white peoplehood, which, as I mentioned above, was being normalized through the populist rhetoric of the New Deal (Guerin-Gonzáles 23). It is of no small coincidence that this would also be the period when the legal sphere would begin its schizophrenic racial definitions of Mexicans, for this would be the period when Mexicans were a racial other in the federal census of 1930.

Especially important is that this was the moment when the legacy of brown radicalism, violence, and leftist politics would haunt the populist dreams of the Mexican American generation that Mario García and Richard García locate in their books on 1930s Mexican political organization and leadership. In this way, the 1930s marked an important liminal juncture, not only for white America but also in the making of our modern understanding of Mexican American collectivity. "Mexican American" collectivity of the period, therefore, was forged out of two interrelated stories of political peoplehood: the populist rhetoric of the 1930s that espoused universal equality and homogeneity, and the legacy of radical politics of the left that fueled the border rebellion in South Texas that the corrido of Gregorio Cortez and other border radicals symbolized. Paredes' cultural work at this time attempted to come to terms with the contradictory formation of Mexican peoplehood and the debates over its very meaning in the United States. He made visible in his works the paradoxical logic of Mexican peoplehood itself, exploring the poetics of Mexican belonging and collectivity. In the end, the irony, we will find, is that despite the fact that Paredes was considered a leader of the Mexican people and most of his cultural production focused on Mexican peoplehood and collectivity, he was, in fact, pessimistic about the logic of peoplehood itself.

Radical Dreams, Mexican Questions

My discussion of Paredes begins by juxtaposing him with another important Chicana leader of the 1930s, Emma Tenayuca. Born one year apart in Texas, the Tejana labor leader Paredes and the Marxist intellectual Tenayuca both passed away in the summer of 1999. I begin this section by putting Paredes and Tenayuca in dialogue with one another in order to examine how the legacy of radicalism affected the political constitution of Mexican peoplehood in the 1930s. Paredes was particularly interested in radical politics and spent much of his life studying the leaders, the corridos, and the history of Mexican radicalism. In many ways, the leitmotif of Parades' cultural work was the dynamics of revolutionary politics and their effects on Mexican collectivity and identity formation. I briefly explain the radical politics that Paredes wrote about and then focus on his most important short story, which he wrote in the 1930s, "The Hammon and the Beans," a poetic work that represents Tenayuca.

When Paredes wrote "The Hammon and the Beans" in the 1930s, Texas had just left a period of drastic geopolitical change, which Richard Flores refers to as the Texas Modern.[5] According to Flores, the years between 1880 and 1900 marked the closing of frontier lands and, with that, the introduction of the railroad and the beginning of commercial farming. In effect, Manifest Destiny laid the ideological path for white American capitalism in nineteenth-century Texas, while, by the turn of the century, Texas underwent the period when Anglos consolidated the lands for economic and political control of the once southwestern territories. We recall here that this was the moment of history that Zavala foresaw as the "bloody period" of political transition for Mexicans in Texas and the southwest. Indeed, Zavala was right. When Zavala died in 1836, Tejano agrarians and Mexican landed elites and politicos still had a power base in the region. However, much like New Mexico's changing economy and the battle between New Mexican and Anglo businessman discussed in chapter 4, so did Texas undergo a battle for control of the emerging Texas markets and lands (Montejano 135). This battle, of course, had drastic effects on the political constitution of Mexican Americans. Between 1900 and 1920 the rate of these changes accelerated greatly, leading to increased geopolitical conflict between Mexicans and Anglos. Richard Flores argues that the Texas Modern gave way to violent conflict, marked by range wars and what would become two of the most important Mexican radical moments in the United States: the writing of the Plan de San Diego and the Sedicioso Movement (43).[6]

Led by Aniceto Pizana, Basilio Ramos, the political writings of Flores Magnon, Luis de la Rosa, and other Partido Libertad Movimiento (PLM) anarchist and Marxist intellectuals in 1915, the Plan de San Diego was an agrarian radical movement whose political goal was to emancipate Mexicans from the grips of the encroaching Anglo capitalist modes of production and to demand democratic enfranchisement for all minorities in the southwest. Though primarily located in South Texas, the leaders of this movement hoped to free the entire southwest from the yoke of U.S. imperialism. The framers of the Plan de San Diego argued that U.S. capitalism spread into the southwest and thereby created class and racial inequalities that were unbearable for Mexicans. The PLM felt that the only way to effectively create political change was to create a collective resistance and thus take up arms and fight for their lands and people through what the Plan felt should be "violent conflict, if necessary." The first Mexican American manifesto to meld populist democratic language and norms to accomplish Marxist ideals of class and land emancipation, the Plan de San Diego hoped to "liberate" Texas, New Mexico, Arizona, Colorado, and California, taking back through violent actions, "the states that the republic of Mexico was robbed in a most perfidious manner by North American Imperialism."[7]

This manifesto was successful in creating an armed resistance. Indeed, emerging from its populist rhetoric of radical Mexican peoplehood, El Sedicioso (the Seditionists) became a legitimate and recognized force of Anglo resistance in the southwest. Informed by the rhetoric of the Plan de San Diego and led by Pizana and de la Rosa, the Sediciosos gathered in order to "challenge the crimes and outrages which were daily being committed on defenseless women and children of our race by the bandits and miserable rangers who guard the banks of the Rio Grande. Just and righteous indignation, which causes our blood to boil and impels us, orders us to punish with all the energy of which we are capable" (Plan de San Diego). In this published manifesto, de la Rosa and Pizana anticipated the leftist rhetoric of populism ("us, "our race," "our blood") in order to highlight the collective solidarity between the Sediciosos and "the Mexican *gente*," for they came together because they felt that "we" Mexicans had had "enough of tolerance, enough of suffering insults and contempt" by Anglos. De la Rosa and Pizana wanted to highlight in their manifesto that Mexicans' collective repression could become the motivation for a collective force of resistance. That is, their racialization and oppression on what was once their land led to what Rogers Smith (*Stories of Peoplehood*) refers to as a "constitutive story," which bound their collective resistance. Repression of the common Mexican individual and land loss becomes the core of their collective existence.

The Sediciosos were successful in putting their words to action. They engaged in more than two dozen battles and raids; burned railroad infrastructures, bridges, the ranches and lands of Anglo ranchers and railroad barons; set branded cattle free; and cut telegraph lines. In effect, they attacked every aspect of Anglo-American expansionism that they felt had led to the racialization of Mexicans in the southwest. Nevertheless, their collective radicalism was short lived. On October 21, 1915, the Sedicisos led their last raid at Ojo de Agua, putting an end to the revolutionary effort to emancipate the Mexicans of the southwest.

Despite the short life of the actual rebellion, stories about the Sediciosos affected Mexican collectivity for generations after their last raid. When Paredes was growing up in South Texas, the corrido "The Seditionists" was a popular folk song that maintained the ideal of radicalism within the Mexican community. Paredes recovered this corrido in his foundational ethnographic study of folk culture, *The Texas-Mexican Cancionero*. Set in South Texas, the corrido "The Seditionists" recounts the exploits of Anziano Pizana, who "singing as he rode along," asks his men, "Where can I find the *rinches* [derogatory name for the Texas Rangers]? I'm here to pay them a visit" (71). In many ways, this corrido is an excellent example of what Popular Front critics call "populist narratives" (Denning, *Cultural Front* 23). It spoke to the concerns of the "common person" of the region and created a poetics of people-making through its themes and motifs. Paredes himself understood its effects on Mexican collectivity in the southwest when he argued that the corrido and its subject, Pizana, answered "deep-seated feelings in a great number of Mexican Americans." Half epic ballad and half lyrical lament, the corrido evokes memory of Pizana's brown radical traditions and its legacy:

> The seditionists are leaving, they have gone into retreat; they have left us red swath to remember them by.

> The seditionists are leaving; they said they would return, but they didn't tell us when because they had no way of knowing. (Paredes, *Texas-Mexican Cancionero*)

Paredes argues that the memory of Pizana and the Sedicioso's radical acts of rebellion continued for decades after the actual moment in history, living on through the corrido and the symbolic "red swath" (87). The last lines are striking because of both the lamentful desire for a radical past and the ambivalence surrounding its return to the Mexican people. The Sediciosos left and did not tell the people of their return precisely because the Sediciosos themselves have no way of "knowing" when they will return. The corrido may inscribe the narrative logic of populism, but it concludes in a rather disjointed manner. By the end of the corrido, the uncertainty of the future prospects of Mexican radicalism ironically situates rebellion as a historical anecdote of the collective past, a historical trope that is left in their memory, not the future of their material collectivity. In this way, the simultaneous historicity of radicalism and its uncertain future helps form an ambivalent collectivity for Mexicans in the 1930s. Radicalism has become an absent presence, living only in the imaginative songs and memories of the collective, emerging as the nostalgia of an agrarian past. Radicalism has become a specter in Paredes' Texas Modern world, haunting the Mexicans whose future can be found in the rhetoric of white American democracy.

The tropes the corrido "Los Sediciosos" evokes serve as a metaphor of Paredes' own cultural work. The unconscious repression of the radical past and the unknowable democratic future haunts the pages of Paredes' fiction. Indeed, nearly all of his fiction represents, in some degree, the legacy of radicalism and the conflicts it creates for Mexicans who must survive in the changing Texas Modern world that hides its imperialist ideologies behind the promise of democratic equality, norms, and ideals that attempt to assimilate Mexicans into the body politic as semicivilized citizens. The opening pages of "The Hammon and the Beans" capture this well:

> Sometimes we joined in the ceremony. . . . That must have been when we had just studied about George Washington in school or recited "The Song of Marion's Men" about Marion the Fox and the British cavalry that chased him up and down the broad Santee. But at other times we stuck out our tongues and jeered at the soldiers. Perhaps the night before

we had hung at the edges of a group of old men and listened to tales about Ancito Pizana. (4)

In this quote, Paredes shows so well that Mexican collectivity, the "we" in the story, was undergoing a drastic transformation. On the one hand, Mexicans were taught the normative stories of democratic peoplehood, and through forceful coercion they learned and recited U.S. history and the founding national stories, as symbolized in "The Hammon and the Beans" and his later novel *George Washington Gómez*. On the other hand, Mexicans held on to a radical past that challenged the universal ideals and norms of democracy through the stories of Ancito Pizana. Indeed, the old stories of Pizana in "The Hammon and the Beans" not only work to create a collective "group," despite the repressive gaze of the military fort that geographically and culturally splits the town in two sections of white and brown, but also incite acts of rebellion against the soldiers; they stick out their tongues. In effect, the opening page of "The Hammon and the Beans" establishes a conflict between two competing stories of peoplehood. The old stories of Pizana keep Mexicans from being completely incorporated as Americans in a town that, though mostly populated by Mexicans, is under Anglo control. And yet, they still desire their autonomy by sticking out their tongues at the U.S. soldiers. To this end, Pizana remains a leader of the people, creating resistance through his absent presence.

This opening scene acts as a springboard into the questions surrounding the political efficacy of leadership and the legacy of Mexican radicalism. The above quote lays the territory for the story's main focus: Chonita. The remainder of the story historically situates the life of this nine-year-old South Texas girl, who is the "poet" and "leader" of the people in South Texas, Jonesville-on-the-Grande. Jonesville-on-the-Grande is the fictional name of the real city, Brownsville, Texas. Set against the backdrop of the Mexican radical movements I have described above, Chonita embodies the legacy and possibility of Mexican radicalism. Chonita's story emerges through the voice of a young boy who lives in the same pueblo. The Mexican town is set against Fort Jones on the Grande, an Anglo-American military base that watches over the border for possible uprisings. Chonita's parents are laborers who are barely able to sustain a living. They take odd jobs at the fort and in the homes of middle-class Mexicans and Anglos in the neighborhood. We also learn that her real father, long dead, may have been a member of the Sediciosos, but the

Texas Rangers lynched him after the rebellions of 1915. Born out of radicalism and violence, colonial South Texas leaves no options for Chonita but to sustain her existence with scraps of food that the soldiers of the fort have left on their plates.

Chonita's economic condition does not dampen her spirit, however. In her mind, she creates a resistant voice against an Anglo capitalist system that has racialized and oppressed the people of her community. In the middle of the story, Chonita lashes out against the Anglo power structures by mimicking the Anglo-American soldiers' eating ritual, as she stands in front of the Mexican boys of the community and yells, "Give me the Hammon and the Beans! Give me the Hammon and the Beans!" Ramón Saldívar argues in the introduction to this story "that her mimicry and her daring are the instruments of her poetry." According to Saldívar, her actions represent the noble possibility of revolutionary social action, deferred (*Chicano Narrative* xxii). At first glance, one could argue that her actions resurrect Ancito Pizana. In this way, through the young life of Chonita, Texas radicalism has a knowable future. Perhaps, then, the prophecy of the corrido, "Los Sedicisocos," finds concrete oppression—radicalism has returned to Texas. The future possibilities of radicalism in the story, however, are complicated by the fact that Paredes based the character Chonita on the 1930s Marxist radical Emma Tenayuca. Indeed, Chonita's actions symbolically resemble the nationally published photo of Tenayuca in 1937, published only a few years before Paredes published his story (Figure 10).

With her fist raised in the middle of the picture, Tenayuca led the pecan sheller's strike and would effectively help the wages and living conditions of thousands of Mexican workers. This is an incredibly important anecdote. To fully explore the embedded contradictions of radicalism and its legacy that Paredes is trying to uproot in "The Hammon and the Beans" and his symbolic use of Tenayuca, it is worth relating the radical thought of Emma Tenayuca through a reading of her published essay "The Mexican Question in the Southwest."

Written by Tenayuca and her husband Homer Brooks in 1939 and published in the *Communist*, "The Mexican Question" is at its most basic level a radical Marxist manifesto that tries to find an emancipatory language for the oppressive situation of Mexicans in the United States. In effect, it tries to create Mexican collectivity through 1930s Popular Front rhetoric espoused by the National Communist Party. As a one of the first Chicana activists, who became the state secretary of the Communist

Figure 10. Emma Tenayuca with fist in air (*San Antonio Light* Collection, 1937)

Party, Tenayuca tried to come to terms with the place that Mexicans would hold, not only in the Communist Party but also within the borders of the United States. Her works reveal a desire to use the radical philosophies of Marx, Stalin, and Lenin to create a collective Mexican people in the geographic region of the southwest. According to her, the heart of Mexican oppression is both the racial and the economic discrimination that originated with the imperialist U.S.-Mexico War, a war, she argues, that was motivated by both racial and geopolitical imperatives. Among the many questions that the essay explores is whether Mexicans consist of a separate geographic nation and people. She concludes that they do not, for Mexicans are linked economically to the Anglo-American working classes and spatially to the land because of the Treaty of Guadalupe Hidalgo. In this way, she is, to a degree, in line with the populist rhetoric of the 1930s Left, which argued in much milder terms that Mexicans are part of the larger collective because of their class positions as workers. To be sure, Tenayuca breaks party lines and Marxist populist rhetoric when she posits that Mexicans are a national minority that have a historical past and a relationship to the land that makes them a distinct people within the larger collective. They are Mexican people first, members of the party second. After establishing Mexicans as a distinct people, however, by the end of the essay, she argues that a collective Mexican people can effectively change the entire U.S. body politic: "The Mexican people's movement in the Southwest will constitute one more important and powerful link in the growing movement for the democratic front in the United States. The achievement of its objectives will be a decisive step forward toward the national unification of the American people" (42).

Though not as blatantly radical as the Plan de San Diego, Tenayuca's populism attempts to insert Mexicans into the geopolitical imagination of the Marxist Left by first constituting them as a people. Only by Marxists embracing Mexicans as a distinct people with a distinct history can Marxism exist as a viable discourse of minority peoplehood. In this way, Tenayuca echoes Kenneth Burke's ideas that we must focus on the ideal of the people and not solely the worker. For Tenayuca, however, the people are not a universal norm; they are not absent of their particular historical and racial characteristics—they are the Mexican people. Only by Marxism embracing their unique history and circumstances of imperialism in the southwest will the populist dreams of Marxism become a materially viable Popular Front for Mexicans in the United States.

Tenayuca's essay finds its roots but also contests a long line of Marxist populist thought and history relating to Mexicans. Certainly, Tenayuca's "Mexican Question" departs from Marx's rhetorical inquiry, "On the Jewish Question" (1847)—a manifesto that was the first to establish the dialectic between the universal worker and ethnic people. Unlike "The Jewish Question" and a number of works that followed about the universal class collective, however, Tenayuca's question challenges the universal ideals set up in Marxist thought that normalizes race and the historical and geographic contingencies that inform Mexican peoplehood. It is particularly interesting that the Marxist roots and historical contradictions that Tenayuca's 'The Mexican Question in the Southwest" reveals began the very same year that Marx wrote "The Jewish Question." During the U.S.-Mexico war, Edgar von Westphalen, Karl Marx's brother-in-law, led a radical Marxist movement in no other than Texas in 1847. A member of the German Socialist Party and a part-time economic philosopher who exchanged ideas with Marx, von Westphalen went to Texas during the U.S.-Mexico War to create a utopian community that was anticapitalist and socialist in nature. His quest for an anticapitalist, socialist Texas community failed, however. The question is whether the community failed because Edgar, like his brother-in-law Karl Marx and colleague Friedrich Engels, did not fully understand the historical, racial, and cultural dynamics of the U.S.-Mexico War or the Mexican people's role as agents of world historical change. Or, as Peter Stallybrass argues, was it because Marx and his colleagues had not yet worked out the dynamics of homogeneity in the making of people? Although Marx was aware of the significance of both the war and ethnic difference in 1847, I suggest that neither Marx, Engels, nor von Westphalen fully considered the ramifications of Mexican racial difference in their radical, communal visions of Texas or the expansion of the United States as a capitalist nation state.

Though grafted to the development of "fresh capital and Anglo bourgeoisie" (as Marx would argue in his letters and in a column in the *New York Daily Tribune* in 1847), Mexicans were, in the last instance, primitive accumulation, not historical agents of a radical movement that would participate in the critique of U.S. capital and create a utopian community; they were historical objects needed for capitalism's rise as the dominant mode of production in the United States and eventually the world. Mexicans' relationship to capitalism, then, was not critical; it was tangential to the global, white proletarian movement.

This is not to say that race questions did not affect Marx's thought and language of capitalism. However, race questions, and for our purposes, the Mexican Question, were not essential to his inquiry into an anticapitalist, radical, utopian, Communist Party. An inquiry into the rights and status of racial others in Marx's thought (here I am thinking of a "Jewish, Irish, Slavic, African, and Asian Question") created a false consciousness about the political public sphere's ability to emancipate racial others and blinded the rise of a universal, radical proletarian class, a "species being" capable of transcending racial distinctions as common workers. Subjects and classes are formed in the sphere of productive relations, while the political merely reflects and mystifies the relations of those subjects and classes.

In this way, Marx, Engels, von Westphalen, and the western Marxist thought that developed in the years that followed did consider race questions, and Marx did represent racial people when discussing changing modes of production and capitalism's rise, but, as I suggest, they did not consider race rights and status as a factor for a radical emancipatory consciousness. This presupposition, they falsely theorized, led to an inquiry predicated on false consciousness and one that worked within the public realm of capitalism, not the anticapitalist space of revolution.[8] I suggest that race questions in Marxist thought, and specifically the Mexican Question, reveals a contradiction that, to some degree, has affected Mexicans' relationship to radical thought for over a century. Tenayuca and later Paredes tried to come to terms with this in their work, and they implicitly revealed that Mexicans remain a specter in Marxist thought and, ironically, to this end, that radical emancipation remains a specter in Mexican peoplehood.

In contradistinction to Marxism's inability to deal with race, Tenayuca's "The Mexican Question" is trying to locate a radical thought that will account for both the rights of racial others and economic emancipation. That is, she is trying to locate a critical race Marxism that accounts for the relationship between these two important aspects of subjectivity and cultural formation. Moreover, she is responding to the Communist Party's race questions of 1930, specifically the "Negro Question," which argued that African Americans consisted of a separate nation in the United States, what many refer to as the "Black Belt thesis." She disagreed with this formulation because it created a segregationist ideology within the popular front's thought. Again it is important to reiterate that Tenayuca's essay should also be read with and against the Anglo-American "Mexican Question" discussed in chapter 3. According to Tenayuca, the "Mexican Question(s)" in Anglo-America concerning the rights and status of Mexicans—Who are the Mexican people? What is their race? What are their rights after the war? How will they affect, "We, the People" of Anglo-America?—were all predicated on ideologies that emerged from geopolitical struggles between Mexico and the United States. Moreover, Tenayuca is trying to negotiate these responses with and against the emergence of LULAC in the 1930s, an organization that, I mentioned, was embracing Anglo-American bourgeois ideologies of peoplehood in hopes of becoming part of "We, the People."

Considering the figure and thought of Tenayuca, the questions surrounding Paredes' characterization of Chonita are puzzling and even contradictory. One must ask why Paredes decided to focus on Tenayuca in this story. What is he representing about radicalism and Mexican leadership? Returning to "The Hammon and the Beans," we begin to find some of the answers. I return to the climactic scene of the story, when Chonita symbolically rises as a leader of the Mexican people. In an act of irony and mimicry of Tenayuca's own work as a leader at the pecan sheller's strike, Chonita in "The Hammon and the Beans" also stands above the Mexican people, who are edging her to "give a speech," as they yell, "Speech. Speech, Speech" (6). This is when Chonita yells, "Give me the Hammon and the Beans! Give me the Hammon and the Beans!" (6). Unlike Tenayuca's heroic acts as a leader of the Mexican people in San Antonio, however, the boys mock Chonita because of her accent and for not speaking correct English. In effect, she is mocked as a leader of the people precisely because she cannot communicate her call for Mexican peoplehood through the master's enlightened tongue, English. Through this episode, we learn that Chonita is not really a leader after all. She may symbolically stand in for radicalism deferred, as Ramón Saldívar notes, but for the people she is speaking to, she symbolizes the radical and "poor" buffoon. Moreover, after her scene of "radicalism," she dies of impoverished conditions. In effect, the incomprehensible language of radicalism cannot sustain her life or class position as a proletariat, nor in the end can the Mexican people understand its meaning. They are not a people, they are a disunified group. What is Paredes suggesting through Chonita's death, then? Is radicalism truly dead? Is what Tenayuca signifies, her idea of the Mexican Question, her desire for a brown radical traditin, incapable of truly emancipating and resisting the normative logic brought about in the material realities of the Texas Modern?

One would think so, if we take into account the discussion of radicalism among the members of the middle-class Mexican American community after Chonita's death. The middle-class Mexicans of the story who lived during the era of the Plan de San Diego have given up on the possibility of the return of a brown radical tradition. Now embracing the ideals of LULAC, they conclude that "people tend to use the word [radical] too loosely," which means that anyone can take a political label and call himself a leader of his people (8). By the end of the story, the realities of radicalism take on an entirely different definition for the Mexicans in it. The only language Mexicans can understand by the end of the story is that radicalism in South Texas is, in fact, a loose signifier that holds no real meaning for their peoplehood. No longer finding peoplehood in the leaders of Pizana or the young hopes of Chonita, they now find its meaning in the bourgeois identity of a doctor, who, they insist, is a "radical" because, ironically, "he pulls up things by the roots" (9). Radicalism gives way to bourgeois identity, and the power lies within the voting booth or in the ability to buy food and antibiotics to fight the fever that killed

Chonita. Radicalism as had been defined by the 1915 Sedicioso Movement is dead in the emerging 1930s middle-class Mexican American generation that Mario García locates in his study.

And yet, with this liberal redefinition of radicalism in the story, we also have the following powerful scene:

> In the later years I thought of her a lot, especially during the thirties when I was growing up. Those years would have been just made for her. Many's the time I have seen her in my mind's eye, in the picket lines demanding not bread, not cake, but the hammon and the beans. But it did not work out that way. (7)

Though Chonita dies in the story, her radical spirit lives within the memory of one individual, a young boy whose nostalgic consciousness desires Chonita to lead the Mexican people out of economic and racial oppression in South Texas. Much like the corrido, "Los Sediciosos," that laments the unknowable future of radicalism, the boy laments the unfulfilled radical life of Chonita. In the end of "The Hammon and the Beans," radicalism remains as a spectral discourse of Mexican peoplehood and only survives in the unconscious representations of an individual, not the collective. Within the material world of the Texas Modern, however, radicalism takes on a new definition that enables the emergence of the "Mexican American," as historians Mario García and Richard García argue in their respective studies. The Mexican American generation emerges, however, by repressing its radical past. As such, brown radicalism haunts only the individual boy, in his dreams, and he can only come to terms with Chonita and her death and all that she signifies through tears. Mourning for what could have been, a brown radical tradition that truly emancipates the people and their land could never survive in the material world of the Texas Modern. The boy's mourning is what keeps him sane in this Texas Modern world, and what is left in his mind is only the discursive fetish that symbolizes brown radicalism, the phrase "the hammon and the beans." With words haunting him, crying calms his soul, so that in the end he feels better, but not whole. Young girls like Chonita will still die in impoverished conditions, and the fort will perpetuate its class and racial hierarchies. In the end, Mexican peoplehood in Jonesville-on-the-Grande is fleeting and partial, only realized in the dreams of the unconscious individual, not the collective.

The unconscious dreams of a radical past are not isolated to "The Hammon and the Beans." In fact, the legacy of radicalism usually manifests itself in Paredes' works through representations of dreams. His first and most celebrated novel, *George Washington Gómez*, illustrates this well in the following dream, which the protagonist Gómez has in the concluding pages:

> He is lying on his stomach at the summit of a hill, watching through a spyglass. The Battle of San Jacinto has just ended with the route of Santa Anna's forces and the capture of the dictator in his underwear. The wild horde of land pirates that form Sam Houston's command have satisfied their blood lust on the Mexican wounded and are now gathered in triumph. The time has come. He gives the command.
>
> There is a barrage of mortar fire from behind the hill, and out of the woods come wave after wave of rancheros, superbly mounted and carrying sabers and revolvers. They are followed by ranks of Mexican soldiers dressed in simple brown uniforms but carrying revolving rifles and hand grenades. He already knows what is to follow. Carnage. Houston is easily captured. Santa Anna is joyous at what he thinks is his deliverance. But his joy does not last long. He is immediately hanged. The Yucatecan traitor, Lorenzo de Zavala, will meet the same fate soon after. Texas and the southwest will remain forever Mexican.
>
> He woke with a start, stared at the unfamiliar ceiling of the bedroom and cursed softly to himself. Again the same mother-loving dream. (281–282)

Written between 1936 and 1939, this episode in the novel is from the last part of the story, entitled "The Leader of His People." Paredes' work is a naturalist novel, in the tradition of Theodore Dreiser's *Sister Carrie* and David Levinsky's *Silas Lapham*, framed as a bildungsroman. The book maps the rise and assimilationist fall of the main character, who is torn between two identities, signified in the names that his family gives him, Gualinto Gómez and George Washington Gómez. "Born a foreigner in his own land" in the same fictional setting as Chonita, Jonesville-on-the-Grande, the young male protagonist struggles with his identity as both George Washington and Gualinto. Paredes's protagonist is "fated to a life controlled by others" after the Texas Rangers (derogatorily, the *rinches*) murder his father in the wake of the Sedicioso Movement (15). Despite the geopolitical struggles that emerge in South Texas during and after the Sedicosiso Movement, his family hopes that he will rise from his surroundings and his father's violent death and become a "leader of his people." His individual ascendance as a person who would free the Mexican people from the impoverished conditions of 1930s Texas never becomes a reality, however. In the end, we are left with an assimilated Mexican American individual who has become a U.S. Army spy and is sent to the South Texas border to watch over radical Mexicans like Tenayuca and Chonita. It is only in his conflicted dreams, as seen above, that George Washington Gómez can imagine himself as a radical leader of the Mexican people, fighting against the liberal and democratic likes of Lorenzo de Zavala and the expansionist policies maintained by Anglo-America. It is telling here that in the concluding pages of the novel, Gómez does not embrace the liberal and democratic ideals of Zavala, whom we considered in chapter 2. Rather, much like the corrido hero, he hopes that he can create a new Texas built on the radical aspirations of Emilio Zapata (Saldívar, *Chicano Narrative* 274). The dream, it would seem, posits for us that only through radicalism can the Mexican people find freedom from Anglo colonialism. However, when George wakes and enters the reality of South Texas, he curses "the same mother-loving dream." He asks himself why he "keep[s] fighting the battles that were won and lost a long time ago?" (273). The world that Gómez must negotiate is one without a people, a world where colonialism shapes the meaning of its political efficacy and its constitution. Much like Chonita in "The Hammon and the Beans," George Washington Gómez represents not only the contradictory category of "the Mexican leader of the people" but also the causes that led to the inability of Mexican individuals to organically rise as leaders within a South Texas world where racism and geopolitical struggles inform the norms of the political.

Learning to Vote

Paredes' cultural works anticipate what historians and social scientists argue about the emergence of modern Mexican democratic peoplehood in the New Deal Era. For Paredes and the historians that followed, this historical period marked the moment when Mexican democratic collectivism and the embrace of liberal norms and ideals in the 1930s emerged from the geopolitical struggles and racial antagonism in the years surrounding the Sedicioso Movement (Johnson 45). "The Hammon and the Beans" demonstrates Paredes' awareness of this transition. What Paredes shows us, however, is that the emergence of democratic collectivism is hardly an answer to Mexican peoplehood and the questions surrounding their rights and status as citizens in the United States. Indeed, Paredes' works demonstrate that democracy, like radicalism, is a normative form of collectivity that never truly leads to political efficacy for Mexicans in South Texas.

The title, *George Washington Gómez: A Mexico-Texan Novel*, is a direct comment on the challenges that democracy creates for Mexicans in the United States. In this way, the book is as much a comment about the failed legacy of radicalism as it is about the discourse that replaces it in 1930s Mexican social thought, democracy. This movement in seen through Paredes' ironic recovery of the symbolic name the protagonist takes in the first pages, George Washington Gómez—a gesture to the first democratic American leader to represent the American people, George Washington. Paredes, however, is not so much interested in ascribing George Washington's foundational qualities of democratic leadership to the Mexican character, George Washington Gómez. Rather by evoking George Washington, the so-called father of the American people, he is trying to explore the paradoxical questions surrounding Mexican democratic representation and peoplehood. Through the main protagonist, Gualinto "George" Washington Gómez, the novel posits for us a fundamental question about Mexican leadership and peoplehood in democratic republics like the United States: Can Gómez represent democratic leadership for the Mexican people by taking on a persona and normative ideal that, up to 1930s, has not guaranteed universal rights and democratic autonomy? In other words, Paredes asks in his book whether democracy is the right path for Mexican America. In some ways, Paredes' works indicate that his answer is no. Indeed, by the end of the novel, Gómez does, in fact, keep the name George Washington, but he is hardly a representative leader of the Mexican people and collectivity. As I mentioned before, he becomes the antithesis of Mexican leadership. He becomes a U.S. soldier-spy, marries the white daughter of a Texas Ranger, and feels that "his" people of South Texas need to get rid of their "Mexican ways." The end of the novel reveals for the reader that he cannot facilitate the emergence of a Mexican nation or lead his people over the Rio Grande to symbolic freedom.

The symbolic naming of George Washington Gómez is not the only critical examination of Mexicans' relationship to democracy in South Texas. The novel also delves into democratic politics and especially Mexican American voting. Showing that voting is the core fundamental contradiction of Mexican democratic peoplehood, Paredes challenges the representational logic of democracy by revealing the racial and power dynamics that taint the act of voting. He does this in the first sections of the book entitled "Jonesville-on-the-Grande," through the character Feliciano, George Washington Gómez's uncle and a former member of the Sedicioso Movement. Feliciano enters George's life in a turbulent manner. After a skirmish with the Texas Rangers, in the last moments of his life, George's father, Gumersindo, asks Feliciano to watch over George and make sure that he becomes a good citizen and leader of white America. Accepting this burden and knowing the secrets of a violent and radical Mexican past, Feliciano takes it upon himself to raise George Washington Gómez. Feliciano believes that this entails leaving his radical past behind him and becoming a successful, middle-class member of the community. His rise as a middle-class member of the community in Jonesville-on-the-Grande crosses paths with the political bosses of South Texas.

One of the most powerful political bosses of the community is Judge Norris, a half-Spanish, half-white Mexican who recruits Feliciano as a member of his political party, "the Blues" and asks him to work as a political mediator for the Mexican people of Jonesville-on-the-Grande. A disenchanted radical, Feliciano at first tells the judge that he knows nothing of democracy. Judge Norris assures Feliciano that there is nothing to it and that he "will learn to vote." Judge Norris is right. Feliciano learns the trade of democracy well. To address Mexican voting regulations in Texas, Feliciano organizes poll tax fiestas and even simplifies the voting process through an idea that Feliciano calls "Arriba los Azules" (47). Addressing the illiteracy of the Mexican people, Feliciano ties little knots in the poll cord to match the ballot. Manipulating the representational act of voting, Feliciano's ingenious idea enables Mexicans to quickly associate which party to vote for when they enter the voting booth, thereby allowing them to associate a given knot with a given candidate. At the voting booths, Feliciano handed Mexicans their poll tax receipts and at the same time told them which knot "represented" Judge Norris. This was incredibly effective, and Judge Norris and the Blues won in a landslide. Through this chapter, Paredes shows us that democracy is not an untainted system of governance. Even the solitary act of voting as a people is subject to manipulation. The knots merely become the representation of a candidate. Mexicans never truly make the informed and "reasoned" decision of who should represent them in government; rather, a mere color marks the vote. A given candidate's political platform never enters this democratic process in South Texas, only the color that represents him. Feliciano reveals for us that democracy is a system used to control the people and power is merely reproduced by those who can control its representational logic.

It is important to point out that *George Washington Gómez's* examination of democracy, voting, and poll taxes is commenting on the real paradoxes of democracy in South Texas and Mexicans' relationship to democratic representation. In the 1930s, Texas Mexicans did have the same full rights as white American citizens; only by paying a poll tax, which ranged between 75 cents and $1.75, could Mexicans buy the right to cast their vote and partake in the "one man, one vote" myth of democracy. In effect, Mexicans had to pay for the guarantees of democratic representation. Democracy was, in the end, merely a commodity for those in power to own and distribute to the people. Mexicans were merely pawns of the democratic system, never truly able to be a part of the form of political organization that was, in theory, supposed to facilitate their collectivity after the death of radicalism marked by the ending of the Sedicioso Movement. The stanzas in Paredes' poem, "The Mexico-Texan," which is the same name as the subtitle of his book, *George Washington Gómez: A Mexico-Texan Novel*, captures this well:

> Elections come round and gringos are loud,
> They pat on he's back and they make him so proud,
> They give him mescal and the barbeque meat,
> They tell him, "Amigo, we can't be defeat."
> But after election he no gotta fran'
> The Mexico-Texan he no gotta lan'.

Published in the LULAC newspapers in 1937, Paredes' poem cynically casts democracy and the act of voting as a failed system, one that manipulates Mexicans with devices such as poll taxes.

Reading Paredes' mimicry of the stereotypical depiction of Texas Mexicans, I am reminded of a picture published two years before his poem in the *San Antonio Light* (Figure 11). The photograph captures a Mexican man dressed as a vaquero, sitting backward on a burro and holding a sign that reads in English, "Judge a Man by His Poll Tax Receipt." Much like the poem, the man represents the paradoxes of democracy and the vexed location that Mexicans hold in this system of governance in the 1930s. In the end, Mexicans never truly are part of democracy because they never truly have a stake in representing themselves as a people; they are merely objects, frozen in a system much like the picture of the Mexican on the burro. Mexicans have no "Ian'" and as such they are racial objects in a network of democratic power. As such, they never hold the position of the full and equal citizen.

That LULAC published the poem in their newspaper is interesting. LULAC found the poll tax unjust for a number of reasons; the most curious was that it was a device to racialize them through the term "Mexican." Paredes uses the term "Mexican" throughout his works in the 1930s. Members of LULAC, however, felt that the term created a racial stigma for Mexicans in the United States. Ironically, they were especially troubled, not just with the poll tax per se but with the fact that the U.S. government wrote the word "Mexican" on the poll tax receipts and therefore defined them as "colored." In 1937 LULAC member A. M. Trevino critiqued this practice and wrote: "If the word 'Mexican' has reference to the nationality or citizenship of the taxpayer, it stands to reason that a person not a citizen of this country cannot participate in the politics of this country. But if the word 'Mexican' has reference to race, then discrimination exists and the laws of the state are being violated" (quoted in Kanellos, *Herencia* 43).

LULAC insisted on maintaining that the Mexican people were white, not colored. Though they felt that racism was an "insidious poison," they fought for their democratic rights by accepting the norms and ideals of democracy as a universal system. As such, they felt that fighting for whiteness as well as assimilation into American society was paramount to the emergence of Mexicans as a democratic people. LULAC ideologically held a blind devotion for democracy and felt that its universal ideals would facilitate the acceptance of "Mexican Americans" as a people in the United States. As Paredes' works demonstrate, however, his fiction challenged the assimilationist policies of LULAC and their blind embrace of American democracy. In fact, Paredes noted in an interview that the assimilation theme and the ending of *George Washington Gómez* was a direct indictment of LULAC policies:

Figure 11. Man on burro (*San Antonio Light* Collection, 1935)

It was what I saw at the time. This was before there was any Chicano movement. The LULACS were trying to teach their children not to speak Spanish. They had a law passed saying that Mexicanos were white, which didn't help us with the issue of segregation in the schools. They could have schools that were half black and half Mexicano, the whites still segregated. The trend was toward assimilation.[9]

LULAC's rhetoric of peoplehood also becomes an illusionary symbol of failed leadership because of their desire for Mexican normalization into white America. Paredes' works reveal a suspicion of Mario García's "Mexican American generation" and their blind devotion to democracy, as many of them saw democracy as the substitution for Mexican ethnic peoplehood. For many LULAC members, the universal norms and ideals of democracy (citizenship, rights, freedom) became the foundational discourse of Mexican collectivity.

Ramón Saldívar astutely points out that Paredes' fiction represents a symbolic resolution to the material realities of South Texas (*Chicano Narrative* 275). I would add that the symbolic resolutions created in his fiction are characteristic of Paredes' cultural work in that it represents the contradiction of representing the partial and fleeting ideal of the people of Mexican America in the 1930s. As I suggest, the 1930s marked an era of heightened Mexican racialization. As such, the ideals of democratic populism or radical politics could not emancipate the racial inequalities that Mexican America dealt with, precisely because the rhetoric of both Marxism and New Deal populism had not created an emancipatory answer for Mexicans as a collective. It is not that Paredes is antidemocratic or even antiradical. Rather, his works reveal that he found that both discourses normalized Mexican identity into a larger homogeneous universal collective, one that did not facilitate a collectivity based on what Renato Rosaldo refers to as "cultural citizenship" (32).

Let us not forget that the 1930s notion of the people was a static ideal based on either a radical collectivism or a democratic populism and left no room for what Paredes spent his lifetime studying, the Mexican "folk" cultures in the southwest. As I sketched out in the introductory section, it is important to reiterate that the people became the central trope of the cultural front of the 1930s. Hundreds of texts represented the people in hopes of defining a collective among a Depression Era that many believed had dismantled the body politic. By representing the people and creating stories of peoplehood that reflected the ideals of the New Deal, cultural workers could then symbolically help in the reconstitution of the nation. However, Michael Denning makes a very important argument that representing the people was a formal and aesthetic problem of the era (*Cultural Front* 67). That is, representing the people, creating stories of peoplehood in the New Deal Era, was contradictory precisely because the notion of the people in the 1930s was a populist fiction of homogeneity. In fact, the populist rhetoric of the New Deal tried to normalize the real ethnic and racial divisions of the era into a static universal. As such, leaders of the era, those responsible for defining peoplehood, did not address the political and economic realities that racial minorities like Mexicans dealt with in the 1930s.

Paredes makes this point in the chapter "La Chilla" in the novel *George Washington Gómez*. "La Chilla" (the squeal) is what Mexicans called the New Deal Era because, as Paredes notes, it was a "euphemism for the most useful of Mexican expressions: *la chingada*" (the fucked) of the 30's: "La Chilla. La Chilla. Rows of vacant store buildings, their empty windows looking like eyeglasses on rows of skulls. And on the sidewalks, in the little lobbies formed by store entrances, groups of dark-skinned men, waiting waiting. For nothing" (197).

For the collective Mexican *chingada* there is no populist rhetoric that can account for their stark absence from the vision of the New Deal. Mexicans spoke Spanish and were brown skinned, and, therefore, it was the white American common man who reaped the benefits of the New Deal, not the Mexican, *la chingada*. Indeed, let us not forget that the New Deal Era would mark the moment when the U.S. government legislated "Mexican repatriation." Authorized by President Hoover, during the 1930s, with this legislative act the United States "repatriated" between 500,000 and two million Mexicans, some of whom had been in the United States for generations. Democracy was hardly embracing Mexicans in the New Deal Era. In this way, by representing Mexican collectivity as fleeting and partial in his cultural work, Paredes is able to call attention to the failed promises of New Deal liberalism, ideals that both the radicals and the LULAC liberals embraced. To this end, it was not that Paredes was against Tenayuca or the other important Mexican leaders of the period; rather, he was against the rhetoric of peoplehood that stood in as substitution for cultural identity and that did not fully account for the racial segregation that Mexicans suffered during this era.

In the end, Paredes was not necessarily interested in forming answers but in asking questions, Mexican Questions that the reader of his works could contemplate and debate.[10] Paredes was aware that peoplehood itself and the stories that reified collectivity were in fact stories, narratives that power holders used to control people to the point that Mexican culture would be stripped of its cultural ideals. This is perhaps why in the years following his writings in the 1930s Paredes would recover the organic narrative form that he felt captured the "base" of Mexican collectivity, Mexican folklore in the United States (Paredes, "Folkbase of Chicano Literature" 7–9). In Mexican folklore, he found the perfect narrative form of organic collectivity, stories that represented the Mexican peoples' collective struggle with humanity, a peoplehood created through the very productive conflict of cultures themselves (13).[11] Before recovering Mexican folklore as an academic at the University of Texas, however, his fictional works of the 1930s struggled to come to terms with the contradictory outcomes that resulted from the dual process of self-making and being-made within the webs of a racial democracy that defined the

Mexican people according to white middle-class populist notions of "the American way of life" (Sussman 234).[12]

Paredes' stories of peoplehood in the 1930s highlight the cultural practices and beliefs of Mexicans produced out of negotiating often ambivalent and contested relations with the democratic state and its hegemonic forms of peoplehood that established the normative criteria of collectivity and belonging within the United States. For Paredes, this negotiated state of ambivalence affected Mexican peoplehood tremendously. In a rather lamentful conclusion of his work on the corrido, Paredes surmised in the 1980s that the legacy of colonialism haunted the collectivity of Mexicans to the point that they were a culture "still searching" for themselves in the United States, a people who Paredes poetically referred to in his poem "Mi Pueblo" as "a certain uncertainty twixt heaven and ruin." Perhaps in the years that followed, Paredes began to see the search ending. For when Paredes passed away in 1999, Mexicans were emerging as the largest minority in the United States and are still growing. Paredes' Greater Mexico was now reaching every part of the United States. Mexicans are perhaps now in a position that Paredes could only hope for in the concluding lines of his poem "Mi Pueblo": [Mexicans are] "out of the abyss and above the summit created by destiny."

Conclusion
Recovering La memoria: *Locating the Recent Past*

I would like to see the people together, and then, if I had great big arms, I would embrace them all. I wish I could talk to all of them again, but all of them together. But, that, only in a dream. . . . Only by being alone can you bring everybody together.

Tomás Rivera. . . . *y no se lo trágo la tierra* (. . . and the earth did not devour him)

I have memories of my own Mexican peoplehood, stories that are deeply rooted in my family's past. Growing up I remember countless stories about my grandparents and parents who, since the nineteenth century, have all at one time in their lives spent many days laboring on white-owned lands in Texas. My family has a long history with lands that are now geographically defined as being within the United States. Either picking cotton or working on rice farms, my family spent their lives trying to escape the memories of the fields or lands they had lost in the war, only to realize that the stories about these fields and lands are ironically what constitutes our family. These stories affected me tremendously. I came to understand who I was each summer I spent with my grandparents, and learning their story I came to understand my place in Mexican America. These recovered memories have now become my story of Mexican peoplehood. Going to the American Legion to listen to *conjunto* and play bingo in El Campo, Texas, with my grandparents, I found that our story of *familia* was, in many ways, one part of a much larger tapestry of stories that constituted our *gente*. The details about individual Mexican families' lives were a bit different, but, in the end, I came to learn that Mexicans' location as a people in the United States has been universally bittersweet. For Mexicans, their peoplehood symbolizes bodily and psychic pain, frustration, exclusion, and racialization. Yet, at the same time, their peoplehood represents belonging, freedom, rights, *familia, el pueblo,* and *la raza.*

Tomás Rivera captures this contradiction so eloquently in his beautifully crafted novel, *. . . y no se lo trágo la tierra* (and the earth did not devour him), when he shows us that the struggle within Mexican America is its dynamic formation as a material Mexican community in the traumatic wake of imperialism (32). The novel traces the psychosocial development of a young nameless character who is trying to recover his past. Through the recovery of his lost memories in the novel, he finds not only himself but most importantly his own peoplehood. The novel, then, is inevitably not about the formation of the "I" but, rather, the recovery of the "we" in Mexican America. Memory of "the lost years" becomes the medium in which we all recover our social imaginary as Mexican. The recovery of an individual's past is what produces our peoplehood.

The recovery of Mexican memories, stories, and its effects on peoplehood is what this book has explored. It is perhaps fitting that I conclude this book about the past with a contemporary Mexican story about recovering Mexican America. It is today in Colorado where I found Judy Baca's *La memoria de la Nuestra Tierra: Colorado* (The Memory of Our Land: Colorado) (Figure 12), a story of peoplehood that illustrates how the mnemonic recovery of Mexican America continues to affect our past and future understanding of the political location of Mexicans in the United States. Dedicated in 2000, *La memoria* is the last public art mural the city of Denver installed in Denver International Airport (DIA). Funded by the grass-roots community organization, the Chicano Arts and Humanities Council, and Denver's Public Arts Council, the digitally produced ten- by fifty-five-foot *La memoria* is in the central public space of DIA's main terminal.

What I found so appealing about *La memoria* is that it visually merges the public spaces of DIA, Colorado, and the nation by merging Mexican lands and Mexican racial bodies with the expansionist history of the United States. *La memoria* is instructive because, like the texts I explore in this book, it represents the ways in which Mexicans continue to engage the public spheres and nineteenth-century geopolitical issues in order to challenge contemporary U.S. democratic culture that continues to question their political and cultural position on U.S. lands. Engaging the pub-

Figure 12. Judy Baca's "La memoria de la Nuestra Tierra," public art installation at Denver International Airport, 2000

lic in order to revitalize twenty-first-century democracy, *La memoria* uses digital technology to confront a U.S. public that has excluded and forgotten the geopolitical design of American democracy through what Judy Baca refers to as "public memory." Baca's conception of "public memory" further substantiates Raúl Villa's argument that "narratives of place" reveal that "the persistence and power of memory is crucial, being simultaneously effective—as practically informing *history* in the politics of communal defense" (235). In this way, *La memoria's* evocation of public memory is a geopolitical civic act that brings forth a counterpolitical message and suggests that Mexican lands and people are not antithetical to the democratic ideals of America. For in *La memoria* they bleed into one another: blood and soil create a new *res publica* within what were once Mexican lands. As a critical site within the public sphere, *La memoria* serves as a model for understanding the possibility of a truly inclusive democracy, one that becomes an actively reflexive political system that engages its imperialist past through the geospatial creation of heterogeneous cultural sites and active citizen participation in public spheres that develop from the material history of the land.

In doing so, the mural radically expands democracy's inclusive and universal ideals through the geopolitical recovery of land and of the Mexican political and cultural workers who once resided on the land in the nineteenth and early twentieth centuries. As I discuss in this book, because of their loss of property rights in the years that followed the Treaty of Guadalupe Hidalgo, their civil right to enter the public sphere was affected, and therefore their voices have historically been relegated to the dustbins of democratic and literary history. They have only now been recovered in this age of the browning of America. In the end, *La memoria* helps us remember both the Mexican cultural workers of this book and the manifest lessons of democracy, thereby relocating a place in the American landscape where Mexicans belong as a people.[1]

Representing Mexicans and Chicanos who have shaped the American landscape, *La memoria de la Nuestra Tierra* interweaves the Colorado landscape with digital images of Aztecs, Mexicans of the Mexican Revolution, Chicana workers, farmers, miners, immigrants, Native cultures, and the Chicano public figures Cesar Chávez, Rudolfo "Corky" Gonzáles, and Reies López Tijerina, who were involved in the land recovery movement of Aztlán during the Chicano civil rights movement. Merging the landscape with historical memory and public figures who have fought for Mexican American civil rights since the nineteenth century, Baca's work blurs the distinction between the land and Mexicans, between the public and the private, between civil rights and land rights in order to make a new place for Mexicans. The images of the Mexicans haunt the brown and gold landscape of mountains, canyons, and plains; their images are specters on the memory of the land. The digitally enhanced ghostly silhouettes of these Mexican figures shimmer when the light from the sun penetrates DIA's mountainous architecture; their translucent bodies symbolically represent their absence from America's democratic history and public culture.

La memoria's visual act of publicity is particularly important, considering that recently within the national public sphere, Mexicans have, once again, become the object of discussions concerning their place in the U.S. political landscape. Take, for example, media giants CNN, ABC News, *Time*, Time.com, and America Online's collaboration of a month-long investigation into the future of American democracy: the making of "Amexica." "The border is vanishing before our eyes, creating a new world for all of us," *Time* would declare on the cover of its special issue on the browning of America (June 11, 2001) (Figure 13). Under the headline, a *Time* photojournalist captures two Mexican children. Staring at the public through sunglasses, the children become haunting images, silently representing the new demographics of an American nation whose economy is fueled by the contradictory empire-building and neoliberal ideals of NAFTA.

As Anglo-America gazes on their brown bodies at newsstands, in supermarket lines, and in their homes, they question how to include these people into the body politic and how this will affect their world. Changing the nationalist signifier "America" to "Amexica" (without the proper accent), *Time* captures the middle-class and mostly white public, freezing their attention in a moment of linguistic terror. The word "America" that has historically symbolized democratic freedom, liberalism, terra cognita (known and mapped landscape), and free-market capitalism morphs into a new symbol, one where the linguistic inclusion of the word "Mexican" changes America's connotations. Terra incognita once again rises within the linguistic meaning of Amexica, and yet another Mexican Question emerges.

After the 2001 visit of Mexico's new president, Vicente Fox, President George Bush, the Spanish-speaking and self-defined "friend of the Mexican people," discussed legislation that would continue to affect this complexion of the United States. After President Fox's appeal for dual citi-

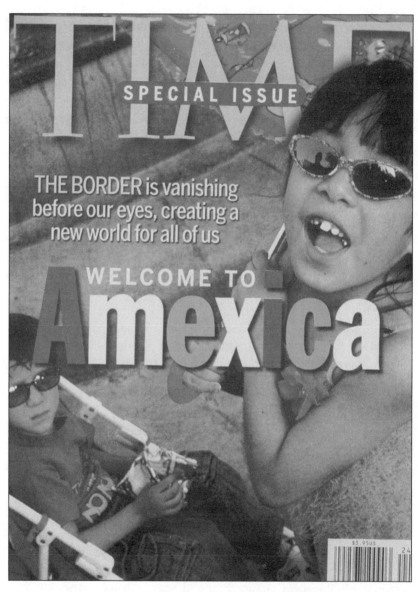

Figure 13. Cover, *Time* magazine, "Welcome to Amexica!" June 11, 2001

zenship for Mexicans residing in America to a joint session of Congress in September of 2001, Bush stated that he wanted to accommodate his friends in Mexico and that if "[Mexicans] are willing to do jobs others in America aren't willing to do, we ought to welcome that person to the country and we ought to make that a legal part of our economy" (*Washington Post*, September 7, 2001).

Covered in every news channel, newspaper, and talk show, Bush argued that Mexicans would do the work that Anglo-Americans would not. They will groom Anglo lawns, raise their children, clean their homes, and pick their produce. Therefore, Bush insists that Americans should include Mexicans in America as laboring citizens; after all, they are already participating in the economy by working the land. According to Bush's "compassionate conservatism," then, the geopolitics of Mexican American inclusion and their increased numbers in the United States is a fiscal matter that is good for the U.S. economy. As such, the border between the two nations becomes a porous membrane that allows Mexican laborers to cross so that they can work U.S. lands. Despite the onset of a new recession, he argued that their presence would only help, not hinder, our progress as a nation.

But in suggesting this legislation and recognizing the fiscal impact of Mexicans in the United States, Bush is also changing the classical concept of the abstracted, disembodied citizen and one of the most important norms of democracy by which the citizen gains universal rights: the American public sphere. In this way, Bush maintains the common solidarity of America by selling two different types of political subjects within the nation's borders. On the one hand, Mexicans are "included" in the public not through traditional republican ideals of property ownership or Enlightened reason; rather, the inclusion occurs through their collective racialized body—a body that labors its way into citizenship status by working the land. Anglo-America, then, can have more leisure time. Mexicans have become a laboring prosthesis for the geo-body politic. Bush also reveals that America is not a democracy of universal equality and egalitarianism; rather, the United States is a capitalist democracy that is built on the backs of racial others whose political subjectivity resembles a laborer tied to the United States' capitalist mode of production, not a free citizen of the state. As such, the prosthetic, laboring Mexican enables Anglos to normalize themselves as a class and citizen designation that is drastically different from that of Mexicans in the body politic. Mexicans are the working arms of the body politic working the land, while Anglos remain figured as the reasoned mind of U.S. democracy (Flores 132). Anglos can enjoy the land, not work it. Moreover, under Bush's proposal, even if Mexicans become the predominant population in the United States, as the census map indicates, they would merely serve as second-class citizens who work the land by picking produce or grooming lawns. In effect, Bush creates third-world rights for Mexican workers, not inclusion as citizens, within the United States' first-world geographic border.

Bush's answer to the Mexican Question, the browning of America's landscape, the making of "Amexica," is to make a more leisurely Anglo-America on the laboring backs of Mexican Americans, whose citizenship remains dubious. When *Time Magazine*, George W. Jr., or the published figures of the census suggest that we are soon to have "Amexica," this poses a challenge to peoplehood in the United States and thus to the common geopolitical solidarity of white America. While the presuppositions of the public sphere warrant Mexican American democratic inclusion, this is counter to a nation's desire to create a country whose people know one another, trust one another, look alike, and feel a sense of solidarity among one another.

And yet, the media have been defining Mexicans as the sleeping giant for over fifty years, objectifying a people according to a rhetorical logic of absent presence. Despite the fact that Mexicans are within the borders of the United States and immigrate everyday to help maintain the U.S. global economy, the U.S. public spheres have rhetorically created an ephemeral existence for Mexicans in the past 150 years. The short-lived memory concerning Mexicans in the public spheres creates a cyclical inquiry into the rights and status of Mexicans in the United States. As I have been suggesting, the inquiries that have recently developed from the demographic "browning of America" are not new: they are nothing more than yet another question about the absent presence of Mexicans in the U.S. landscape that began in the nineteenth century. And again these questions arise within the terra incognita of our globalized, deterritorial public spheres.

Today, Mexican's relationship to the national public sphere acquires new meaning through the neoliberal rhetoric of NAFTA and conservative anti-immigration legislation. Media publics in the age of NAFTA do not want to remember that Mexico has geographically and economically participated in the rise of the United States as an imperial and economic power. NAFTA-generated publics are perhaps not so (post)nationalist after all. The borders of the nation are still patrolled under Operation Gatekeeper, as are the discursive borders of the public sphere. Parochial discourses of America's economic exceptionalism inflect the national public's lack of memory. The result of this is that Mexicans remain objects of inquiry within the public sphere, never able to fully represent themselves as a people in the nation. Mexicans merely embody a question in the public sphere.

One must ask, therefore, if the national public sphere's understanding of its landscape reveals what Friedrich Nietzsche refers to as "active forgetting" (7). In this way, forgetfulness is reflexive and occurs so that people can cover up the scars of the past, for remembering would only open up its wounds of imperialism. Indeed, I am suggesting that the public sphere does not solely forget how the landscape of the U.S. body politic has been mapped simply because transnational economic imperatives affect the public's ability to rationalize, remember, and critically create discourses of influence. Rather, the national public sphere works according to a logic of active forgetting. The American public actively forgets the imperialist and racial discourses that develop within the public sphere in order to maintain its semblance of universal inclusion and democratic egalitarianism. The land, in theory, must remain free and democratic for all people, for it is the basis of democracy. In this way, a democratic public continues to question but never truly resolves its imperial past precisely because it does not remember the history of the land and its relationship to the public's constitution itself. Active forgetting ensures that the territorial presuppositions of the Mexican Question will remain alive in American democracy. In the case of the recent browning of America, active forgetting allows European Americans to answer the Mexican Question by maintaining the political landscape of white European people. Mexican people will be included in the U.S. landscape, but only as workers. Americans actively forget that the Treaty of Guadalupe Hidalgo ended an imperialist war and would both cede millions of acres to the United States and create an artificial border between the United States and Mexico. This is the history of the United States, and this is the impetus behind Mexican immigration.

But for Mexican people in the United States, the land has an alternative public memory. And this is exactly why *La memoria's* mnemonic revision of the landscape is so important during this moment. As a site that visually represents the temporal past of Mexican peoplehood, *La memoria* collides the private history of racial others within a late-capitalist space that defines time according to transnational or global flight schedules. With each shimmering landscape panel of the mural, the Denver public is reminded of its spatiality and temporality and its inability to remember the past. At one of the busiest airports in the world, the mural has an infinite number of public subjects to impress. In this way, *La memoria* is a landmark in Chicano public art in that its geopolitical strategies of publicity make Mexicans in the United States *the* public site of civic debate for an infinite number of publics—whether local, national, or global. The mural's initial spatial act of publicity browns DIA's white architecture, but as a public site creating public memory for local, national, and global spaces, the mural browns Colorado, the United States, and the world through historical images that literally reflect from the digitally inscribed photos and landscape. The mural, then, inevitably expands democratic peoplehood with each passenger's gaze, creating public memory about Mexicans where there was once none.

It should not go without saying that Chicano murals have been critical in representing Mexican peoplehood for generations. Indeed, what is so important about Chicano public art, Eva Sperling Cockroft and Holly Barnet-Sánchez argue, is that it "provides society with the symbolic representation of collective beliefs as well as re-affirmation of the collective sense of [a Chicano] self" (5).[2] Chicano murals such as the East Los Streetscapers's *La familia*, the Common Arts' *Song of Unity*, Antonio Bernal's *The Del Rey Mural*, and Barbara Carrasco's *The History of L.A.: A Mexican Perspective*, to name a few, visually ask us to redefine the relationship between the public, culture, and democracy. As such, they challenge the very concept of the public and the philosopher who made the idea of the democratic public so important in our understanding of democracy: Jürgen Habermas. Chicano murals demonstrate, however, that the notion of the public did not surface only within the geopolitical confines where bourgeois white Europeans resided, who through the exclusion of women and racial others would become the political norm of democratic culture through self-abstraction. Although Chicano muralists' strategies of publicity fall within Habermas's political notion of deliberative democracy, the works have drastically expanded the idea of the public and its relationship to democratic peoplehood, translating the public into a geographic space where Mexican people can create recognition by responding to the Mexican Question's imperialist ideologies.

Baca's work is unique among Chicano murals because of her radical democratic strategies of collectivity, for she makes the landscape and space central to her story of the emergence of Mexican peoplehood. Indeed, *La memoria*'s acts of publicity are much more temporally reflexive and nuanced to the geopolitical questions that inform ethnonationalist identities that the universal public sphere that nineteenth-century republicanism so desired. As Baca herself would argue, public art must create civic dialogue, debate, and democratic ideals. For Baca, the public sphere is fundamental to the "health of a democracy" (quoted in "The Globe Is Her Canvas" 3) and the formation of Mexican peoplehood.

If the national public sphere that objectifies Mexicans' works according to a geopolitical logic of active forgetting, *La memoria*'s strategies suggest that public memories of the *ethnos*, land, and democracy are interrelated and created in a similar fashion. The mural conveys that Mexicans are not passive subjects being discussed and shaped by and for white America. Although white America constitutes one of the many publics the mural addresses, Baca reached out to over four thousand members of the Mexican American public, held classes and seminars, talked to their political leaders, and created public spheres where Mexicans in the United States can actively engage in her vision of the mural. In every way, the mural was a public act, created out of the history of Mexicans who are demographically changing the new complexion of America's landscape.

La memoria is much more than an act of "counterpublicity," then. With each brown, digital image of the landscape, Mexicans in the United States become public subjects for civic memory, and their spectral bodies become the mediating discourse of territorial, embodied, and democratic recognition. *La memoria*, the U.S. presence of Mexicans in this NAFTA era, is no longer an amnesiac inquiry of deterritorialization that objectifies or normalizes Mexicans and their land for global capitalist flows. *La memoria*'s Mexicans are no longer outside of the map; the land has memory, and so, too, should all of us.

The mnemonic recovery of the recent Mexican past is a decolonial struggle against the imperialist presuppositions of demography and the national public spheres that are trying to define what the browning of America means for the millions of Mexican people located in the United States, on its borders, or as transnational subjects who migrate between Mexico and the United States. The 2000 census's demographic numbers with which I began this book mark a liminal moment in our social imaginary that has yet to fully reveal its cultural effects on the everyday material realities of Mexicans and Anglos in the United States. The history that will write our era as the emergence of Mexican America is still unfolding. In the end, then, it is in the realm of culture where Mexicans in the United States will be able to recover the paths to their peoplehood and will help us map our recent past and create the future history of Mexican America.

Notes

INTRODUCTION

1. For press information see www.adaywithoutamexican.com.

2. I am well aware that "democracy" has become a relative term and that its meaning is complicated. My interests are in how the norms and ideals of democracy (rights, the people, citizenship, etc.) are realized and understood through the imaginative production of cultural forms in the public spheres. Although the cultural forms I study do not adhere to one definition or ideology of democracy, they suggest that democracy is a political system whose meaning is in flux and is constantly debated. Hence, one could argue that the logic and meaning of democracy reveals itself in a given culture's rhetorical search for that meaning, a journey mediated by the imaginative productions of a given culture. This is what I mean by the term "democratic culture."

3. There have been a number of recent studies on peoplehood. "Peoplehood" is in many ways the current nomenclature for what the Greeks referred to as *demos*. It encompasses both a political and a cultural collectivity of a given democratic nation-state. Departing from studies of the liberal individual subject, political philosophers have taken aim at the cultural logic behind the term "the people," a core concept in the development of democratic nation-states. Political thinkers such as Rogers Smith (2003), David Lie (2004), Michael Hardt and Antonio Negri (2004), Kathleen Wilson (1998), Craig Calhoun (2002), and Charles Taylor (2004) argue, though in different degrees, that "people-making" is a highly complicated endeavor that, as Lie says, reveals much about the formation of liberal democratic collectivization. In other words, they are interested in the logic that made possible the phrase "We the People," which is now so synonymous with democratic societies. Moreover, they have found that "story" or "narrative" is an essential element in creating an individual's social imaginary and thus their sense of belonging within a given group. That is, cultural works are the mediums by which a people come to understand its very make-up as part of this or that collective. My use of the term "stories of Mexican peoplehood" departs from the Chicano critics, Américo Paredes (1993), José Limon (1998), and Richard Delgado (1989), who have been interested in the poetics of Mexican peoplehood in all of their works. Chicano critic Tomás Rivera (1993) has in-

fluenced my thought on the cultural function of political collectivity in Mexican cultures in his essays on community. As I describe in the pages that follow, I use the term "community" to refer to the complicated ways in which Mexican cultural workers imagine their political and cultural peoplehood in democratic culure. Stories of Mexican peoplehood refer to cultural works that are specifically interested in the normative constitution of Mexicans as a political and racial group. As such, my use of the term departs from that used by Smith (2003), Hardt and Negri (2004), Calhoun (2002), Taylor (2004), and Cornelius Castoriadis (1987). However, unlike these political philosophers, I am interested in cultural dynamics that influence the norms of Mexican peoplehood.

4. For the importance of the concept of peoplehood in political culture, see Wilson, *Sense of the People* (1998).

5. For a discusssion of "minority peoplehood," see David Lie, *Modern Peoplehood* (1994), p. 248.

6. See Wilson, *Sense of the People* (1998), pp. 20–21.

7. Cynthia Brewer and Trudy A. Suchan, *Mapping Census 2000* (2001).

8. Here I am taking the title of Otto Santa Ana's book, *Brown Tide Rising* (2002).

9. For an interesting discussion that studies the relationship between democracy, the census, and the formation of the political subject, see Jeremy Black, *Maps and Politics* (2000).

10. The number of people of Mexican origin in 2000 was 20.6 million, but this number does not fully account for the possibly 5 million Mexican immigrants who reside in the United States or live on both sides of the border. Nevertheless, based on these official numbers, Mexican-origin peoples comprised 58 percent of the nation's Latinos. The Mexican population increased by 7.1 million between 1990 and 2000 (the largest growth of all Latino groups). Among the remaining Latinos in 2000, 3.4 million were Puerto Rican, 1.2 million were Cuban, 1.7 million were Central American, 1.4 million were South American, 765,000 were Dominican, 100,000 were Spaniards, and 6.1 million were of other Hispanic origins. See U.S. Census Bureau Publications, available at http://www.census.gov/Press-Release/www/2001/cb01–81.html

11. From Sergio Arau's Tivoli talk in Denver, Colorado, on September 30, 2004.

12. I borrow the term "incorporation" from Raymond Williams. Explaining the importance of the term for minority peoples in the United States, Joel Pfister (*Individuality Incorporated*, 2004, p. 27) argues as follows: "In elaborating Antonio Gramsci's theory of hegemony, Raymond Williams developed the concept of "incorporation" to better chart how complexly dynamic hegemonic orders often try to incorporate, control or transform 'alternative or directly oppositional politics and culture'—ostensibly free play free thinking free speech—frequently by attempting to produce 'forms of counter-culture,' channel its critique,

or commodify (subsidize) its 'rebellions.'" Through the concept of "incorporation," power structures may seem democratically responsive or pluralistic rather than uncompromisingly repressive. This is the hegemonic logic behind such concepts as "Manifest Destiny" and the "Mexican Question," which I discuss at length in chapter 3.

13. My initial ideas of terra incognita began when I read Mary Pat Brady's "Full of Empty" (2002).

14. I borrow "topospatial" from José David Saldívar's *Border Matters* (1997), p. 79; he points out that there is a profound interaction between space, history, geography, psychology, politics, nationhood, and imperialism, and one must define space as not just a "setting" but as a formative presence within culture.

15. I use "geopolitics" to confront and analyze the geographical imagination of the state, its foundational myths, and the political norms and ideals that develop from America's territoriality. As such, I explore the interrelationship between "geo" and "political" in order to analyze the mutually constitutive relationship between the construction of political cultures and geographic discourses. What is of interest to me, then, is how geography and politics became so important in the project of democratic culture. Equally important, though, is how this relationship was normalized in order to elide the racial inquests that mediate its contradictory logic. See the introduction in Gearóid Tauthail and Simon Dalby, eds., *Rethinking Geopolitics* (1998) for a recent example of the relationship between the geographic imagination and the formation of political cultures. See also David Jacobsen's *Place and Belonging* (2002).

16. See Michael Omi and Howard Winnant, *Racial Formation in the United States* (1994), pp. 3–24, for an important examination of race and collectivity.

17. See Jacobsen, *Place and Belonging* (2002) for a discussion of these men's' desire to forge a relationship between land and democracy.

18. As I show in chapter 3, the United States also argued that Mexicans' inability to work the land into a viable capitalist resource fueled the rhetoric of filibusterers and was used to argue that Mexicans were unfit for democracy. Hence, Mexicans relationship to the land become central to how they should be viewed as political subjects.

19. See the epilogue to K. Anthony Appiah and Amy Gutman, *Color Consciousness* (1998), p. 181.

20. I am well aware of the distinctions between republican and liberal notions of democracy. I follow Charles Taylor (2002) and Michael Sandel (1998) in their point that modern democracy does not follow the exclusive logic of one element of democracy, but, rather, at any given point in history, democracy's "elements," be they liberal, capitalist, republican, or federalist—make up the contours of our democratic culture. This is not to say that there are not tensions that develop within our democratic culture between these varying ele-

ments. Indeed, in the chapters that follow, I explore the tensions between some of these elements.

21. See Étienne Balibar, *Politics and the Other Scene* (2002) for a discussion about the *ethnos/demos* split.

22. One can surmise, then, how this exclusionary logic creates an *ethnos* who, though he holds a racially marked body, is rhetorically invisible in political culture, while the white *demos* uses its racial invisibility for power in the public sphere.

23. See Charles Taylor, "The Dynamics of Exclusion" in *Modern Social Imaginaries* (2004).

24. See, for example, Richard Rodriguez, *Brown* (2002).

25. I owe much of my ideas of historical time to one of the many illuminating conversations with Patty Limerick.

26. *La memoria* represents a moment when the natural order of domination is interrupted by the publics formed on the part of those who have no part (Isen 2002, pp. 275–277; Rancière 1998, pp. 38–39). *La memoria* reveals a moment when Mexicans in America engaged and exposed the oppressive technologies of American public culture; they realized themselves as public subjects as well as changed the very contours of democracy (Ranciere 1998, pp. 23–45). *La memoria* emerges out of this public act as self-inclusion.

27. For an excellent discussion of culture and democracy, see the introduction by Russ Castronovo and Dana Nelson, eds., in *Materializing Democracy* (2002).

28. I do not use the term "disagreement" to signify its standard English connotations. As opposed to consensus democratic theories, I argue that disagreements are what define and develop political ideologies in a democracy. See Jacques Rancière (1998) for my use of the term "disagreement."

CHAPTER 1

1. See Sheldon Wolin's *Tocqueville between Two Worlds* (2001), pp. 4–9.

2. The two versions are Lorenzo de Zavala, *Viage de los Estados Unidos del Norte America*, 1834, and Zavala, *Viaje de Los Estados-Unidos del Norte America*, 1846. See the 2005 English translation, *Journey to the United States of America*, edited and introduced by John-Michael Rivera, 2005.

3. Ramón Gutiérrez's *Corn Mothers* (1991) is an excellent exception to this trend.

4. See Carl Gutiérrez-Jones, *Rethinking the Borderlands* (1995).

5. See Juan Gómez-Quiñones, "On Culture," (1977), pp. 29–47.

6. In this way, I follow Kirsten Gruesz Silva's argument that the Monroe Doctrine is essential for understanding early literary production of Latino authors. See Gruesz Silva, *Ambassadors of Culture* (2002).

7. For the role of religion in Mexican democracy, see Roderic L. Camp, *Poli-*

tics in Mexico (2003), and Charles Hale, *Mexican Liberalism in the Age of Mora 1821–1853* (1968).

8. Another important narrative about U. S. democracy is Ramón de la Sagra's travel narrative, *Cinco meses en los Estados-Unidos de la América del Norte desde el 20 de abril al 23 de setiembre de 1835* (1835), published one year after Zavala's *Journey*.

9. There were hundreds of travel narratives and magazine articles about Mexico and its lands in the nineteenth century, published in the years after the U.S.-Mexico war. With the exception of Philip Freneau's poetry and travel essays, most Anglo-American travel narratives to Mexico were published after 1834. See Eric Wertheimer's *Imagined Empires* (1999).

10. For a discussion of American and European travel narratives to Mexico, see Gilbert González and Raúl A. Fernández, *A Century of Chicano History* (2003), pp. 72–83.

11. For a discussion of *theoria's* relationship to political culture, see Wolin, *Tocqueville between Two Worlds*, pp. 113–127.

12. See Gener M. Brack's *Mexico Views Manifest Destiny, 1821–1846* (1975), pp. 20–22.

13. J. Hector St. John de Crèvecoeur, Letters *from an American Farmer and Sketches of Eighteenth-Century America* (1981); Janina W. Hoskins, ed., *Lafayette in America* (1983); Alexis de Tocqueville, *Democracy in America* (1961).

CHAPTER 2

1. The "greaser" has a long history in American culture. There were many movies, novels, and cartoons that used this term. See Arthur Pettit's *Images of the Mexican in Fiction and Film* (1980), pp. 22–61, for an extended analysis of the "greaser."

2. My use of fiction in this chapter counters Richard Ohmann's fictional story (*Selling Culture*, 1998) that begins his Marxist study of middle-class America and magazine culture. As I show in the following pages, I depart from Ohmann's myopic class analysis in my fictional story in order to capture the "imaginative" ways in which white middle-class American social structures develop within and against the frontier and the Mexicans who live on these lands.

3. See Arturo J. Aldama, *Disrupting Savagism* (2001), for an excellent discussion of the savage in colonial discourse. Although his idea is more predicated on postcolonial theories, his book was very helpful in my own "political" suppositions of the idea of savage.

4. Although I evoke Stephen Greenblatt's now famous term, "self-fashioning," I am more indebted to Jürgen Habermas's *The Structural Transformation of the Public Sphere* (1991) in this chapter, as well as the study as a

whole. His exploration into the public sphere and how reading sentimental novels helped constitute subjectivity is what I am thinking about in my study of magazine culture. I depart from Habermas, however, in his final argument about the refeudalization of the public sphere.

5. I was able to locate these articles through searches in the database Making of America at Cornell University and University of Michigan. Although they are not exact, the numbers that I give are modest.

6. Here I am suggesting that the literary public sphere is the space where national discourses are institutionalized. In this way, public sphere institutions, like magazines, not only help form the nation but also help create the individual private citizen's role as a member of that nation. This chapter is a study of the process as it relates to the institutionalization of the Mexican Question in the public sphere and how this pervasive discourse affected nationalist and citizen subjectivity. See Michael Warner's *The Letters of the Republic* (1990) and Craig Calhoun's "Nationalism and the Public Sphere" (1977) for a discussion of the relationship of the public sphere institutions and nationalism.

7. Kenneth Robert Olwig, *Landscape, Nature, and the Body Politic* (2002), and Anders Stephanson, *Manifest Destiny* (1995), discuss republican thought and expansion.

8. This second question was fundamental to democratic culture of the time, In 1849, for example, Senator John C. Calhoun wondered whether the political norms and ideals of democracy could accommodate the expanding nation into the territories of the west, as he inquired if the U.S. "constitution extended to the territories or does it not extend to them." Calhoun's question was not isolated, and it reveals how the territorial growth of the United States would supplant foundational questions about the capacity of democracy itself and its ability to deal with the new lands that they had forcefully acquired. In the end, Calhoun felt that democracy could deal with the new landscapes, for the racial mission of the United States enabled him to rectify that expansion and democracy were not contradictory, they were complementary. Indeed, Calhoun would argue in February 11, 1847, in the *Congressional Globe* that "we must march from ocean to ocean. . . . We must march from Texas straight to the Pacific Ocean. . . . It is the destiny of the white race, it is the destiny of the Anglo-Saxon Race." In effect, Calhoun already knew the answer to his question. The mission of the Anglo-Saxon race, as a people who made up the *demos*, is the answer to the rhetorical dimensions of democratic expansion.

9. This contradicts the argument that the United States created a historical amnesia about the war. Indeed, there was an effort to change the "imperialist" presuppositions of the U.S. conquest of Mexico in the public sphere.

10. For a discussion of the relationship of benevolence and American democracy, see Andrew Burstein, *Sentimental Democracy* (1999).

11. See Michael Denning, *Mechanic Accents* (1998), for a discussion of the

importance of the dime novel in American popular culture, as well as Shelley Streeby, *American Sensations* (2003).

12. See Richard Griswold Castillo, *The Treaty of Guadalupe Hidalgo* (1990), for an excellent analysis of the treaty. See also Juan Gómez-Quiñones, *Roots of Chicano Politics* (1994), p. 212.

13. See Martha Menchaca, *Recovering History, Constructing Race* (2001), and.Deena González, *The Treaty of Guadalupe Hidalgo, 1848* (1982).14. See Guadalupe Luna, "Beyond/Between Colors" (1999).

15. See Paula Rebert, *La gran linea* (2001), pp. 23–45.

16. See Étienne Balibar, "What Is a Border" in *Politics and the Other Scene* (2002).

17. Thomas Janvier is another example of a writer using this type of fiction.

18. See the collected works of Maria Cristina Mena edited by Amy Doherty (1997).

19. See Shawn Smith, *American Archives* (1999).

CHAPTER 3

1. For the sake of space, I will abbreviate María Amparo Ruiz de Burton to Ruiz, which was her maiden last name.

2. The Ruiz letters are cataloged at the Huntington Library: Collection of Eighty-One Letters to General Mariano Guadalupe Vallejo, 1858–1890. Although my analysis of the influence of race, republicanism, gender, and sexuality are different from his mostly biographical work, I found his research invaluable.

3. The Spanish phrase "no-ismo" has been a hard usage to translate from her letters. Working with Dr. Nicolás Kanellos (University of Houston), and comparing her use of "ismo" with other letters to Vallejo, I have concluded that "ismo" refers to republicanism, which she sees as not simply a form of government but as a theory; she uses these two terms in two letters written the same year to describe republicanism and its relation to other theories. See letter dated February 27, 1869. In this letter she comments on the hypocrisy of the "followers of republicanism" [Apóstoles de Republicanismo] and their inability to understand more "sublimo teorias."

4. Although Ruiz used various racial terms to define herself, her letters indicate that "Mexican" became her term of choice.

5. Certainly, Mexican men were the objects of racist discourse, and as Linda Gordon argues in *The Great Arizona Orphan Abduction* (2001), men were much more racialized than Mexican women, who were sexualized and often married into Anglo families. I explore the elite Mexican women's appropriation of the sexual aspects of the Mexican Question in the final pages of this chapter.

6. See L. H. Hewitt, "The Maid of Monterey, Arranged for Guitar," 1851. The song is as follows:

She casts a look of anguish,
On dying and on deed,
Her lap she made the pillow,
Of those who groaned and bled.
And when the dying soldier
For one bright gleam did pray,
He blessed the Senorita,
The Maid of Monterey.
She gave the thirsty water
And dress'd the bleeding wound:
And gentle prayers she uttered
For those that sighed around.
And whom the bugle sounded,
Just at the break of day,
We bless'd the Senorita,
The Maid of Monterey.
For, tho' she lov'd her nation
And pray'd that it might live:
Yet-for the dying foeman
She had a tear to give.
Then, here's to that bright beauty
Who drove death's pang away.
The meek-eyed Senorita,
The Maid of Monterey.

For an excellent analysis of Ruiz, see José Aranda, *When We Arrive* (2003), pp. 89–92.

7. Antonia Castañeda's work on Mexican women and the land has been invaluable for my understanding of the gendered dimensions of the Mexican Question. Especially helpful was Casteñeda's "Malinche, Califia y Toypurina," which is an unpublished working paper. Without her assistance, this chapter would have never been completed. I thank her and all of the Chicana feminists who have done groundbreaking work in this area; this includes Mary Pat Brady (2002, 2003), Alicia Gaspar de Alba (1998), Deena González (1999), and Emma Pérez (1999).

8. For an excellent examination of John Gast's work and the cultural rise of Manifest Destiny, see Stephanson, *Manifest Destiny* (1995), pp. 66–67.

9. I have located hundreds of instances of the term "Mexican Question" in nineteenth- and early-twentieth-century cultural forms, the first of which was published in the *United States Magazine and Democratic Review* in 1845. The term itself is an expansionist inquest into the democratic rights and racial status of Mexicans in the United States, and, as such, reveals the contradiction between

nineteenth-century racial ideologies, territorial expansion, and the universal norms and ideals of American democracy.

10. This trope was also seen in Latin American literature of the nineteenth century and was called "blanqueamiento." I thank distinguished professor of Spanish, Nicolás Kanellos, University of Houston, for his help on this draft and ideas of race changes.

11. By the 1870s the southwest was considered "public domain," and Anglo-Americans were free to take anything from these lands. A number of maps showed this public space and were widely circulated throughout New England, but one of the most popular was Thompson's "National Map of Public Domain, 1873," created one year after Ruiz's novel was published.

12. Although I do not agree with their points about the novel's representation of the Civil War and African Americans, I find their introduction to *Who Would Have Thought It?* (p. xviii), a brilliant analysis.

13. Douglass was perhaps aware that the lands ceded to the United States after the war would become slave states.

14. This may also have to do with the fact that Mexicanos were racialized as having African American blood and "Negroid features." See Arnoldo De León, *They Call Them Greasers* (1983), p. 45. Also see Martha Menchaca's excellent study of Mexican racial classification, *Recovering History, Constructing Race* (2002).

15. For a detailed discussion of the rise of scientific racism, see Maurice L. Wade, "From Eighteenth- to Nineteenth-Century Racial Science" (2003), pp. 27–44.

16. I thank Jon Smith for pointing this out. I would also like to thank him for reading this chapter so carefully. Extending the Kantian duality between the phenomenal and noumenal, I am saying here that *Who Would Have Thought It?* represents the phenomenal body as the false signifier of racial and political ontology and thus challenges the white, disembodied, and metaphysical norms and ideals of public sphere inclusion. In contrast, the noumenal "blood" of the body is the realm of the thinkable, a metonym for the political and racial ontology of the "Spanish-Mexican" citizen, and thus enables the possibility of Mexican American political inclusion through a similar metaphysical abstraction as white Americans. The noumenal body is cognizable, and thus embodiment is thinkable. See Kant, *Critique of Pure Reason* (1965), p. 255.

17. Pat Hilden pointed this out when I gave a talk at the University of Oregon. Also, see Phillip Deloria, *Playing Indian* (1998).

18. See, for example, William R. Lighton, "The Greaser" in *Atlantic* (1899).

19. Note that Lola is defined as Mexican and Spanish interchangeably in the novel after this point.

20. Here is a prime example of the "Spanish-Mexican" terminology used in the novel.

21. For an excellent analysis of Mexican women and Anglo men relations in the nineteenth century, see Deena González, *Refusing the Favor* (1999).

22. This biblical metaphor of "one flesh" was a common phrase used by southern and northern politicians in the age of expansion. The Whig Alexander H. Stephens of Georgia, for example, employed it to describe Texans as Anglo-Saxons: "They are from us; bone of our bone, and flesh of our flesh." What is important to point out here are the embodied discourses that describe political solidarity. See Nancy Isenberg, *Sex and Citizenship in Antebellum America* (1998), p. 250.

CHAPTER 4

1. The term "Los Bilitos" in the title to this chapter refers to Louis Leon Brauch's handwritten manuscript, "'Los Bilitos': The Story of Billy the Kid and His Gang As Told by Charles Frederick Rudulph—a Member of Garrett's Historical Posse."

2. On the social bandit, see Eric Hobsbawm, *Bandits* (1969), pp. 17–29.

3. See John M. Nieto, *The Language of Blood* (2004).

4. Miguel Antonio Otero's three-volume autobiography, *Otero: An Autobiographical Trilogy* (1974), details this "metamorphosis."

5. Otero's *The Real Billy the Kid* (1998) was originally printed by Rumford Press in Hartford, Connecticut. The papers that document the activity of this now-defunct press—held at Harvard University—unfortunately do not mention the Otero book or any relationship of Otero with the publisher. R. R. Wilson published two other works in 1936: a book on fur trading in the southwest and a small collection of Walt Whitman's poetry. According to various on-line catalogs and the Otero family papers held in New Mexico, *The Real Billy the Kid* was printed in limited numbers, and of the original print run there are only 118 in public circulation.

6. See Philip Fisher for a discussion of Turner and the expansionist crisis of democracy.

7. Some Mexican American elites sided with the Santa Fe Ring. However, the ring itself was mostly controlled by Anglo elites who used these Mexican American elites to gain the Mexican natives' sympathies during a time of empire building. See Mount Graeme, "Nuevo Mexicans and the War of 1898" (1983).

8. This is demonstrated throughout editorials in *La opinion* (1878), the most widely circulated daily, in the months of July and August.

9. *New Mexico Blue Book, 1856–1888* (1882).

10. See, for example, Albert E. Hyde, with pictures by J. N. Marchand, *The Old Regime in the Southwest* (1899).

11. Like his autobiography, *The Real Billy the Kid* allows Otero to explain why statehood was impossible for a Mexican to accomplish.

12. See John R. Chávez, *The Lost Land* (1984), for example.

13. I conducted an interview with Anaya through the mail, in which I wrote him questions about Billy the Kid and the play he wrote, and he sent these questions back with his answers.

CHAPTER 5

1. For a discussion of the corrido's people-making effects within Chicano culture, see José Limón, *Mexican Ballads, Chicano Poems* (1992); Ramón Saldívar, *Chicano Narrative* (1990); and Hector Pérez, "Voicing Resistance on the Border" (1998).

2. This poetic act of embodying print culture and thus taking on the characteristics of a democratic citizen is not new to American public culture. No other than Ben Franklin's epitaph would liken his figure to a man of print, who literarily embodies a book and printing press. I bring up Franklin because this posthumous relationship between poetics and the democratic citizen is so intriguing to me and has a long history in American democratic culture.

3. See Michael Denning, *The Cultural Front* (1997), for a discussion of these writers and populism.

4. See Mario García, *Mexican Americans* (1989), p. 132.

5. See Richard Flores, "Mexicans in a Material World: From John Wayne's *The Alamo* to Stand-up Democracy on the Border," p. 187.

6. For a discussion of the importance of the 1911 Congresso, see José Limón, "El Primer Congreso Mexicanista de 1911" (1974).

7. For an excellent discussion of this period, see Benjamin Heber Johnson, *Revolution in Texas* (2004).

8. It was not simply a question of race versus class in Marx's thought; rather, it was a tension between a discourse presupposed on the natural rights of the public sphere and one based on the systematic change of the capitalist mode of production. This tension was magnified when Marx and Marxism tried to deal with difference, be it racial, gendered, or sexual.

9. Quoted in Leticia Falcon, *Gente Decente* (1998), p. 234.

10. June Howard, *Form and History in American Literary Naturalism* (1985), p. 43, argues that this is a rhetorical technique of naturalist fiction.

11. For a discussion of the importance of the corrido in the formation of Mexican collectivity and humanity, see Américo Paredes, *The Texas-Mexican Cancionero* (1976), p. xviii.

12. This is not to say that neither folklore nor the corrido influenced his work. Indeed, Limón makes a compelling argument that the corrido affected

Paredes' early work, as well as Chicano poetics as a whole. See Limón, *Mexican Ballads, Chicano Poems* (1992).

CONCLUSION

1. Baca's mural was not the first to engage the Chicano community in its aesthetic creation. Partly based on Siqueros's *New Democracy* (1944), the mural *La mujer* in Hayward, California, was one of the first to bring the Chicano community into its creation and political message. For further information, see Shifra M. Goldman's (1982) discussion of this mural. For further information on Baca's communal mission, see the website of the Social and Public Art Resource Center (SPARC) at www.sparcmurals.org and Judy Baca's website at www.judybaca.com

2. For further scholarship on the significance of public art and in the Chicana and Chicano communities, see Alicia Gaspar de Alba, *Chicano Art* (1998), and Eva Cockroft et al., *Signs from the Heart* (1977).

Bibliography

ABQ Journal (July 13, 1997).

Agamben, Giorgio. *Homo Sacer: Sovereign Power and Bare Life.* Stanford: Stanford University Press, 1998.

Alarcón, Daniel. *The Aztec Palimpsest: Mexico in the Modern Imagination.* Tucson: University of Arizona Press, 1997.

Alarcón, Norma. "Chicana Feminism: In the Traces of 'The Native Woman.'" In *Between Woman and Nation: Nationalism, Transnationalism, Feminisms, and the State.* Edited by Caren Kaplan, Norma Alarcon, and Minoo Moallen, pp. 63–72. Durham, N.C.: Duke University Press, 1999.

Aldama, Arturo J. *Disrupting Savagism: Intersecting Chicana/o, Mexican Immigrant, and Native Struggles for Self-Representation.* Durham, N.C.: Duke University Press, 2001.

Almaguer, Tomás. *Racial Fault Lines: The Historical Origins of White Supremacy in California.* Berkeley: University of California Press, 1994.

Anderson, Benedict. *Imagined Communities: Reflections on the Origin and Spread of Naturalism.* New York: Verso, 1991.

Anderson, Benedict. *Imagined Communities: Reflections on the Origin and Spread of Nationalism.* New York: Verso, 1991.

Ankersmit, F. R. *Aesthetic Politics: Political Philosophy beyond Fact and Value.* Stanford: Stanford University Press, 1996.

Appiah, K. Anthony, and Amy Gutman. *Color Consciousness: The Political Morality of Race.* Princeton, N.J.: Princeton University Press, 1996.

Aranda, José. *When We Arrive: A New Literary History of America.* Tucson: University of Arizona Press, 2003.

Averill, Charles. *The Mexican Ranchero; or, The Maid of Chapparal.* Boston: F. Gleason, 1848.

Balibar, Étienne. *Politics and the Other Scene.* London: Verso Press, 2002.

Barrera, Mario. *Race and Class in the Southwest: A Theory of Racial Inequality.* Notre Dame, Ind.: University of Notre Dame Press, 1979.

Bauer, Ralph. *The Cultural Geography of Colonial American Literatures.* Cambridge: Cambridge University Press, 2004.

Bederman, Gail. *Manliness and Civilization: A Cultural History of Race and*

Gender in the United States, 1880–1917. Chicago: University of Chicago Press, 1995.

Billington, Ray Allen, ed. *Frontier and Section: Selected Essays of Frederick Jackson Turner.* Englewood Cliffs, N.J.: Prentice Hall, 1961.

Black, Jeremy. *Maps and Politics*. Chicago: University of Chicago Press, 2000.

Bordo, Susan. *Unbearable Weight: Feminism, Western Culture, and the Body*. Berkeley: University of California Press, 1995.

Bourdieu, Pierre. *Outline of a Theory of Practice*. London: Cambridge University Press, 1977.

Bourke, John. "The American Congo." *Scribner's Magazine* (1894): 32–49.

Brack, Gener M. *Mexico Views Manifest Destiny, 1821–1846: An Essay on the Origins of the Mexican War*. Albuquerque: University of New Mexico Press, 1975.

Brady, Mary Pat. *Extinct Lands, Temporal Geographies: Chicano Literature and the Urgency of Space*. Durham, N.C.: Duke University Press, 2002.

Brady, Mary Pat. "'Full of Empty': Creating the Southwest as 'Terra Incognita.'" In *Nineteenth-Century Geographies: The Transformation of Space from the Victorian Age to the American Century*, edited by Helena Mitchie and Ronald R. Thomas, 251–265. New Brunswick, N.J.: Rutgers University Press, 2003.

Brauch, Louis Leon. "'Los Bilitos': The Story of Billy the Kid and His Gang As Told by Charles Frederick Rudulph—a Member of Garrett's Historical Posse." Handwritten manuscript. New Mexico, R.R. Wilson, 1881.

Brewer, Cynthia, and Trudy A. Suchan. *Mapping Census 2000: The Geography of U.S. Diversity*. Washington, D.C.: U.S. Department of Commerce, Economics and Statistics Administration, U.S. Census Bureau, 2001.

Brewerton, Douglas G. "Incidents of Travel in New Mexico." *Harper's New Monthly Magazine* 47 (1854): 577–587.

Briones, Brigida. "A Carnival Ball at Monterey in 1829." *Century Magazine* (1890): 468–469.

Briones, Brigida. "A Glimpse of Domestic Life in 1827." *Century Magazine* (1890): 470.

Burgett, Bruce. *Sentimental Bodies: Sex, Gender and Citizenship in the Early Republic*. Princeton, N.J.: Princeton University Press, 1998.

Burstein, Andrew. *Sentimental Democracy: The Evolution of America's Romantic Self-Image*. New York: Diane, 1999.

Calhoun, Craig, ed. *Habermas and the Public Sphere*. Cambridge, Mass.: MIT Press, 1997.

Calhoun, Craig. "Imagining Solidarity: Cosmopolitanism, Constitutional Patriotism, and the Public Sphere." *Public Culture* 14, no. 1 (2002): 147–171.

Calhoun, John C. *Congressional Record.* Washington, D.C.: U.S. Government Printing Office, July 29, 1849.

Camp, Roderic L. *Politics in Mexico: The Democratic Transformation.* New York: Oxford University Press, 2003.

Casteñeda, Antonia. "Malinche, Califia y Toypurina: Of Myths, Monsters, and Embodied History." Unpublished paper. 2003.

Castillo, Richard Griswald. *The Treaty of Guadalupe Hidalgo: A Legacy of Conflict.* Norman: University of Oklahoma Press, 1990.

Castoriadis, Cornelius. *The Imaginary Institution of Society.* Cambridge, Mass.: MIT Press, 1987.

Castronovo, Russ. *Necro-Citizenship: Death Eroticism and the Public Spheres in the Nineteenth-Century United States.* Durham, N.C.: Duke University Press, 2001.

Castronovo, Russ, and Dana D. Nelson, eds. *Materializing Democracy: Toward a Revitalized Cultural Politics.* Durham, N.C.: Duke University Press, 2002.

Chávez, John R. *The Lost Land: The Chicano Image of the Southwest.* Albuquerque: University of New Mexico Press, 1984.

Child, Lydia Marie Francis. *A Romance of the Republic.* Lexington: University of Kentucky Press, 1997.

Cleaves, W. S. "The Political Life of Lorenzo de Zavala." Master's thesis, University of Texas, 1931.

Clifford, Michael. *Political Genealogy after Foucault: Savage Identities.* New York: Routledge, 2001.

Cockroft, Eva Sperling, and Holly Barnet-Sánchez. *Signs from the Heart: California Chicano Murals.* Albuquerque: University of New Mexico Press, 1993.

Cockroft, Eva, John Pitman Weber, and James Cockroft. *Toward a People's Art: The Contemporary Mural Movement.* Albuquerque: University of New Mexico Press, 1977.

Cohen, Nancy. *The Reconstruction of Liberalism, 1865–1914.* Chapel Hill: University of North Carolina Press, 2002.

Cooper, James Fenimore. *Notions of the Americans: Picked Up by a Travelling Bachelor.* Albany: State University of New York Press, 1991.

Crane, Gregg D. *Race, Citizenship and Law in American Literature.* New York: Cambridge University Press, 2002.

Crane, Stephen. "A Man and Some Others." *Century* 53, no. 4 (1897): 600–607.

Crane, Stephen. *Stephen Crane in the West and Mexico.* Edited by Joseph Katz. Kent, Ohio: Kent State University Press, 1970.

Crane, Stephen. *The University of Virginia Edition of the Works of Stephen Crane.* Edited by Fredson Bowers. 10 vols. Charlottesville: University of Virginia Press, 1969.

Crèvecoeur, J. Hector St. John de. *Letters from an American Farmer and Sketches of Eighteenth-Century America*. Edited with an introduction by Albert E. Stone. New York: Penguin Books, 1981.

Cullen, Jim. *The Civil War in Popular Culture: A Reusable Past*. Washington, D.C.: Smithsonian Institution Press, 1995.

Cushing, Caleb. "Mexico." *Democratic Review* (1846): 342–358.

de la Sagra, Ramón. *Cinco meses en los Estados-Unidos de la América del Norte desde el 20 de abril al 23 de setiembre de 1835*. N.p., n.d.

De León, Arnoldo. *They Call Them Greasers: Anglo Attitudes toward Mexicans in Texas, 1821–1900*. Austin: University of Texas Press, 1983.

Delgado, Richard. "Storytelling for Opposionists and Others: A Plea for Narrative." *Michigan Law Review* 87 (1989): 2411–2441.

Delgado, Richard, and Jean Stefancic, eds. *The Latino/a Condition: A Critical Reader*. New York: New York University Press, 1998.

Deloria, Philip. *Playing Indian*. New Haven, Conn.: Yale University Press, 1998.

Denning, Michael. *The Cultural Front*. New York: Verso, 1997.

Denning, Michael. *Mechanic Accents: Dime Novels and Working Class Culture in America*. New York: Verso, 1998.

"The Depredations on the Rio-Grande: A Tale of Two Cities." *Appleton's* (March 1873): 432–434.

Douglass, Frederick. *The Life and Writings of Frederick Douglass*. Edited by Philip S. Foner. New York: International Publishers, 1950.

Downes, Paul. *Democracy, Revolution, and Monarchism in Early American Literature*. New York: Cambridge University Press, 2002.

Dreiser, Theodore. "Who Challenges the Social Order?" *Survey* 50 (May 1923): 175.

Dyer, Richard. *White*. New York: Routledge, 1997.

Eberly, Rosa. *Citizen Critics: Literary Public Spheres*. Urbana: University of Illinois Press, 2000.

Emerson, Edward Waldo, and Waldo Emerson Forbes Emerson, eds. *The Journals of Ralph Waldo Emerson*. 10 vols. Boston: Houghton Mifflin, 1909–1914.

Engels, Frederick. "Democratic Pan-Slavism." *Neue Rheinische Zeitung* 22 (Feb. 1849).

Falcon, Leticia. *Gente Decente: A Borderlands Response to the Rhetoric of Dominance*. Austin: University of Texas Press, 1998.

Fanon, Frantz. *Black Skin, White Masks*. New York: Grove Press, 1967.

Feller, Daniel. *The Jacksonian Promise: America, 1815–1840*. Baltimore: Johns Hopkins University Press, 1995.

Felski, Rita. *Beyond Feminist Aesthetics: Feminist Literature and Social Change*. Cambridge: Harvard University Press, 1989.

Fisher, Philip. *Still the New World: American Literature in a Culture of Crative Destruction.* Cambridge: Harvard Univesity Press, 1999.

Fishkin, Shelley. *From Fact to Fiction.* New York: Oxford University Press, 1985.

Fishkin, Shelley. *Was Huck Black?* New York: Oxford University Press, 1993.

Fitch, George. "How California Came into the Union." *Century Magazine* (1890): 775–792.

Flores, Richard. "Mexicans in a Material World: From John Wayne's *The Alamo* to Stand-up Democracy on the Border." In *Materializing Democracy: Toward a Revitalized Cultural Politics,* ed. Russ Castronovo and Dana D. Nelson, pp. 95–115. Durham, N.C.: Duke University Press, 2002.

Flores, Richard. *Remembering the Alamo: Memory, Modernity, and the Master Symbol.* Austin: University of Texas Press, 2002.

Foley, Neil. *The White Scourge: Mexicans, Blacks, and Poor Whites in Texas Cotton Culture.* Berkeley: University of California Press, 1997.

Foner, Eric. *Reconstruction: America's Unfinished Revolution, 1863–1877.* New York: Harper Perennial, 2002.

Forest, John D. *Miss Ravenal's Conversion from Secession to Loyalty.* New York: Rinehart, 1955.

Foucault, Michel. *The History of Sexuality,* Vol. 1. New York: Vintage, 1990.

Foucault, Michel. *Technologies of the Self.* Cambridge, Mass.: MIT University Press, 1988.

Gaines, Kevin. *Uplifting the Race: Black Leadership, Politics and Culture in the Twentieth Century.* Chapel Hill: University of North Carolina Press, 1996.

Gaonkar, Dilip Parameshwar, and Benjamin Lee, eds. *New Imaginaries.* Durham, N.C.: Duke University Press, 2004.

García, Mario. *Mexican Americans.* New Haven, Conn.: Yale University Press, 1989.

García, Richard. *Rise of the Mexican American Middle Class: San Antonio, 1929–1941.* College Station: Texas A&M Press, 1991.

Garrett, Pat, and Ash Upson. *The Authentic Life of Billy the Kid: The Noted Desperado of the Southwest, Whose Deeds of Daring and Blood Made His Name a Terror in New Mexico, Arizona and Northern Mexico.* Norman: University of Oklahoma Press, 2000. Originally published 1882.

Garza-Falcón. *Gente Decente: A Borderlands Response to the Rhetoric of Dominance.* Austin: University of Texas Press, 1998.

Gaspar de Alba, Alicia. *Chicano Art: Inside/Outside the Master's House—Cultural Politics and the CARA Exhibition.* Austin: University of Texas Press, 1998.

Gatens, Moira. *Imaginary Bodies: Ethics, Power and Corporeality.* New York: Routledge, 1996.

"The Globe Is Her Canvas." *Los Angeles Times* (August 2001).

Goldman, Shifra M. "Mexican Muralism: Its Social-Educative Roles in Latin America and the United States." *Aztlán: International Journal of Chicano Studies Research* 1–2 (1982): 111–131.

Gómez-Quiñones, Juan. "On Culture." *Chicano-Requeña 5,* no. 2 (Primavera 1977): 29–47.

Gómez-Quiñones, Juan. *Roots of Chicano Politics, 1600–1940.* Albuquerque: University of New Mexico Press, 1994.

Gonzáles-Berry, Erlinda. "Introduction." *Recovering the U.S. Hispanic Literary Heritage,* Vol. 2. Houston: Arte Publico Press, 1996.

González, Deena J. *Refusing the Favor: The Spanish Mexican Women of Santa Fe, 1820–1880.* New York: Oxford University Press, 1999.

González, Deena J. *The Treaty of Guadalupe Hidalgo, 1848: Papers on the Sesquicentennial Symposium, 1848–1898.* Las Cruces, N.M.: Dona Ana Historical Society, 1982.

González, Gilbert, and Raúl A. Fernández. *A Century of Chicano History: Empire, Nations, and Migration.* New York: Routledge, 2003.

González, Jovitá. *Caballero: An Historical Romance.* College Station: Texas A&M Press, 1996.

Gordon, Linda. *The Great Arizona Orphan Abduction.* Cambridge: Harvard University Press, 2001.

Graeme, Mount. "Nuevo Mexicans and the War of 1898." *New Mexico Historical Review* 58, no. 4 (1983): 388–389.

Gruesz Silva, Kirsten. *Ambassadors of Culture: The Trans-American Origins of Latino Writing.* Princeton, N.J.: Princeton University Press, 2002.

Gruesz Silva, Kirsten. "Utopía Latina: The Ordinary Seaman in Extraordinary Times." *MFS: Modern Fiction Studies* 49, no. 1 (2003): 54–83.

Gubar, Susan. *Race Changes: White Skin, Black Face in American Culture.* New York: Oxford University Press, 2000.

Guerin-Gonzáles, Camille. *Mexican Workers and American Dreams: Immigration, Repatriation, and California Farm Labor, 1900–1939.* New Brunswick, N.J.: Rutgers University Press, 1996.

Gutiérrez, David. *Walls and Mirrors: Mexican Americans, Mexican Immigrants and the Politics of Ethnicity.* Berkeley: University of California Press, 1995.

Gutiérrez, Ramón. *When Jesus Came, the Corn Mothers Went Away: Marriage, Sexuality and Power in New Mexico, 1500–1846.* Palo Alto, Calif.: Stanford University Press, 1991.

Gutiérrez-Jones, Carl. *Critical Race Narratives: A Study of Race, Rhetoric and Injury.* New York: New York University Press, 2001.

Gutiérrez-Jones, Carl. *Rethinking the Borderlands: Between Chicano Culture and Legal Discourse.* Berkeley: University of California Press, 1995.

Habermas, Jürgen. *Between Facts and Norms: Contributions to a Theory of Law and Democracy.* Cambridge, Mass.: MIT Press, 1996.

Habermas, Jürgen. *The Inclusion of the Other.* Cambridge, Mass.: MIT Press, 1998.

Habermas, Jürgen. *The Structural Transformation of the Public Sphere: An Inquiry into a Category of Bourgeois Society.* Cambridge, Mass.: MIT Press, 1991.

Hale, Charles. *Mexican Liberalism in the Age of Mora, 1821–1858.* New Haven, Conn.: Yale University Press, 1968.

Hardt, Michael, and Antonio Negri. *Multitude: War and Democracy in the Age of Empire.* New York: Penguin Press, 2004.

Hartnett, Stephen John. *Democratic Dissent in the Cultural Fictions of Antebellum America.* Urbana: University of Illinois Press, 2002.

Harvey, David. *Spaces of Hope.* Berkeley: University of California Press, 2000.

Hass, Lisbeth. *Conquests and Historical Identities in California, 1769–1936.* Berkeley: University of California Press, 1995

"A Heathen Nation within Our Borders." *Ladies Repository* 17 (1857): 269–272.

Hero, Rodney E. *Latinos and the U.S. Political System.* Philadelphia: Temple University Press, 1992.

Hewitt, L. H. "The Maid of Monterey, Arranged for Guitar," 1851

Hietala, Thomas R. *Manifest Destiny: Anxious Aggrandizement in Late Jacksonian America.* Ithaca, N.Y.: Cornell University Press, 1985.

Higuera, Prudencia. "Trading with the Americans." *Century Magazine* (1890): 193

Hobbes, Thomas. *Leviathan.* New York: Penguin, 1982.

Hobsbawm, Eric. *Bandits.* New York: Pantheon, 1969.

Hoganson, Kristin L. *Fighting for American Manhood: How Gender Politics Provoked the Spanish-American and Philippine-American Wars.* New Haven, Conn.: Yale University Press, 1998.

Holland, Catherine. *The Body Politic: Foundings, Citizenship and Difference in the American Political Imagination.* New York: Routledge, 2001.

Honig, Bonnie. *Democracy and the Foreigner.* Princeton, N.J.: Princeton University Press, 2001.

Horsman, Reginald. *Race and Manifest Destiny: The Origins of American Racial Anglo-Saxonism.* Cambridge: Harvard University Press, 1981.

Hoskins, Janina W., ed. *Lafayette in America: A Selective List of Reading Materials in English.* Washington, D.C.: Library of Congress, 1983.

Hough, Emerson. *The Story of an Outlaw.* New York: Cooper Square Press, 2001.

Howard, June. *Form and History in American Literary Naturalism.* Chapel Hill: University of North Carolina Press, 1985.

Hyde, Albert E., with pictures by J. N. Marchand. *The Old Regime in the Southwest: The Reign of the Revolver in New Mexico.* New York: The Century Company, 1899.

Isen, Engine. *Being Political: Genealogies of Citizenship.* Minneapolis: University of Minnesota Press, 2002.

Isenberg, Nancy. *Sex and Citizenship in Antebellum America.* Chapel Hill: University of North Carolina Press, 1998.

Jacobsen, David. *Place and Belonging.* Baltimore: Johns Hopkins University Press, 2002.

James, Henry. *The Bostonians.* New York: Oxford University Press, 1998.

Johannsen, Robert. *To the Halls of Montezumas: The Mexican War in the American Imagination.* New York: Oxford University Press, 1988.

Johnson, Benjamin Heber. *Revolution in Texas: How a Forgotten Rebellion and Its Bloody Suppression Turned Mexicans into Americans.* New Haven, Conn.: Yale University Press, 2004.

Kanellos, Nicolás. *Herencia.* New York: Oxford University Press, 2005.

Kanellos, Nicolás. *Thirty Million Strong: Reclaiming the Hispanic Image in American Culture.* Golden, Colo.: Fulcrum, 1998.

Kant, Emmanuel. *Critique of Pure Reason.* Translated by N. Kemp Smith. New York: Dutton, 1965.

Kaplan, Amy. *The Anarchy of Empire in the Making of U.S. Culture.* Cambridge: Harvard University Press, 2005.

Kolodny, Annette. 1975. *The Lay of the Land: Metaphor as Experience and History in American Life and Letters.* Chapel Hill: University of North Carolina Press.

Las Vegas Optic (August 5, 1881): 19.

Las Vegas Optic 3(15) (1897): 11.

Lie, David. *Modern Peoplehood.* Cambridge: Harvard University Press, 2004

Lighton, William. "The Greaser." *Atlantic Monthly* (July 1899): 986–1021.

Limerick, Patricia. *All Over the Map: Rethinking American Regions.* Baltimore: Johns Hopkins University Press, 1996.

Limón, José. *American Encounters: Greater Mexico, the United States and the Erotics of Culture.* New York: Beacon, 1998.

Limón, José. *Dancing with the Devil: Society and Cultural Poetics in Mexican American South Texas.* Madison: University of Wisconsin Press, 1994.

Limón, José. "El Primer Congreso Mexicanista de 1911: A Precursor to Contemporary Chicanismo." *Aztlan* 5, no. 1 (1974): 85–117.

Limón, José. *Mexican Ballads, Chicano Poems: History and Influence in Mexican American Social Poetry.* Berkeley: University of California Press, 1992.

López, Haney Ian F. *White by Law: The Legal Construction of Race.* New York: New York University Press, 1996.

Lott, Eric. *Love and Theft: Blackface Minstrelsy and the American Working Class.* Oxford: Oxford University Press, 1993.

Lummis, Charles. "The Land of Poco Tiempo." *Scribner's* 10 (1891): 760–771.

Luna, Guadalupe. "Beyond/Between Colors: On the Complexities of Race: The Treaty of Guadalupe Hidalgo and *Dred Scott v. Sanford.*" *Miami Law Review* (July 1999): Rev. 575.

Mares, E.A. "The Wraggle-Taggle Outlaws: Vicente Silva and Billy the Kid as Seen in Two Nineteenth Century Documents." In *Pasó Por Aquí: Critical Essays on the New Mexican Literary Tradition, 1542–1988,* edited by Erlinda Gonzalez-Berry, 29–55. Albuquerque: University of New Mexico Press, 1989.

Marx, Karl. "On the American Civil War; on Intervention with Mexico." In *Marx and Engels Collected Works.* London: Lawrence and Wishart, 1983.

Marx, Karl. "On the Jewish Question." In *The Marx-Engles Reader,* edited by Robert Tucker, 158–191. New York: Norton, 1972.

McClintock, Anne. *Imperial Leather: Race, Gender, and Sexuality in the Colonial Conquest.* New York: Routledge, 1994.

Melendez, Gabriel A. *So All Is Not Lost: The Poetics of Print in Nuevomexicano Communities, 1834–1958.* Albuquerque: University of New Mexico Press, 1997.

Mena, María Cristina. *The Collected Stories of Maria Cristina Mena.* Edited by Amy Doherty. Houston: Arte Publico Press, 1997.

Menchaca, Martha. *Recovering History, Constructing Race: The Indian, Black and White Roots of Mexican Americans.* Austin: University of Texas Press, 2001.

"Mexicans and Their Country." *Atlantic* 28 (1860): 23–41.

"The Mexican War: Its Origin and Conduct." *Democratic Review* 20 (1847): 291–299.

"Mexico." *Atlantic* 28 (1860): 235–247.

Monroy, Douglas. *Thrown among Strangers: The Making of Mexican Culture in Frontier California.* Berkeley: University of California Press, 1990.

Montejano, David. *Anglos and Mexicans in the Making of Texas, 1836–1986.* Austin: University of Texas Press, 1987.

Montgomery, Charles. *The Spanish Redemption: Heritage. Power and Loss on New Mexico's Upper Rio Grande.* Berkeley: University of California Press, 2003.

Mora-Torres, Juan. *The Making of the Mexican Border: The State, Capitalism, and Society in Nuevo León, 1848–1910.* Austin: University of Texas Press, 2003.

Morrison, Michael. *Slavery and the American West.* Chapel Hill: University of North Carolina Press, 1997

Mohanram, Radhika. *Black Body: Women, Colonialism, Space.* Minneapolis: University of Minnesota Press, 1999.

Nash, Gerald D. "New Mexico in the Otero Era: Some Historical Perspectives." *New Mexico Historical Review* 67, no. 1 (1989): 1–13.

Negt, Oskar, and Alexander Kluge. *Public Sphere and Experience: Towards an*

Analysis of the Proletarian and Bourgeoisie Spheres. Minneapolis: University of Minnesota Press, 1996

Nelson, Dana. *National Manhood: Capitalist Citizenship and the Imagined Fraternity of White Men.* Durham, N.C.: Duke University Press, 1998.

New Mexico Blue Book, 1856–1888. Compiled by R. G. Ritch, Secretary of the Territory of New Mexico 1882.

Nieto, John M. *The Language of Blood: The Making of Spanish-American Identity in New Mexico, 1880's to 1930's.* Albuquerque: University of New Mexico Press, 2004.

Nietzsche, Friedrich. *Basic Writings of Nietzsche.* New York: Modern Library, 2000.

Niles National Register 70 (June 1848): 68.

Noriega, Chon, Curator. *From the West: Chicano Narrative Photography.* Seattle: University of Washington Press, 1995.

"The Occupation of Mexico." *Democratic Review* (1847): 381–390.

Ohmann, Richard. *Selling Culture: Magazines, Markets and Class at the Turn of the Century.* New York: Verso, 1998.

Olwig, Kenneth Robert. *Landscape, Nature, and the Body Politic: From Britain's Renaissance to America's New World.* Madison: University of Wisconsin Press, 2002.

Omi, Michael, and Howard Winnant. *Racial Formation in the United States: From the 1960s to the 1990s.* New York: Routledge, 1994.

O'Neil, John. *Five Bodies: The Human Shape of Modern Society.* Ithaca, N.Y.: Cornell University Press, 1985.

O'Sullivan, John. "Annexation." *Democratic Review* (1845): 234–254.

O'Sullivan, John. "The Mexican Question." *North American Review* (1845): 434–445.

Otero, Miguel Antonio II. *Otero: An Autobiographical Trilogy,* Vols. 1–3. New York: Arno, 1974.

Otero, Miguel Antonio II. *The Real Billy the Kid: With New Light on the Lincoln County War.* Introduced and edited by John-Michael Rivera. Houston: Arte Publico Press, 1998. Originally published by R. R. Wilson, 1936.

Owen, Robert Dale. "Recallings from a Public Life II: Texas and the Peace of Guadalupe Hidalgo." *Scribner's Magazine* (1878): 868–878.

Padilla, Genaro. *My History, Not Yours: The Formation of Mexican American Autobiography.* Madison: University of Wisconsin Press, 1993.

Paredes, Américo. *Between Two Worlds.* Houston: Arte Publico Press, 1991.

Paredes, Américo. "The Folkbase of Chicano Literature." In *Modern Chicano Writers,* edited by Joseph Sommers and Tomás Yharra-Frausto, 4–17. Englewood Cliffs, N.J.: Prentice Hall, 1979.

Paredes, Américo. *Folklore and Culture on the Texas-Mexican Border.* Austin: Center for Mexican American Studies, University of Texas at Austin, 1993.

Paredes, Américo. *George Washington Gómez: A Mexico-Texan Novel.* Houston: Arte Publico Press, 1990.

Paredes, Américo. *The Hammon and the Beans and Other Stories.* Houston: Arte Public Press, 1994.

Paredes, Américo. *The Texas-Mexican Cancionero: Folksongs of the Lower Border.* Urbana: University of Illinois Press, 1976.

Paredes, Américo. *Uncle Remos con Chile.* Houston: Arte Publico Press, 1993.

Paredes, Américo. *With His Pistol in His Hand: A Border Ballad and Its Hero.* Austin: University of Texas Press, 1958.

Paredes, Raymond. "The Evolution of Chicano Literature." In *Three American Literatures: Essays in Chicano, Native American, and Asian-American Literature for Teachers of American Literature*, ed. Houston Baker, 33–79. New York: Modern Language Association, 1982.

Patterson, Anita Haya. *Democracy, Race and the Politics of Protest.* New York: Oxford University Press, 1997.

"Peace—And What Next?" *Putnams' Monthly Magazine* (1848): 292–299.

Pereles, Alonso. "The Evolution of Mexican-Americans." In *Herencia*, ed. Nicolás Kanellos, 152–156. New York: Oxford University Press, 2002.

Pérez, Emma. *The Decolonial Imaginary: Writing Chicanas into History.* Bloomington: Indiana University Press, 1999.

Pérez, Hector. "Voicing Resistance on the Border: A Reading of Américo Paredes' *George Washington Gómez*." *MELUS: Journal of the Society for the Study of Multi-Ethnic Literature of the United States* 23 (1998): 27–48.

Perea, Juan. "Fulfilling Manifest Destiny: Conquest, Race, and the Insular Cases." In *Foreign in a Domestic Sense: Puerto Rico, American Expansion, and the Constitution*, edited by Christina Duffy Burnett and Burke Marshall, pp. 140–167. Durham, N.C.: Duke University Press, 2001.

Pettit, Arthur. *Images of the Mexican American in Fiction and Film.* College Station: Texas A&M Press, 1980.

Pfister, Joel. *Individuality Incorporated: Indians and the Multicultural Modern.* Durham, N.C.: Duke University Press, 2004.

Pilcher, James. "Outlawry on the Mexican Border" *Scribner's Magazine* 50 (July 1891): 78–87.

"Politics in Mexico," *North American Review* 31 (1830): 110–154.

Powell, Emily. "A Modern Knight: Reminiscences of General M. G. Vallejo." *Harper's New Monthly Magazine* 86 (1893): 786–789.

Pratt, Mary Louis. *Imperial Eyes: Travel Writing and Transculturation.* New York: Routledge, 1999.

Price, Janet. *Feminist Theory and the Body.* New York: Routledge, 1999.

Ramírez, Francisco. "Editorials." In *Herencia*. Edited by Nicolás Ganellos. New York: Oxford University Press, 2002.

Rancière, Jacques. *Disagreement: Politics and Philosophy*. Minneapolis: University of Minnesota Press, 1998.

Rebert, Paula. *La Gran Linea: Mapping the United States–Mexico Boundary, 1849–1857*. Austin: University of Texas Press, 2001.

Reid-Pharr, Robert F. *Conjugal Union: The Body, the House and the Black American*. Oxford: Oxford University Press, 1999.

Rivera, John-Michael. "Miguel Antonio Otero II, Billy the Kid's Body and the Fight for New Mexican Manhood." *Western American Literature* 35, no 1 (Spring 2000): 31–56.

Rivera, Tomás. *Tomás Rivera: The Complete Works*. Edited by Julian Olivares. Houston: Arte Publico Press, 1993.

Robertson, Jamie. "Stephen Crane, Eastern Outsider in the West and Mexico." *Western American Literature*. 13 (1978): 243–258.

Robinson, Cecil. *Mexico and the Hispanic Southwest in American Literature*. Tucson: University of Arizona Press, 1977.

Rodriguez, Richard. *Brown: The Last Discovery of America*. New York: Viking Press, 2002.

Rogoff, Irit. *Terra Infirma: Geography's Visual Culture*. New York: Routledge, 2000.

Rosaldo, Renato. "Cultural Citizenship, Inequality, and Multiculturalism." In *Latino Cultural Citizenship: Claiming Identity, Space, and Rights*, edited by William Flores and Rina Benmayor, 27–38. New York: Beacon Press, 1997.

Rosenus, Alan. *General M. G. Vallejo and the Advent of the Americans*. Albuquerque: University of New Mexico Press, 1995.

Ruiz de Burton, María Amparo. *Conflicts of Interest: The Letters of María Amparo Ruiz de Burton*. Edited by Rosura Sánchez and Beatrice Pita. Houston: Arte Publico Press, 2001.

Ruiz de Burton, María Amparo. *The Squatter and the Don*. Edited and introduced by Rosaura Sánchez and Beatrice Pita. Houston: Arte Publico Press, 1997. Originally published by C. Loyal, 1885.

Ruiz de Burton, María Amparo. *Who Would Have Thought It?* Houston: Arte Publico Press, 1995. Originally published by J. P Lippincott, 1872.

Saldívar, José David. *Border Matters: Remapping American Cultural Studies*. Berkeley: University of California Press, 1997.

Saldívar, José David. *The Dialectics of Our America: Genealogy, Cultural Critique and Literary History*. Durham, N.C.: Duke University Press, 1991.

Saldívar, Ramón. "The Borderlands of Culture: Américo Paredes' *George Washington Gómez* and Chicano Literature at the End of Century." In *The American Literary History Reader*, edited by Gordon Hutner, 42–72. New York: Oxford University Press, 1995.

Saldívar, Ramón. *Chicano Narrative: The Dialectics of Difference*. Madison: University of Wisconsin Press, 1990.

Sánchez, Rosaura, and Beatrice Pitt, eds. *Conflicts of Interest: The Letters of María Amparo Ruiz de Burton*. Houston: Arte Publico Press, 2001.

Sánchez-Eppler, Karen. *Touching Liberty: Abolition, Feminism, and the Politics of the Body*. Berkeley: University of California Press, 1997.

Sandel, Michael. *Democracy's Discontent: America in Search of a Public Philosophy*. New York: Belknap Press, 1998.

Santa Ana, Otto. *Brown Tide Rising: Metaphors of Latinos in Contemporary American Public Discourse*. Austin: University of Texas Press, 2002.

Schneirov, Matthew. *Dream of a New Social Order: Popular Magazines in America 1893–1914*. New York: Columbia University Press, 1994.

Seguín, Juan. *Personal Memoirs*. San Antonio, 1858.

Seltzer, Mark. *Bodies and Machines*. New York: Routledge, 1992.

Sierra, Justo. "Noticia su vida y escritos." In Lorenzo de Zavala, ed., *Obras*, 189–232. México: Editorial Porrúa, 1976.

Silber, Nina. *The Romance of Reunion: Northerners and the South, 1865–1900*. Chapel Hill: University of North Carolina Press, 1997.

Slotkin, Richard. *Gunfighter Nation: The Myth of the Frontier in Twentieth-Century America*. New York: Harper, 1992.

Smith, Rogers. *Civic Ideals: Conflicting Visions of Citizenship in U.S. History*. New Haven, Conn.: Yale University Press, 1997.

Smith, Rogers. *Stories of Peoplehood: The Morals and Politics of Political Membership*. Cambridge: Cambridge University Press, 2003.

Smith, Shawn. *American Archives: Gender, Race and Class in Visual Culture*. Princeton, N.J.: Princeton University Press, 1999.

Stallybrass, Peter. "Marx and Heterogeneity: Thinking the Lumpenproletariat." *Representations* 31 (Summer 1990): 69–95.

Stephanson, Anders. *Manifest Destiny: American Expansion and the Empire of Right*. New York: Hill and Wang, 1995.

Streeby, Shelley. *American Sensations: Class, Empire, and the Production of Popular Culture*. Berkeley: University of California Press, 2003.

Sussman, Warren. *Culture as History: The Transformation of American Society in the Twentieth Century*. New York: Pantheon, 1984.

Tatum, Charles. *Chicano Literature*. Boston: Twayne, 1982.

Tatum, Stephen. *Inventing Billy the Kid: Visions of the Outlaw in America, 1881–1981*. Albuquerque: University of New Mexico Press, 1982.

Tauthail, Gearóid, and Simon Dalby, eds. *Rethinking Geopolitics*. New York: Routledge Press, 1998.

Taylor, Charles. *Modern Social Imaginaries*. Durham, N.C.: Duke University Press, 2004.

Taylor, Charles. "The Dynamics of Democratic Exclusion." *Journal of Democracy* 14, no. 4 (2002): 147–171.

Tenayuca, Emma, and Homer Brooks. "The Mexican Question in the Southwest." *Communist* (1939).

Thirty-Four 35 (June 1880): 1–7.

Tocqueville, Alexis de. *Democracy in America*. New York: Vintage, 1961. Originally published 1835.

Trollope, Frances Milton. *Domestic Manners of the Americans*. London, 1832

Turner, Frederick Jackson. *The Frontier in American History*. New York: Dover, 1996.

Tuska, Jon. *Billy the Kid: His Life and Legend*. Albuquerque: University of New Mexico Press, 1997.

Vallejo, Guadalupe. "Ranch and Mission Days in Alta California." *Century Magazine* (1890): 183–190.

Vallejo, Mariano Guadalupe. *Memorias*. University of California, Berkeley, Bancroft Collection, Box 32-45.

Vargas, Zaragosa. "Tejana Radical: Emma Tenayuca and the San Antonio Labor Movement during the Great Depression." *Pacific Historical Review* 66 (Nov. 1997): 553–560.

Vélez-Ibáñez, Carlos G. *Border Visions: Mexican Cultures of the Southwest United States*. Tucson: University of Arizona Press, 1997.

Villa, Raúl. *Barrio-Logos: Space and Place in Urban Chicano Literature and Culture*. Austin: University of Texas Press, 2000.

Wade, Maurice. "From Eighteenth- to Nineteenth-Century Racial Science: Continuity and Change." In *Race and Racism in Theory and Practice*, edited by Berel Laming, pp. 27–44. Oxford: Rowman and Littlefield, 2003.

Wairda, Howard J. *The Soul of Latin America: The Cultural and Political Tradition*. New Haven, Conn.: Yale University Press, 2003.

"The War: The New Issue." *American Review* (1848): 105–117.

Warner, Michael. *The Letters of the Republic: Publication and the Public Sphere in Eighteenth-Century America*. Cambridge: Cambridge University Press, 1990.

Warner, Michael. *Publics and Counter Publics*. New York: Zone Books, 2002.

Weber, David. *The Mexican Frontier, 1821–1846: The American Southwest under Mexico*. Albuquerque: University of New Mexico Press, 1982.

Webster, Daniel. *The Writings and Speeches of Daniel Webster*. National ed. 18 vols. Boston: Little, Brown, 1903.

Wertheim, Stanley, and Paul Sorrentino, eds. *The Crane Log: A Documentary Life of Stephen Crane, 1871–1900*. New York: G. K. Hall, 1994.

Wertheimer, Eric. *Imagined Empires: Incas, Aztecs and the New World of American Literature, 1771–1876*. Cambridge: Cambridge University Press, 1999.

Wilson, Kathleen. *The Sense of the People: Politics, Culture and Imperialism in England, 1715–1785*. Cambridge: Cambridge University Press, 1998.

Wolin, Sheldon. *Tocqueville between Two Worlds: The Making of a Political and Theoretical Life*. Princeton, N.J.: Princeton University Press, 2001.

Woodhull, Victoria. *The Victorian Woodhull Reader*. Edited by Madeleine B. Stein. Weston, Conn.: M.&S. Press, 1974.

Wollstonecraft, Mary. *A Critical Edition of Mary Wollstonecraft's* A Vindication of the Rights of Woman, with Strictures on Political and Moral Subjects. Edited by Ulrich H. Hardt. New York: Whitson, 1982.

Young, Elizabeth. *Disarming the Nation: Women's Writing and the American Civil War*. Chicago: University of Chicago Press, 1999.

Zavala, Lorenzo de. *Ensayo historico de las revoluciones de México*. 1830.

Zavala, Lorenzo de. *Journey to the United States of America*. Edited and introduced by John-Michael Rivera. Houston: Arte Publico Press, 2005.

Zavala, Lorenzo de. *Viage de los Estados Unidos del Norte América*. Paris: Imprenta de Decourchant, 1834. Reprinted as *Viaje de los Estados-Unidos del Norte América*. Mérida de Yucatán: Castillo, 1846.

Index

Adams, Henry, 96; and *Democracy*, 109
Adams, John, 12, 48
Aesthetic representation, 46
Alarcón, Norma, 68
Alberdi, Juan Bautista, 47
Alemán, Lucas, 48
"The American Congo" (Bourke), 71, 73
Amexica, 169–170
Anaya, Rudolfo, 134
Anderson, Benedict, 64
Ankersmit, F. R., 46
Antiliberal, 45
Arau, Sergio, 1; *A Day without a Mexican* (film), 2–6
Atlantic, 54, 61
Austin, Stephen F., 49
Autoethnographic expression, 30–31
Averill, Charles, 65

Baca, Judy, 166
Balibar, Étienne, 14
Bauer, Ralph, 31
Beveridge, Senator Albert, 118
Billy the Kid, 110; and dime novels, 123, 124; and Mexican people-hood, 111–114, 121; and the Mex-ican Question, 124; as social ban-dit, 111–112,123–124
Binational, 106–109

Blackwood, Mary Josephine, 114
Blackwood, Page, 114
Blood, 100–101; and Mexican people-hood, 101–103; v. body, 101
Body, 83; and blood, 101–103; dis-ease of, 93; and metamorphosis, 91; and peoplehood, 93–94; and the Reconstruction Era, 92; and Republicanism, 83–84; and sexual-ity, 87–88; and womanhood, 85–87
Borderlands, 60, 71; and magazine culture, 70; and the Mexican Ques-tion, 73; and overdetermination, 71–72
Bourdieu, Pierre, 42
Bourke, John G., 71, 73–74
Brooks, Homer, 148
"Browning of America," 6
Burke, Kenneth, 141
Bush, George W., 169–170; and the Mexican Question, 172

Calhoun, John C., 69–70, 182n. 8
Califas, 88
Californios, 102
Capitalism, 80; and Mexico, 42; and U.S., 80
Casteñeda, Antonia, 88
Castoriadis, Cornelius, 3
Census, 6–8, 7 *fig. 2*, 178

Century, 75
Chicano identity, 25
Civil War, 95
Communist, 148
Communist Party, 148, 151; and the "Black Belt thesis," 152; and the "Negro Question," 152
Congressional Record, 69
Conjunto, 165
Cooper, James Fenimore, 41
Corrido, 137; "Con su pluma en su mano," 137–139; and Gregorio Cortez, 138; as story of peoplehood, 138, 145, 146; temporality of, 137
Cortez, Gregorio, 142
Crane, Stephen, 75–77
Creole, 31; and racialization, 32
Crèvecoeur, John Hector, 41
Cultural citizenship, 162
Cushing, Caleb, 60

Delgado, Richard, 2
Democracy, 12, 18, 59, 177; and colonialism, 28
Democratic Review, 43, 60
demos, 12–13, 54, 177; and *ethnos/demos* split, 14
Denver International Airport, 166
"The Depredations on the Rio Grande" (Pilcher), 71
Dime novels, 124; and masculinity, 125; and territorial politics, 127. *See also* Billy the Kid
Disturnell, J., 66; and Mapa de los Estados Unidos de Mejico (1847–1848), 67
Douglass, Frederick, 96–97
Dreiser, Theodore, 155

El clamor publico, 11
Emerson, Ralph Waldo, 40

Engels, Friedrich, 68, 69–70
Enlightenment and Jeffersonian ideology, 60
Ethnos, 13

Fernández, Raúl, 26
Fiction, 181n. 2
Fifteenth Amendment, 85,86
Flores, Richard, 143
Foley, Neil, 97
Folk culture, 78
Foucault, Michel, 101
Fourteenth Amendment, 84, 86
Fox, Vicente, 169

G. Stocking Map of Acquisitions and Territory of the United States, 1870–1885, 72
Gachupines, the, 31, 32
Gadsden Purchase of 1853, 70, 117
García, Mario, 142
García, Richard, 142
Garrett, Pat, 123, 127
Gast, John, 88, 89
Gente de razón (people with reason), 20, 86, 103–104
Geopolitics, 59, 108, 179n. 15; and *Who Would Have Thought It?* 99, 100
"The Gold Vanity Set" (Mena), 78
Gómez-Quiñones, Juan, 25–26, 66, 68, 74
González, Deena, 66
González, Gilbert, 25
González, Jovitá, 106
Grant, Ulysses S., 96
Greaser, 11, 131, 181n. 1; and "The Greaser," 55, 56
"The Greaser" (Lighton), 50, 51–54, 55
Gubar, Susan, 92

Guerrero, Vicente, 35
Gutiérrez-Jones, Carl, 2, 25

Habermas, Jürgen, 17, 33, 127; and
the public sphere, 17–18
Habitus, 42
Hinojosa, Tish, 136–139
Holland, Catherine, 10
Hough, Emerson, 126, 132
House magazines, 56

Imagined community, 64
Incorporate, 8; as concept, 178n.12

Jackson, Andrew, 35, 48
Jacksonian America, 29, 40
Jefferson, Thomas, 12, 60
Jim Crow, 141
Johannsen, Robert, 62

Kant, Emmanuel, 185n. 3

La Malinche, 88
Lafayette, Marquis de, 41
League of Latin American Citizens
(LULAC), 20, 142, 159–161
Levinsky, David, 155
Leyenda Negra, 44
Liberal state, 45
Liberalism, 50
Lighton, William, 54–56; "The
Greaser," 62
Limón, José, 71, 137
Lincoln, Abraham, 15, 16, 100, 114
Luna, Guadalupe, 86
Luna, Tranquilo, 122

Magnon, Flores, 144
"A Man and Some Others" (Crane),
75–77
Manhood, 113, 132; and culture,
113; and territorialism,

113–114. *See also* Otero,
Miguel Antonio
Manifest Destiny, 11–14; and democ-
racy, 12; and John O'Sullivan,
58–59
Manners, 41–42
Marx, Karl, 68–69; "On the Jewish
Question" (1847), 150–151
Marxism, 149–150
McSween, Alexander, 121
Mena, Maria Christina, 78–81; and
"The Gold Vanity Set," 78
Menchaca, Martha, 66
Mexican Constitution of 1824, 26
Mexican peoplehood, stories of, 2, 5,
10, 28, 128–129; and aesthetics,
45; criticism on, 177; and dime
novels, 127; and magazines, 56
"Mexican Question," 11, 54, 55, 56,
58, 59, 61, 86, 100, 130, 184n. 9;
as defined by John O'Sullivan, 59;
definition 54; and "the Indian
Question," 100; and masculinity,
132; and the "Negro Question,"
98–99; and stories of peoplehood,
54
"The Mexican Question" (O'Sullivan), 59
*The Mexican Ranchero or The Maid
of the Chapparal: A Romance of
the Mexican War* (Averill), 65–67
Mexican repatriation, 163
Mexican-American generation, 142,
154
Monroe Doctrine, 26, 48; and neo-
colonialism, 26–27
Murals, 174
Murrieta, Joaquín, 133

Narrative and people-making, 5
Natural rights, 60
"Negro Question," 96–97

New Deal, 140–141; and concept of the people, 141

New Democracy (Sigueros), 188n. 1

New Mexico, 112–114; masculinity, 132–133; and metamorphosis, 112; and race, 131–133; as territory, 117–119

Nietzsche, Friedrich, 173

North American Free Trade Agreement (NAFTA), 16; and public sphere, 23, 169–171

Northwest Ordinance of 1787, 58

Obregón, Pablo, 48

"The Occupation of Mexico" (anonymous), 64

"One flesh," 108, 186n. 22

Operation Gatekeeper, 173

O'Sullivan, John, 58, 70; and "Annexation" 56, 60; and "The Mexican Question," 56, 60; U.S./Mexico relations, 61–62

Otero, Miguel Antonio, 113–115; and masculinity 112–113; and the Mexican Question, 130–132; *The Real Billy the Kid*, 117; and Theodore Roosevelt, 118

"Outlawry on the Mexican Border" (Pilcher), 71

Owens, Robert, 70

Paine, Thomas, 12

Paredes, Américo, 136; and brown radicalism, 139; and folklore, 163; *George Washington Gómez* 146, 155–157; "The Hammon and the Beans," 143, 146–147; and the Mexican Question, 140; *Mi Pueblo*, 163–164; peoplehood and democracy, 157–158

Partido Libertad Movimiento (PLM), 144

Pedraza, Manual Gómez, 35

People v. De La Guerra, 86, 103

Peoplehood, 2–4, 166, 177; democratic, poetics of, 139; and embodiment, 86–87; invisibility of, 4–5; and modernity, 140; and populism, 141

Perales, Alonso S., 15; "The Evolution of Mexican Americans," 15–16

Pérez, Emma, 25

Phrenologist, 63

Pilcher, James, 71

Pita, Beatrice, 95

Pizana, Aniceto, 144

Plan de San Diego, 144, 150

"Political reality," 46

"Politics in Mexico" (anonymous), 43

Polk, James, 25

Popular Front, 148, 162

Populism, 162

Pratt, Mary Louis, 28

Private sphere, 94–95

"Public domain," 74, 77, 93

"Public memory," 168

Public sphere, 17, 83–84; and Jürgen Habermas, 17–18; literary, 90, 182n. 9; and stories of peoplehood, 18

Racialization, 63; and whiteness, 94

Ramírez, Francisco, 11–14

Ramos, Basilio, 144

Remington, Frederic, 77

"Republic of Sierra Madre," 84

Republicanism, 83–86, 90, 97, 122; and liberalism, 179n. 20; and John Lock, 60; and Mexicans, 84

Res publica, 168

Richardson, Bill, 133

Rivera, Tomás, 165–166

"Romance to reunion" novel, 107

Roosevelt, Theodore, 75; and *How the West Was Won*, 75–76, 113

Rosa, Luis de la, 144
Ruiz de Burton, María Amparo, 85–87; as "The Maid of Monterey," 88, 184n. 6; and Mexican peoplehood, 97; and the Mexican Question, 108; and republicanism, 98; and sexuality, 87–88; *The Squatter and the Don*, 98; and stereotype, 89; *Who Would Have Thought It?* 87–88

Saldívar, José David, 71
Sánchez, Rosaura, 95–96
Sánchez-Eppler, Karen, 91–92
Santa Fe Ring, 119–120, 186n. 7
Schwartzenegger, Arnold, 1
Scribner's, 70
Sediciosos, the, 144; corrido "Los Sediciosos," 145–146
Seguín, Juan, 20, 49
Self-fashioning, 181n. 4
Silva-Gruesz, Kirsten, 10
"Social bandit," 111–112
Social imaginary, 3, 166; and the public sphere, 18
Spanish colonialism in Mexico, 31–39, 46; and racial ideology, 31
Spanish Fantasy Heritage, 104, 131
Stallybrass, Peter, 151
Stereotyping, 43; in U.S. magazines, 62
Sussman, Warren, 140

Tatum, Chuck, 79
Taylor, Charles, 14
Tenayuca, Emma, 69, 143, *149 fig. 10*; and "The Mexican Question," 148–152
Terra incognita, 54
Territorialism, 112; and masculinity, 132; and New Mexico, 117–118, 129

Texas, 47–50
Texas colonization, 47; Texas Colonization Act, 48
Texas Modern, 143–144
Theoria, 37–40, 42
Topospatial, 10, 179n. 14
Tocqueville, Alexis de, 41, 48; *Democracy in America*, 41
Transculturalization, 28
Travel writing, 36–39; and *theoria*, 37
Treaty of Guadalupe Hidalgo, 1, 8, 25; and Mexican identity formation in the U.S., 66–68; in magazine culture, 64–65; and racial democracy, 11–14
Trist, Nicholas, 65; as character in Averill's *The Mexican Ranchero . . .*, 66
Trollope, Fanny, 41; *Domestic Manners of the Americans*, 41
Tunstall, John H., 120
Turner, Frederick Jackson, 115–116; and manhood, 116

United States Magazine, 63
United States/Mexican War of 1848, 8, 63, 68; and magazine culture, 61
United States Census Map, 1870, 9
United States Census Map of Latino Population 2000, 7–8

Vallejo, Guadalupe (Platon), 104
Vallejo, Mariano Guadalupe, 82–84
Voting, 158–160

Washington, George, 157; as icon, 157–158
"We, the People," 12–13, 141
Webster, Daniel, 40
Westphalan, Edgar von, 150–151
Wisconsin Organic Act of 1836, 117

Woodhull, Victoria, 84
Wollstonecraft, Mary, 84–85
Womanhood, 85; and the body, 85; and racial politics, 84
Worker's Progress Alliance, 141

Zapata, Emilio, 156
Zavala, Lorenzo de, 24; and manners, 41; and Mexican Constitution of 1824, 26; and Mexican stereotype, 43; and political reality, 46; and public sphere, 39; and slavery, 44; and story of peoplehood, 29, 46; and theoria, 37–40, 42; *Viage de los Estados Unidos del Norte América* (Journey to the United States of America), 24–32

About the Author

John-Michael Rivera is Assistant Professor of English and Director of Undergraduate Studies at the University of Colorado at Boulder. Working as an archivist, he has critically introduced and edited Lorenzo Zavala's *Journey to the United States* and Miguel Antonio Otero's *The Real Billy the Kid*. He has also published articles in the areas of Chicano and cultural studies, political philosophy, and cultural geography.